REDIRECTIONS IN CRITICAL THEORY

Truth, Self, Action and History, previously linchpins of philosophical and literary critical discourses, have been steadily deprived of their stabilizing functions in a plural theoretical age. The essays in *Redirections in Critical Theory* seek to reanalyse and reconstruct major figures and configurations of the past, asking questions often neglected or overlooked by a readership ever in pursuit of new theorctical directions.

In this volume, Christopher Norris re-examines the work of William Empson and his treatment of the sublime. Nick Heffernan explores the 'truth' to their moment of the events of May 1968 in France, and places the writings of Gilles Deleuze and Felix Guattari in this specific poststructuralist historical context. Steve Giles analyses Chekhov's later plays and theorizes what it means to 'be in a state of crisis'. And finally, Sara Danius takes up Fredric Jameson's own invitation, in *The Political Unconscious*, to be read and tested both theoretically and against his interpretive practice.

Redirections in Critical Theory brings together established critics and new names in the field of theory who re-examine key debates on discourses often said to be deprived of any stable terminology. It will be an important text for students of literature, critical theory and philosophy.

Bernard McGuirk is Reader in Romance Literatures at the University of Nottingham, where he is Head of the Graduate School of Critical Theory. He has published widely on modern literature.

REDIRECTIONS IN CRITICAL THEORY

Truth, Self, Action, History

Edited by Bernard McGuirk

London and New York

First published 1994
by Routledge
11 New Fetter Lane, London EC4P 4EE

Simultaneously published in the USA and Canada
by Routledge
29 West 35th Street, New York, NY 10001

Typeset in Baskerville by Intype, London

Printed and bound in Great Britain by T.J. Press (Padstow) Ltd,
Padstow, Cornwall

Printed on acid free paper

British Library Cataloguing in Publication Data
A catalogue record for this book is available from the British Library

Library of Congress Cataloging in Publication Data
Redirections in Critical Theory: Truth, Self, Action, History / edited
and with an introduction by Bernard McGuirk
p. cm.
Includes bibliographical references and index.
1. Criticism. 2. Critical theory. I. McGuirk, Bernard.
PN98.S6R43 1993
801'.95–dc20 93–14031

ISBN 0–415–07756–7

CONTENTS

v

NOTES ON CONTRIBUTORS

Christopher Norris is Professor of Philosophy at the University of Wales in Cardiff. His more recent books include *Deconstruction and the Interests of Theory* (1988), *Spinoza and the Origins of Modern Critical Theory* (1990), *What's Wrong with Postmodernism* (1991), *Uncritical Theory: Postmodernism, intellectuals and the Gulf War* (1992), and *The Truth About Postmodernism* (1993).

Nick Heffernan is Lecturer in American Studies at Nene College, Northampton. He is currently doing research on the cultural aspects of Fordism and post-Fordism.

Steve Giles is Lecturer in German and Critical Theory at the University of Nottingham. He is the author of *The Problem of Action in Modern European Drama* (1981) and editor of *Theorizing Modernism* (1993).

Sara Danius is a graduate student in the Programme in Literature at Duke University. She is the co-translator of Fredric Jameson's *The Political Unconscious* into Swedish. Currently she is working on the relations of modernist aesthetics and technology.

INTRODUCTION

Bernard McGuirk

Redirections at once seek new trajectories and derive from prior movements. Truth, self, action, history, previously linchpins of philosophical and literary critical discourses, have been ever more deprived of their stabilizing functions amidst the multiplicities of a plural theoretical age. Yet as terms, and as values, they have not disappeared; neither have their roles been reallocated as relative turning-points in a metaphysics generally lacking such prime movers. The essays that follow reflect both current developments and reassessments, offering fresh insights and, at the same time, re-evaluations of major issues of the avowedly theoretical era of the late twentieth century. For a decade, the key word in the realm of criticism has been the prefix 'post-': poststructuralism, postmodernity, postfeminisms and so forth. The historical moment of a century moving towards its close, however, cannot be confined to such a postscript. For writing and speaking, thinking and showing move ever on. Intellectual exchange anticipates and activates, as well as reflecting upon, social change. In a climate of often headlong theorizing rhythms, these essays seek to resituate, reanalyse, restructure and reconstruct major figures and configurations of the past.

The first contribution is an important reassessment, by Christopher Norris, of the work of William Empson. The study covers the whole range of Empson's critical writing but invites us to re-examine such works as *Seven Types of Ambiguity, The Structure of Complex Words, Argufying, Some Versions of the Pastoral*, in the light of contemporary theoretical concerns. Norris reminds us that, for Empson, 'criticism is most usefully employed in making rational sense of semantic complications that would otherwise open the way to all manner of mystified quasi-religious doctrine or "paradoxical" pseudo-wisdom'. In the process, he stresses the

> need to distinguish between Empson's strikingly down-to-earth treatment of the sublime and those other (postmodernist or deconstructive) readings that emphasize its aporetic character, its paradoxical claim to 'present the unpresentable', or its power to discompose all the normative categories of thought and perception.

In short, Norris 'sees little virtue in theories that equate the most valuable forms of critical insight with a knowledge that lies somehow beyond the reach of rational analysis, or in a realm of "paradox", "aporia" or flat contradiction where reason fears to tread'.

From his opening comparison of Empson's stance with the arguments of Donald Davidson's 'On the very idea of a conceptual scheme', Norris pursues a wide-ranging and combative series of juxtapositions of Empson's ideas with those of New Critics, neo-Christians, Marxists, structuralists and poststructuralists, ever with a view to demonstrate that, for Empson, 'criticism is simply not doing its job if it fails to make a bridge between "technical" interests and issues of a real-world moral and practical kind'.

While, polemically, focusing on aspects of Empson's work which distinguish his thought from that of such as I. A. Richards and Cleanth Brooks, Norris situates Empson close to philosophers in the Anglo-American 'analytical' tradition (Frege, Russell, Quine) and moves on to outline his 'rational humanist' position. One of the most telling of the comparisons Norris makes is with Mikhail Bakhtin's 'sociological poetics'. Yet even here Empson's rigorous pursuit of fitting the 'relevant historico-semantic' text or context into 'a "grammar" of implicit semantic equations' is set up as a project of the theoretical exposition of 'Truth' values. Finally, Christopher Norris makes an eloquent culminating plea in support of his view that *The Structure of Complex Words* 'is by far the most original and substantial effort of literary theory to have appeared in this country during the past fifty years'.

The 'truth' to its moment – the events of May 1968 – of the critical enterprise of Gilles Deleuze and Felix Guattari is the subject of Nick Heffernan's study. Tracing how they 'successfully assimilated Lacanian theory in order to turn it against itself in defence of the spirit of 1968' in *Anti-Oedipus*, he goes on to illustrate how their project broadened, developed and changed in *A Thousand Plateaus*. The dissolution of subjectivity is 'dramatized' for Heffernan, by the peculiar parallel dissolving of the political into the aesthetic, and vice versa. By situating the Deleuze and Guattari enterprise in its specific poststructuralist historical context, he is able both to trace its demise and, at the same time, to argue for its enduring suggestivity in an era already being classified as post-theoretical.

The underlying assumption that modernity consists in fragmentation and crisis has operated at the level both of general theories (socio-political, cultural, aesthetic) and of specific analyses of individual texts. Steve Giles, in his study of Chekhov's late plays, sets out to theorize what it means to 'be in a state of crisis'. In the process he explores the relationship between paradigm and change largely within a framework of Hegelian theory, juxtaposing his case-study of Chekhov with other models such as the theatre of Büchner and Ibsen with a view to demonstrating a 'final implosion' of the structuring concepts of 'freedom, volition, decision and will'. In short, we are offered here a prefiguration of the modernist abolition of action and self and, concomitantly, a scrutinizing of the concepts of truth and history which all the essays in this volume address.

Finally, Sara Danius, in a meticulous response to Fredric Jameson's own invitation, in *The Political Unconscious*, to be read and tested both theoretically and against his interpretive practice, pursues the case-study of Joseph Conrad. She argues that Jameson's readings are never applications of, but always extensions to, theory. First, however, she offers a thoroughgoing political analysis of Jameson's Marxism as it purports to transcend the theory–practice dichotomy, a tactic designed to reconcile her own treatment of the philosophy of history and textual interpretation as inseparable discursive activities. At the same time, however, she is careful to point out the vulnerabilities of Jameson's and, indeed, her own enterprise. We are left in no doubt that insight is as bedevilled by blindness in the theorizing of history as it has been shown to be – amongst others – in the discourses of truth, of self and of action.

It was originally intended that this volume would appear with Pinter Press as part of a project presenting Nottingham Studies in Critical Theory. This explains the format of *Redirections in Critical Theory: Truth, Self, Action, History*, consisting as it does of two extensive essays by established scholars – one external and one internal to the University of Nottingham Postgraduate School of Critical Theory – and two by former postgraduate members of the School. In Spring 1991, Pinter withdrew from Humanities publishing, and this volume was transferred to Routledge with Pinter's Humanities list.

1

WILLIAM EMPSON AND THE CLAIMS OF THEORY

Christopher Norris

When is a theorist not a theorist? Perhaps when, like William Empson, he starts out by writing an extraordinary first book (*Seven Types of Ambiguity*)[1] which raises all manner of subtle and far-reaching theoretical questions, but then lives on to develop a hearty dislike of the modern 'Eng. Lit.' industry, its ethos of geared-up professional expertise and – most especially – its tiresome display of bother-headed 'theoretical' concern. Such was certainly Empson's response to just about every school or movement of literary theory, from the American New Criticism to structuralism and deconstruction. For a while he made a point of keeping up with these developments, reviewing any books that came his way (though rarely with much enthusiasm), and at least hanging on to the basic conviction – so strong in *Seven Types* – that 'theory' was a worthwhile pursuit just so long as it helped us to puzzle out the sense of some otherwise mysterious passage, and didn't fly off at a speculative tangent, or become tied up in philosophical problems of its own ingenious creating. After all, as he wrote in *Seven Types*,

> [n]ormal sensibility is a tissue of what has been conscious theory made habitual and returned to the pre-conscious, and, therefore, conscious theory may make an addition to sensibility even though it draws no (or no true) conclusion, formulates no general theory, in the scientific sense, which reconciles and makes quickly available the results which it describes.
>
> (p. 254)

At this time Empson was mainly concerned to head off the objections of those posturing aesthetes ('Oxford' types as he tagged

1

them) who would no doubt regard his book as a monstrous piece of clanking theoretical machinery, an approach that threatened to 'kill the plant' – or destroy the very sources of poetic response – by 'pruning down too far toward the emotional roots'. In face of such attitudes Empson felt justified in adopting a stance of sturdy 'Cambridge' rationalism, an outlook informed by his own keen interest in mathematics, theoretical physics, and the scientific disciplines in general. To this extent at least 'theory' was useful: as a means of persuading oneself and others that poetry – even 'obscure' modern poetry – was best approached with the intellect fully engaged, and without giving way to an aestheticist mystique that would leave readers entirely at the mercy of this or that irrational prejudice. In short, 'it is necessary to protect our sensibility against critical dogma, but it is just because of this that the reassurance given by some machinery for analysis has become so necessary in its turn' (*ST*, p. 253). For otherwise one might as well admit that criticism – especially Empson's kind of criticism – performs a great disservice to poetry by analysing that which of its very nature resists the best efforts of analytic commentary.

It is worth looking more closely at Empson's arguments here since they help to explain both his early, positive attitude to 'theory' and the reasons for his subsequent lack of sympathy for what others were attempting to do under the same broad description. In *Seven Types* he takes the view that, if poetry makes sense, then its sense-making properties are likely to be continuous with those of our everyday 'prosaic' understanding, even if raised to a much higher power of semantic or syntactic condensation. At any rate it is better to work on this assumption – to press as far as possible towards analysing the character and sources of poetic 'emotion' – than to take easy refuge in the wholesale aestheticist creed which elevates the mysterious nature of poetry to a high point of critical doctrine. Thus:

> [t]hings temporarily or permanently inexplicable are not, therefore, to be thought of as essentially different from things that can be explained in some terms you happen to have at your disposal; nor can you have reason to think them likely to be different unless there is a great deal about the inexplicable things that you already know.
>
> (*ST*, p. 252)

In other words, there is something wrong – philosophically suspect – about the attitude that treats poetry as somehow vouch-
safing imaginative truths, insights or orders of 'paradoxical'
wisdom that inherently transcend the powers and capacities of
rational thought. Critics who take this line are in much the
same position as cultural relativists who argue that there exist
languages, world-views, scientific paradigms, 'universes of discourse' or whatever that differ so radically from our own (modern
Eurocentric) standpoint that there can, in principle, be no question of 'translating' reliably between them, or at any rate of
knowing for sure that such translation has in fact occurred.[2] For
you could only be in a position to assert this incommensurability-
thesis if you had at least understood sufficient of the language
or world-view in question to register the problems of achieving
any reasonably accurate or truthful grasp. And then of course
the thesis would self-deconstruct, since the very fact of claiming
to be in such a position, i.e., to *know* where the difficulties arose,
would constitute a standing reproof to the claims of any wholesale
cultural-relativist outlook.

This is not to deny – as Empson readily admits – that there
may be 'things temporarily or permanently inexplicable', whether
these have to do with some radically alien set of cultural beliefs,
practices, or life-forms, or perhaps (his more immediate concern)
with some passage of especially opaque poetry that turns out to
baffle the best efforts of rational prose commentary. But to take
these exceptional cases as the norm is to fall into the same
error that anthropologists, philosophers, historians of science and
others make when they conclude on the basis of such localized
(however well-documented) problems that translation between
languages and cultures is a radically impossible enterprise; that
different 'language games' or 'forms of life' are incommensurable
one with another; that there is no judging between various scientific 'paradigms' or 'discourses' since they each set their own,
strictly immanent or *sui generis* terms for understanding; or that
knowledge (including scientific knowledge) is always a product
of the dominant conventions, the professional codes of practice
or research programmes that effectively determine what shall
count as such at any given time. These arguments are open to the
obvious rejoinder, as above: that without at least some measure of
shared understanding across and between languages, disciplines
and cultures the sceptic's positions would be strictly unintelligible,

since they would lack any means of making their point with respect to *particular* or well-attested cases of misunderstanding.[3] In short, this attitude of out-and-out cultural relativism is self-refuting in so far as it trades on a generalized refusal to acknowledge the terms on which *all* understanding necessarily proceeds, at least in so far as it hopes to make sense in the forum of accountable public debate.

Such – in broad outline – is the case advanced by the philosopher Donald Davidson in his well-known essay 'On the Very Idea of a Conceptual Scheme'.[4] His main targets here are the various forms of currently fashionable cognitive scepticism, among them Whorfian ethno-linguistics (where 'truth' and 'reality' are held to be constructed entirely in and through language),[5] Quine's ultra-empiricist attack on the analytic/synthetic distinction (along with his consequent denial of the possibility of 'radical translation'),[6] Feyerabend's anarchist philosophy of science (which throws out all validity-conditions save those adopted more or less at whim on the part of this or that localized short-term collective),[7] and other such versions of the basic idea that all knowledge is mediated by 'conceptual schemes' (language games, 'forms of life', etc.) which differ so fundamentally in respect of their sense-making criteria that nothing could justify our claiming to compare them, or to understand, interpret or criticize one in terms of the other.[8] To this catalogue Davidson might well have added poststructuralism, postmodernism, Foucauldian 'genealogy' (or discourse theory), and at least one variety of deconstruction as practised by (mainly American) literary critics.[9] For with these thinkers also it is a high point of doctrine that 'truth' is nothing more than what counts as such according to the codes, cultural conventions, power/knowledge interests, 'intertextual' relationships and so forth which make up the conditions of intelligibility within this or that field of 'signifying practice'. And he (Davidson) would surely have much the same point to make against this latest efflorescence of epistemic scepticism in a textualist or literary-rhetorical mode. For they all raise the question – wholly unanswerable on their own terms – of just what constitutes a valid (or even meaningful) interpretation when all 'discourses' come down to a play of strictly incommensurable language-games with no rational grounds for adjudicating the issue between them.

It seems to me that Empson is within sight of this question

when he devotes the last chapter of *Seven Types* to a defence of 'analytic', as opposed to subjective or 'appreciative' criticism. For the main purpose of verbal exegesis, as he sees it, is to offer a 'machinery' of rational understanding which may not satisfy the aesthete (on grounds of tact, sensibility or mere good taste), but which can at least give heart to the critic in search of more solid grounds for debate. And this machinery is necessary, he writes,

> partly so as to look as if you knew what you were talking about, partly as a matter of 'style', and partly from the basic assumption of prose that all parts of speech must have some meaning. (These three give the same idea with increasing generality.) Otherwise, one would be constantly stating relations between unknown or indefinite objects, or only stating something *about* such relations, themselves unknown or indefinite, in a way which probably reflects accurately the nature of your statement, but to which only the pure mathematician is accustomed. So that many of my explanations may be demonstrably wrong, and yet efficient for their purpose, and vice versa.
>
> (*ST*, p. 253)

Or again: the situation with criticism is much like that in the sciences, where intuition may go a long way – may indeed be indispensable when it comes to assessing the truth-claims of rival, equally plausible theories – but where one still needs the 'machinery' of rational argument by way of making good some particular claim.

Hence the alternating process, as Empson describes it, between commentary of a broadly 'appreciative' kind and commentary that ignores the rules of good taste and presses as far as it can towards a limit-point of lucid, rational understanding.

> When you have made a quotation, you must first show the reader how you feel about it, by metaphor, implication, devices of sound, or anything else that will work; on the other hand, when you want to make a critical remark, to explain *why* your quotation takes effect as it does, you must state your result as plainly (in as transferable, intellectually handy terms) as you can.
>
> (p. 250)

What this amounts to (as perhaps one might have expected, given

5

Empson's early and continued interest in mathematics and the natural sciences) is a theory of criticism that minimizes – even looks like collapsing – the difference between problems of literary interpretation and problems in the nature of scientific reasoning. His poems of this period show Empson puzzling in much the same way about just how far the more advanced (i.e., speculative) models and metaphors of modern science find expression through modes of 'poetic' reasoning that tend to jump over the logical relations required of a straightforward demonstrative sequence of argument.[10] But it is equally important to recognize that Empson is very far from regarding this as a one-way relation of dependence, a version of the argument (much touted by recent 'radical' philosophers of science) that scientific discovery is ultimately reliant on imaginative 'leaps' that somehow elude all the standard protocols of method and verification.[11] For he is just as keen to make the point that criticism will amount to nothing more than a species of aestheticist self-indulgence if it doesn't give *reasons* – sound analytical reasons – for coming up with this or that ingenious piece of closely wrought verbal exegesis. The one idea that he won't entertain is that poetry somehow expresses a wisdom – an order of 'higher', paradoxical, or purely intuitive thought – beyond the reach of rational analysis. And this was a conviction that stayed with Empson right through to the books and essays of his last period.

In *Seven Types* it produces the strong rationalist conviction that poetry ought to make sense according to the best, most rigorous (if 'prosaic') standards of hard-pressed analytic commentary. Thus

> explanations of literary matters ... , involving as they do much apparently random invention, are more like Pure than Analytical Geometry, and, if you cannot think of a construction, that may show that you would be wise to use a different set of methods, but cannot show the problem is of a new kind.
>
> (pp. 252–3)

What I think this means – and the meaning is far from self-evident – is that theory works best if allowed to settle down into a generalized sense that adequate explanations ought to be available, even in cases of 'obscure' modern verse where the meaning (in Wallace Stevens's pregnant phrase) 'resists the intel-

6

ligence almost successfully'. In other words, criticism has to operate on the principle that any poem worth the effort of detailed
exegesis will most likely make sense in rationally accountable
terms, and that where such efforts fail – or find themselves at
last driven back upon talk of 'deep' symbolism, obscure private
motives, paradoxical truths or whatever – then one can always go
back and try another analytical 'construction'. Thus

> [any] advance in the machinery of description makes a
> reader feel stronger about his appreciations, more reliably
> able to distinguish the private or accidental from the criti-
> cally important or repeatable, more confident of the reality
> (that is, the transferability) of his experiences; adds, in
> short, in the mind of the reader to the things there to be
> described, whether or not it makes those particular things
> more describable.
>
> (p. 254)

For it is Empson's firm belief that the only way to read intelli-
gently is to keep the reasoning faculties fully in gear and not to
go along with emotive, symbolist, Jungian or other such doctrines
that would sever all links between poetic language and the language of plain-prose reason. This is not to say that there may not
be passages, and among them passages of genuinely powerful,
haunting or profound poetry, which in the end turn out to elude
all the critic's dogged sense-making efforts. Such was Empson's
experience with the lines from Wordsworth's 'Tintern Abbey'
which he puzzled over at length in *Seven Types* and took up again
– hoping to explain the puzzlement – in a chapter of his later
book *The Structure of Complex Words*.[12] But instances like this,
though not at all uncommon, were best regarded as exceptions
that in some sense proved the rule, or cases that could only be
dealt with adequately by keeping one's rational defences up and
not (so to speak) admitting defeat at the first hurdle.

Such was at any rate the lesson that Empson drew from the
scientific disciplines – especially the advances in theoretical physics – that dominated the Cambridge intellectual scene during his
student years. It was an outlook as remote as possible from the
kinds of extreme cognitive scepticism or the varieties of relativist
doctrine which nowadays pass (at least among literary theorists)
as the last word in *au courant* philosophy of science. Small
wonder, as I have said, that Empson found himself increasingly

at odds with an enterprise (that of professional 'Eng. Lit.') whose
drift he perceived as getting further and further out of touch
with the interests of science and – more urgently – the needs of
enlightened rational understanding. Not that this involved the
kind of vulgar positivist conception of science and truth that
literary theorists are apt to hold up as a justification for their
own more 'sophisticated' views. (Barthes's *Critique et vérité* has a
good deal to answer for here,[13] along with the anti-cognitivist bias
of American New Criticism and – albeit from a very different
angle – F. R. Leavis in his absurd crusade against science during
the 'two cultures' debate with C. P. Snow.) On the contrary:
Empson saw very clearly that such a model was out of the question, not only for literary criticism but even (or especially) for
the kinds of scientific enquiry that most engaged his speculative
interest. In *Seven Types*, as indeed in his poems of the period,
Empson shows himself fully up-to-date with ideas – like Heisen-
berg's Uncertainty Principle – which had already done much to
problematize the relation between knower and known, or scientific observation and the order of 'objective' reality. All of which
tended to complicate his view that verbal analysis was the right
way for criticism to go, or at any rate a method that would serve
critics better than the lame retreat into various kinds of emotivist,
irrationalist or aestheticist doctrine. For very often one had to
concede, as he put it, that 'the act of knowing is itself an act of
sympathizing; unless you are enjoying the poetry you cannot
create it, as poetry, in your mind' (*ST,* p. 248).

On the one hand this meant that any claims for 'analytical' as
opposed to 'appreciative' criticism had better take account of
these deep-laid problems and not pin their faith to an old-
fashioned positivist paradigm which no longer possessed much
credibility even among scientists. Such would be the view that
'the mind, otherwise passive, collects propositions about the outside world' (p. 248); a view whose application to poetry would at
least have the negative virtue of showing up its inbuilt limitations,
or 'reduc[ing] that idea of truth (much more intimately than
elsewhere) to a self-contradiction' (p. 249). But this is no reason
– so Empson maintains – to go along with the prevalent idea
of poetry as somehow enjoying a special dispensation from the
standards of rational accountability or plain good sense. Least of
all could it justify what Empson regards as the desperate recourse
to emotivist doctrines that entirely sever the link between poetry

and other (scientific, philosophical or everyday) uses of language. This last had been the view of I. A. Richards, argued in a series of influential books, notably his *Principles of Literary Criticism* (1927).[14] On Richards's view, it was simply a muddle – a species of category-mistake – to worry about the status of poetical truth-claims as if they aspired to the condition of a constative (i.e. factual or assertoric) truth. Poems were valuable chiefly for their power of evoking a complex *emotional* response in the reader's mind, a state in which the chaos of our humdrum, day-to-day experience could achieve a mometary 'equipoise' or balance of diverse (normally conflicting) psychological impulses. The greatest poetry, according to Richards, is the product of 'exceptional experiences' in the lives of 'exceptional individuals'. Its power to communicate such privileged moments comes from the poet's peculiar gift for condensing a range of otherwise confused or contradictory emotions into a verbal form that achieves the maximum degree of lucidity and poise. But it can do so only on the condition that readers approach it in the proper frame of mind, that is to say, by suspending the standards appropriate to other (truth-functional) kinds of discourse, and effecting that 'complete severance of poetry from belief' which Richards (like the early T. S. Eliot) considered the *sine qua non* of its survival in a scientific age.

What this amounts to is a modern restatement of Matthew Arnold's case in 'The Study of Poetry', retaining the stress on literature's vital role as a force for cultural renewal, but adopting the language of behaviourist psychology to back up its claims. The march of science had left small room for those forms of collective belief or imaginary projection that had once made it possible to feel at home in an otherwise hostile or indifferent universe. Poetry can 'save' us, Richards believes, but only if we learn to read it aright, and give up thinking of poetic truth as in any way subject to the normal criteria of factual or veridical discourse. This means accepting that poets deal only in varieties of 'pseudo-statement', sentences which share the grammatical *form* but not – he insists – the assertoric *force* of genuine propositions. Otherwise poetry must forfeit all claim to be taken seriously in an age when science has pressed so far towards defining the terms of rational debate in every other realm of enquiry. Richards would seem to have arrived at this conclusion by endorsing the logical-positivist argument in its strongest (and least tenable) form, i.e. that the only propositions which really made sense were those that squared with the world-view of modern scientific reason, or which lent themselves to verification in accordance with principles derived from that programme. Thus truth-values would apply to just two classes of utterance: empirical truths-of-observation on the one hand and purely analytic (hence empty or tautologous) statements of logical necessity on the other. Hence Richard's unfortunate retreat – as Empson saw it – into a form of dead-end 'emotivist' doctrine that attempted to save appearances by cutting poetry off from any semblance of rational sense.

The American New Critics, Wimsatt and Brooks chief among them, did nothing to challenge this anti-cognitivist bias despite their taking issue with Richards's 'affective' or psychologistic premises.[15] What they managed, in effect, was a wholesale transfer of priorities from the realm of subjective reader-response to that of the poem as 'verbal icon', an inwrought structure of paradox, irony, or multiple meaning under whatever favoured designation. It would then become possible – so they hoped – to place criticism on a properly disciplined or methodical footing by avoiding the appeal to reader-response with all its impressionistic vagaries, and attending instead to the 'words on the page', or those various privileged figures and tropes that characterized poetic language. But they retained from Richards the same root conviction that poetry wasn't in the business of offering arguments, advancing truth-claims, or in any way providing fit material for the purposes of logico-semantic analysis. Indeed their whole approach was premised, like his, on a principle of non-continuity between poetry and other kinds of discourse, a *de jure* principle which required – among other things – that critics should respect the (supposedly) autonomous character of poetic language and form, and thus guard against the manifold 'heresies' of paraphrase, biography, historical source-hunting, sociological background-studies and so forth. What these approaches had in common was a tendency to substitute content-analysis (or an unseemly rush from words to world) for the effort of detailed rhetorical exegesis which alone provided an adequate grasp of the poem's meaning and structure. And this applied above all to the 'heresy of paraphrase', the idea that one could so far separate 'form' and 'content' as to offer a plain-prose summary which fleshed out the poem's meaning in conveniently simplified terms. In which case – according to the New Critics – one might as well give up reading poetry altogether, since any difference between it and the various discourses that attempted to analyse, describe or explain it could only be a matter of degree, not a qualitative difference, and would therefore tend to reduce or disappear as soon as one applied the requisite analytic skills. Only by respecting the uniqueness of poetry – its resistance to paraphrase and other such reductive ploys – could criticism make out a convincing case for the continued value of literary studies in an age of rampant scientism or technocratic reason.

Thus the New Critics followed Richards in this respect at least: they drew a firm line between the rational prose virtues that (supposedly) governed their own interpretive procedure and the realm of poetic meaning where issues of truth and falsehood – or of argumentative warrant – no longer had any significant role to play. For Empson, on the contrary, there seemed little point in pursuing an 'emotive' (or non-cognitivist) theory of poetic language whose effect – as he saw it – was to isolate literature in a self-enclosed realm of feelings or affects which bore no relation to wider practical or socio-political concerns. In *Seven Types* the main thrust of this argument is against the kind of woolly-minded 'appreciative' criticism which shies away from verbal analysis for fear of harming our delicate intuitive responses. Empson puts this case most forcefully in a 1930 article responding to John Sparrow's polemical attack on Richards, Cambridge, and the newly emergent 'school' of tough-minded analytic criticism.[16] Where Sparrow goes wrong – in company (one might add) with many reviewers of *Seven Types* – is in trying to separate enjoyment from analysis, or judgements of value (supposedly arrived at on the basis of 'pure intuition') from the process of patiently figuring out what this or that passage actually means. But he ignores all the evidence, as Empson argues, that 'those who judge in literary matters by "intuition" always assume a legacy of analysis, and complain when it is carried further'. Thus Sparrow treats 'beauty' as a simple noun, a non-natural attribute (like 'goodness' in G. E. Moore's ethical theory) which somehow typifies our best, most responsive and rewarding moments of experience, but which cannot be in any way explained or analysed beyond making the right appreciative noises. To Empson, this seemed nothing more than an easy escape-route, a retreat not only from problems in the realm of aesthetics or literary theory, but also from those

11

very real difficulties which arose at every point in the effort to understand other people's motives and intentions. In short, it is an outlook which 'stultifies the intelligence, abolishes criticism, makes most of the facts about beautiful things unintelligible, and leaves us with a sense that the whole thing is a necromancy to which any charlatan may have the password'.[17] Thus Sparrow is here cast as a typical 'Oxford' aesthete, a critic who refuses to examine the sources of his own emotive reactions, and who therefore remains entirely at the mercy of whatever irrational prejudice may happen to capture his mind. Whereas it is the great virtue of 'analysis', as Empson sees it, to make us more aware of those prejudicial blind-spots and thus more capable of thinking our way through and beyond them.

All the same Empson is willing to concede that there *is* something deeply problematic about the claims of analytical criticism, especially when these are combined – as in Richards – with a sense that poetry needs to preserve its mysterious, 'inexplicable' power if it is ever to provide the imaginative sustenance required in a post-religious world of drastically naturalized meanings and values. To Sparrow this seems nothing more than a cheat on Richards's part, a means of smuggling myth and magic back in by the back door while exploiting the appeal of a 'method' that trades on its pseudo-scientific credentials. For Empson, conversely, the issue about 'analysis' must be seen as one of those deep and *inescapable* problems which arise as soon as one reflects on the nature and limits of human understanding. In fact his rejoinder to Sparrow at this point reads like a synopsis of what Kant has to say in that section of the First *Critique* devoted to the 'Antinomies of Pure Reason'.

> The prime intellectual difficulty of our age is that true beliefs may make it impossible to act rightly; that we cannot think without verbal fictions; that they must not be taken for true beliefs, and yet must be taken seriously; that it is essential to analyze beauty; essential to accept it unanalyzed; essential to believe that the universe is deterministic; essential to act as if it was not. None of these abysses, however, opened under Mr Sparrow's feet.[18]

Empson's point is that you won't avoid these problems – whether in ethics, epistemology, aesthetics, or literary criticism – by adopting the kind of blinkered emotivist outlook which counts them irrelevant for the purposes of ordinary, day-to-day human understanding. For the result of such thinking, as shown by Sparrow, is to fall back on vague appeals to 'intuition' that make no allowance for the reasoned appraisal of motives, meanings and intentions. So the puzzle about analytic criticism is often within reach of larger questions as to how we can cope with those various vexing antimonies (free will *versus* determinism, etc.) which don't disappear through a simple application of intuitive or commonsense criteria.

On this point Empson is fully in agreement with Richards, whatever his differences elsewhere: that the 'scientific' method which Sparrow so despises is better than any amount of 'appreciative' waffle since it does at least try to sort these problems into some kind of humanly intelligible sense. Richards is right to take a robust line on the question of reader-response (or affective psychology), and is also quite justified – Empson thinks – in treating poetry as fit material for tests under near-laboratory conditions, tests which take it pretty much for granted (1) that there is no ultimate mystery about poems, (2) that their language is continuous with the language of straightforward prose communication, and therefore (3) that any failures of readerly grasp can best be understood – and hopefully remedied – by examining the various causal factors (social, cultural, psychological, etc.) which may be shown to have brought them about. All this strikes Empson as far preferable to Sparrow's squeamish protests on behalf of an obscurantist ethos which amounts to little more than a species of 'Oxford' high-table snobbery. Where he *will* take issue with Richards – increasingly so in his articles and reviews of the next two decades – is over the argument that criticism can only practise these needful therapeutic skills on condition that it treat poetry as an 'emotive' form of utterance, a language-game devoid of truth-telling warrant, cognitive interests, or veridical force. Only thus, Richards thinks, can poetry 'save' us from the encroachments of science in an age given over to positivist conceptions of meaning and method. That criticism should emulate these methods – that is to say, turn itself into a branch of behavioural psychology – is a development that Richards can happily endorse since it promises to place literary studies on a footing with the other, more prestigious 'sciences of man'. But there would be no point in mounting such a strong neo-Arnoldian case for the high destinies of poetry if it weren't for this saving difference between poetic and other (referential or truth-functional) varieties of discourse. For on Richards's view – again carried over from the logical positivists – it is impossible to conceive how poetry could ever be taken seriously except by suspending those otherwise normative conditions for valid utterance and treating it as a language of 'pseudo-statements' devoid of any genuine propositional force.

In his rejoinder to Sparrow there are signs already that Empson is unwilling to take his doctrine on board. He concedes that the emotivist argument might be more 'decently plausible' when applied to painting or the other visual arts since here 'the modes of satisfaction are little understood, and are far removed from the verbal system on which the discursive intelligence usually supports itself.'[19] But it shouldn't be so attractive to literary critics whose main business, after all, is to explain as best they can how language works, including the language of poetry, and who therefore shouldn't rest content with 'explanations' which in fact explain nothing bar their own deep puzzlement. This was why Empson went on, in *The Structure of Complex Words*, to develop a theory of multiple meaning that would offer precisely a working account of that 'verbal system on which the discursive intelligence usually supports itself'. *Seven Types*, he came to feel, had rather fudged this issue by ranging its examples on a vaguely defined scale of 'increasing logical and psychological complexity', with a clear implication that the best, most rewarding cases were those that involved a downright clash of contradictory beliefs or attitudes. Thus the Seventh Type is the kind that occurs 'when the two opposite meanings of the word, the two values of the ambiguity, are the two opposite meanings defined by the context, so that the total effect is to show a fundamental division in the writer's mind' (*ST*, p. 192). But there is a problem with this if you believe, like Empson, that criticism is most usefully employed in making rational sense of semantic complications that would otherwise open the way to all manner of mystified quasi-religious doctrine or 'paradoxical' pseudo-wisdom. For it did seem to many readers of the book that Empson was implying an equation – or at any rate a strong elective affinity – between full-blown cases of the Seventh Type and states of psychological conflict in the poet which most often resulted from some 'deep' clash of unconscious motives or desires. And many of his examples – especially the closing *tour de force* on George Herbert's 'The Sacrifice' – tended

14

to support this impression in so far as they focused on religious poetry where the orthodox (Christian devotional) reading came up against the signs of neurotic self-doubt engendered by adherence to a harshly paradoxical creed.

Hence the final image of Christ in Herbert's poem:

> scapegoat and tragic hero; loved because hated; hated because godlike; freeing from torture because tortured; torturing his torturers because all-merciful; source of strength to all men because by accepting he exaggerates their weakness; and, being outcast, creating the possibility of society.
>
> (*ST,* p. 233)

It is clear enough, from this passage and others like it, that Empson not only viewed such paradoxes as a great source of poetic concentration and power, but had also come to think of them – no doubt in consequence of reading some of Freud's late essays – as compulsively repeating a primal scene of repressed sacrificial guilt and desire which was played out over and again in the consciousness of latter-day 'civilized' reason.[20] Thus 'Herbert deals in this poem, on the scale and by the methods necessary to it, with the most complicated and deeply-rooted notion of the human mind' (p. 233). This idea is taken up in *Some Versions of Pastoral* (1935), where it becomes a kind of ground-bass or running theme for the various stages of thematic transformation – again laid out on a scale of increasing psychological complexity – that characterize the history of 'pastoral' writing in Empson's massively extended definition of that term.[21] Indeed, one could argue that Empsonian pastoral is not so much a genre or literary 'form' as a standing possibility for endless variation on a basic structure of feeling, a technique of self-complicating irony ('putting the complex into the simple') whose instances range from the highly conventional – the Renaissance courtier-as-swain – to a poet like Marvell, suggesting profound philosophical puzzles in a style of relaxed contemplative ease, or again works like *The Beggars' Opera* or *Alice in Wonderland* where Empson finds a cluster of deeply ambivalent (not to say perverse) motives gathering around the figures of MacHeath, the sacrificial victim-hero and Alice, the child as idealized image of adult fantasy-projection. Such is presumably what Empson means when he talks (*à propos* the Seventh Type) about ambiguities that in the end have to do with 'the most complicated and deeply-rooted notion of the

15

human mind'. For behind all these variants – even the 'simplest' – there is more than a hint of the primal scene evoked in Empson's analysis of Herbert, a scene that many readers will nowadays associate with René Girard and his dark meditations on 'mimetic rivalry' and the origin of human social institutions in the act of (real or imaginary) parricide that first gave rise to the bonding-through-guilt of the parties to that fabulous event.[22]

However, there is still some doubt in Empson's mind as to whether such 'deep' ambiguities should really be thought of as fit material for the literary critic's purpose. Neil Hertz, in his article 'More lurid figures', has some shrewd things to say about the sense of gathering tension and excitement that overtakes Empson's writing as he approaches the 'secret places of the Muse', a domain where the ground rules of logic appear to be suspended, where the law of contradiction no longer holds, and where one ought to feel 'something of the awe and horror which are felt by Dante finally arriving at the most centrique part of earth, of Satan, and of hell' (*ST*, p. 196). For indeed one can view the whole book as building up to those extraordinary instances of the Seventh Type, cases that offer the maximum resistance to any reading premised on rationalist ideas of language, truth and logic. No doubt Hertz is right when he suggests that these pages convey a sense of threshold or liminal experience, an 'allegory of reading' (in de Man's terminology) or an 'end-of-the-line' encounter (Hertz) which can only find voice through such a rhetoric of crisis whose nearest equivalent is the Kantian or Romantic sublime.[23] At least this would explain something of Empson's disquiet as he moves into regions of conflict, paradox or advanced logical disorder where the conscious mind seems increasingly out of its depth. One could then perhaps read the essay on Marvell in *Some Versions* as a kind of pastoral self-reassurance on Empson's part, a reminder that poetry can evoke mental states which are 'neither conscious nor not conscious', which involve all manner of subliminal ideas or thoughts beyond reach of lucid awareness, but which none the less provide an apt stimulus for the poet's 'conceited' metaphysical style. 'Here as usual with "profound" remarks the strength of the thing is to combine unusually intellectual with unusually primitive ideas; thought about the conditions of knowledge with a magical idea that the adept controls the external world by thought' (*SVP*, p. 99). Many readers have felt that the essay, like the poem, has a sense of exhilaration which comes of its somehow holding these anti-monies in a state of rapt, near-mystical repose, a mood rather seldom to be found in Empson's criticism. After all, 'the chief point of the poem', as he reads it, 'is to contrast and reconcile conscious and unconscious states, intuitive and intellectual modes of apprehension . . . like the seventh Buddhist heaven of Enlight-enment' (p. 99).

It seems to me that this impression has a lot to do with Empson's strongly felt need, in the early criticism, to find some way beyond all those problems thrown up by the depth-psychological approach, problems that had scarcely been laid to rest in the reply to Sparrow or the closing chapter of *Seven Types*. At least on this occasion – in the reading of Marvell – Empson seems largely untroubled by such problems and ready to follow out the poem's suggestions for a life of unimpeded harmonious balance between instinct and reason, will and self-knowledge, unconscious impulse and reflective awareness. So there is maybe something a bit too portentous – a slight misjudgement of tone – about Hertz's reading of the Seventh Type as an approach to the 'secret places of the Muse' that brings Empson out in the company of de Man and other such essayers of language at the limit. In fact his more usual way of handling these 'deep' ambiguities is to admit that they may point back to some kind of 'deep' psychological disturbance or 'primitive' (prelogical) confusion, but then suggest various ways to fit them into a ration-ally intelligible structure. Thus 'although such words appeal to the fundamental habits of the human mind, and are fruitful of irrationality, they are to be expected from a rather sophisticated state of language and feeling' (*ST*, p. 195). It is at this point precisely that ambiguities of the Seventh Type may be seen to shade off into a version of pastoral, or a mode of understanding which treats them reflexively as topics for the play of self-con-scious speculative thought.

Again, these ideas are often within reach of something very like the Kantian sublime, a topos much invoked by present-day theorists of a deconstructive or postmodern bent.[24] That is to say, they figure at the limit-point where thought comes up against some obstacle, some overwhelming force or check to its powers of cognitive grasp, such that the mind at first fails to discover any adequate (conceptual or linguistic) means of representation, but then turns this failure around, so to speak, by finding *within itself* the autonomous potential – the capacity for creative self-renewal – which transforms such experiences into a source of moral and imaginative strength. Empson's chapter on Marvell offers several striking examples, among them *The Ancient Mariner* (where 'so long as the Mariner is horrified by the creatures of the calm he is their slave; he is set free to act, in the supreme verses of the poem, as soon as he delights in them') and the story by Poe where 'the sailor in *The Maelstrom* is so horrified as to be frozen, by a trick of neurosis, into idle curiosity, and this becomes a scientific interest in the portent which shows him the way to escape from it' (*SVP*, p. 101). Like 'The Garden' – though in a more dramatic fashion – these works communicate a powerful sense that the mind somehow contains all of nature, is able to comprehend or 'control' it through thought, so that differences between subject and object (or conscious and unconscious knowledge) are momentarily suspended in a state of achieved reflective equilibrium. All of which would tend to support Hertz's claim that Empson was at this time much engaged with issues in the region of the Kantian sublime.

But it is also worth noting how he gives the whole topic a markedly different philosophical slant by stressing those elements of conscious, rational, 'witty' or reflective self-knowledge that enable these poets to attain something like a perspective atop all the vexing antinomies that would otherwise threaten to 'freeze' thinking in a state of self-induced neurotic deadlock or disabling aporia. For here, as in *Seven Types*, Empson sees little hope for improved understanding in the kind of criticism that seeks out 'deep' conflicts – whether of a psychological or an epistemological order – with a view to pointing up the inherent limitations of rational-discursive thought. This is why he prefers to treat of the sublime (or its pastoral equivalent) as essentially a matter of 'putting the complex into the simple', of discovering some social-communicative basis for experiences that would otherwise occupy the realm of private neurosis or psychopathology. This 'grand theme' may have its 'root in magic' but is still very strong, Empson suggests, 'among the mountain climbers and often the scientists' (*SVP*, p. 100). In other words, it is a source of very real practical (at times, life-saving) benefits which probably have to do with our capacity – especially when under pressure or in circumstances of extreme physical danger – to perform highly complex mental operations that are only called 'intuitive' for lack of any adequate descriptive or analytical machinery. At any rate there does seem a need to distinguish between Empson's strikingly down-to-earth treatment of the sublime and those other (postmodernist or deconstructive) readings that emphasize its aporetic character, its paradoxical claim to 'present the unpresentable', or its power to discompose all the normative categories of thought and perception.

This difference is well brought out in Empson's gloss on the notion of 'transcendence' as it figures in the famous lines of Marvell describing the state of contemplative repose to which pastoral ideally gives access. ('The Mind, that Ocean where each kind / Does streight its own resemblance find; / Yet it creates, transcending these, / Far other worlds, and other Seas, . . .') His main point is that the paradoxes here can best be interpreted by trying to sort them into some kind of rational sense, even while conceding – as the poem powerfully suggests – that there may be states of mind ('unconscious', 'preconscious' or whatever) that lie beyond reach of knowing exegesis or plain-prose commentary. What seems to be involved at this point, according to Empson, is

> a transition from the correspondences of thought with fact to those of thought with thought, to find which is to be creative; there is necessarily here a suggestion of rising from one 'level' of thought to another; and in the next couplet not only does the mind transcend the world it mirrors, but a sea, to which it is parallel, transcends both land and sea too, which implies self-consciousness and all the antinomies of philosophy. Whether or not you give *transcendent* the technical sense 'predicable of all categories' makes no great difference; by including everything in itself the mind includes as a detail itself and all its inclusions.
>
> (*SVP*, pp. 104–5)

This passage comes as close as any to capturing the subtle transformation that the sublime undergoes when brought into contact with the Pastoral complex of themes, metaphors, or structural ironies. That is to say, there is a shift of philosophical viewpoint which also entails a certain shift of register or tone, a marked disinclination to dwell on the deeper, darker sources of the sublime experience, and a corresponding stress on those aspects that belong to the order of conscious, reflective self-knowledge. In part this has to do with Empson's often-stated principle that the mind has to labour against sizable odds of prejudice, self-ignorance, or irrationality, and that criticism should therefore do its best to cast light on these blind spots wherever they occur, rather than make matters worse by adopting its own kinds of obfuscatory rhetoric. Such, as we have already seen, is his attitude when dealing with ambiguities of the Seventh Type, and it is an outlook carried over into Pastoral by way of the various adaptive strategies (or techniques for 'putting the complex into the simple') which characterize that protean genre. But there is also, I think, a much stronger claim involved here, one that amounts to something more than just a matter of temperamental bias (i.e. Empson's characteristic 'tone' of sturdy commonsense rationalism), or a bottom-line pragmatist ground of appeal (his feeling that critics are best employed making 'decently intelligible' sense of any puzzles or obscurities that come their way). What is really at stake in all this is the question whether language can provide a basis for the kind of rationalist interpretive 'machinery' that Empson wishes to build on it. And indeed, the whole development of his critical thinking after *Seven Types* and *Some Versions* can be seen as an attempt to answer this question in a way that would hold up philosophically as well as helping with interpretive problems as and when they arise.

Pastoral would figure from this point of view as a cover term or conveniently loose generic description for the kinds of text that enabled Empson to address matters of depth psychology (or downright conflicts of motive and meaning) without giving way to an irrationalist persuasion that such cases must exceed all the powers of analytic thought. He thinks it important to maintain this position since otherwise one is left, in literature as in life, at the mercy of deep-laid impulses or drives that supposedly resist any form of self-enlightening explanatory grasp. As Empson puts it in a characteristic passage towards the close of *Seven Types*:

> human life is so much a matter of juggling with contradictory impulses . . . that one is accustomed to thinking people are probably sensible if they follow first one, then the other, of two such courses; any inconsistency that it seems possible to act upon shows that they are in possession of the right number of principles, and have a fair title to humanity. Thus any contradiction is likely to have some sensible inter-

pretation; and if you think of interpretations which are not sensible, it puts the blame on you.

(p. 197)

As I have said, this adds up to an attitude fairly remote from the brooding intensity or 'end-of-the-line' meditation that critics like Hertz and Paul de Man have discovered in Empson's early criticism.[25] There are two main points that such readings tend to ignore. The first has to do with his principled assumption that any conflicts uncovered by the depth-hermeneutical approach will most likely turn out to have some 'sensible' (i.e., rationally explicable) meaning, as for instance when writers have to cope with the demands of opposed or contradictory value-systems and do so by keeping both in play through devices like ambiguity, pastoral, double irony, multiple plots and so forth. From which it follows – secondly – that Empson sees little virtue in theories that equate the most valuable or furthest-reaching forms of critical insight with a knowledge that lies somehow beyond reach of rational analysis, or in a realm of 'paradox', 'aporia' or flat contradiction where reason fears to tread.

In his middle-period essays and reviews this aversion was most often expressed with regard to the American New Criticism and its bad habit – as Empson thought – of raising paradox into an absolute measure of poetic worth. The effect of this doctrine was to deny poetry any cognitive, assertoric, or truth-telling force and treat it as a purely rhetorical construction out of the various privileged tropes and figures that comprised the New Critical lexicon.[26] What Empson chiefly objects to here is the whole dogmatic apparatus of checks and prohibitions which theorists like W. K. Wimsatt ran up around the tenets of 'old' New Critical orthodoxy. In particular he rejects the twofold ban on 'intentionalist' readings and those that have resort to *paraphrase*, or any kind of plain-prose rendition, in the attempt to clarify nuances of meaning and style. In both cases, so Empson argues, these critics are perversely denying themselves access to a level of everyday interpretive competence which operates in *all* varieties of human social exchange, from casual talk to the most complex forms of literary communication. The only result of setting up these absurd 'heresies' is to trivialize poetry and criticism by sealing them off within a realm of purely aesthetic meanings and values, a domain of 'pseudo-statements' where poets are assumed

21

not to mean what they say in any serious sense, and where questions of argumentative validity (or truth and falsehood) cannot be raised without falling foul of one or another prohibition.

> Consider the Law, which might be expected to reject a popular fallacy; it recognizes amply that one can tell a man's intention, and ought to judge him by it. Only in the criticism of literature, a thing delicately concerned with human intimacy, are we told that we must give up all idea of knowing his intention.[27]

And the effect is even worse, as Empson came to feel, when this self-denying ordinance is joined on to an irrationalist craze for 'paradoxical' meanings (or deep symbolist interpretations) which make a full-scale programme of rejecting the appeal to normative standards of debate. For it then becomes possible for the high priests and mystagogues of Eng. Lit. fashion – mostly 'neo-Christians' of varying doctrinal adherence – to impute all manner of repellent theological beliefs under cover of a theory (the 'intentional fallacy') that prevents the author from *arguing back* to any real or convincing effect.

That Empson felt obliged to take some of the blame for this bad state of affairs is evident in his 1963 review of an essay on George Herbert by T. S. Eliot, undoubtedly the single most influential figure in the neo-Christian crusade. After all, he now reflects, *Seven Types* had got itself pretty deep into paradox and kindred forms of irrational rhetoric, not least in those climactic pages on Herbert that represent ambiguity at its furthest (and undoubtedly most intriguing) reach. Empson's later thoughts are worth noting at length since they bring out his reasons for rejecting this approach on moral, intellectual, and scholarly grounds.

> I put 'The Sacrifice' last of the examples in my book, to stand for the most extreme kind of ambiguity, because it presents Jesus as at the same time forgiving his torturers and condemning them to eternal torture. It now strikes me that my attitude was what I have come to call 'Neo-Christian'; happy to find such an extravagant specimen, I slapped the author on the back and egged him on to be even nastier . . . [Rosamund] Tuve seemed disposed to treat me as a pagan stumbling towards the light. Clearer now

about what the light illuminates, I am keen to stumble away from it.[28]

But in fact, if one then turns back to the offending pages, it soon becomes clear that Empson is not really doing himself justice – or has at any rate misremembered certain crucial details – in issuing this retrospective *mea culpa*. For the reading of Herbert by no means goes along with an irrationalist mystique that would elevate paradox (or the mysteries of Christian atonement) to the status of sublime or transcendent truths beyond reach of rational criticism. Indeed, the predominant tone of these pages is one of quizzical detachment mixed with a certain anthropological interest in the way such ideas – 'deep-rooted' but none the less repulsive – can exert a hold upon even the most subtle intelligences. Moreover, the effect is to credit Herbert himself with a degree of civilized, self-distancing irony that operates (like Pastoral) to place these harshly paradoxical notions in a larger context of socialized meanings and values. Thus

> the various sets of conflicts in the Christian doctrine of the Sacrifice are stated with an assured and easy simplicity, a reliable and unassuming grandeur, extraordinary in any material, but unique as achieved by successive fireworks of contradiction, and a mind jumping like a flea.
>
> (*ST*, p. 226)

Such is indeed, as Empson views it, the chief virtue of the so-called 'metaphysical' style: this capacity to handle deep-seated conflicts of motive and belief by treating them not as profound (paradoxical) truths beyond reach of further analysis, but as puzzles best approached in a spirit of open-minded readiness for public debate.

So it is Empson's main objection to Wimsatt and the other guardians of New Critical orthodoxy that their precepts, if acted upon consistently, would leave no room for this kind of dialogical engagement, or indeed for any criticism that treated poetry as more than a pure, self-occupied play with its own tropological conventions. That is to say, one could always invoke the 'intentionalist fallacy' against any critic who presumed to find *arguments* (or propositional content) in poetry, and who then went on – like Empson – to suggest how these arguments might link up with questions of a psycho-biographical or wider socio-cultural

23

import. And the 'heresy of paraphrase' would likewise come in handy for discrediting the notion – such a staple of Empson's approach in *Seven Types* – that one can make at least a decent shot at explaining what poems are about by offering a simplified prose restatement of the passage in question (or multiple attempts to tease out the sense), and leaving the reader to sort these efforts into some kind of working synthesis. That there is no good reason *in principle* why this method shouldn't succeed – no reason, that is, having to do with poetry's uniquely 'paradoxical' mode of utterance, or its belonging to a realm of autonomous values discontinuous with the interests of plain-prose discourse – is an argument everywhere implicit in Empson's quarrel with the New Criticism. In *Seven Types*, writing in an age of happy innocence before these 'bother-headed' theories cropped up, he just takes it pretty much for granted that critics are in the business of hunting out authorial intentions, and that where those intentions prove hard to establish – as happens with cases of 'advanced logical or psychological disorder' – then one had best cast around for some 'rational' explanation that at least gives the author full credit for not taking refuge in this or that half-baked 'paradoxical' creed. Otherwise criticism is liable to fall into a kind of reverse-Pastoral strategy, 'putting the simple into the complex', or making authors out to be more simple-minded – more completely at the mercy of irrational promptings – than need be supposed on a fairly basic principle of interpretive charity.

Empson made the point again in his 1950 contribution to a *Kenyon Review* symposium on 'verbal analysis' or the style of intensive close reading which he, more than anyone, had been instrumental in promoting.

> These extra meanings are present, [Empson writes], not in any deep unconscious, but in the preconscious levels where we handle lexicon and grammar, in our ordinary talk, at the speed we do (surely the various current uses of the word must be in the mind somehow, or how can we pick out the right one so quickly?)[29]

This passage takes up several arguments that are there implicitly in *Seven Types* but which only emerge to full view when Empson finds himself obliged to defend them in face of neo-Christian, New Critical and other such emergent irrationalist trends. They include (1) the continuity principle, that poetic understanding is

24

not *essentially* different from the kinds of 'everyday' linguistic grasp required to make sense of straightforward communicative discourse; (2) the idea that criticism (like linguistics) had best focus on the 'preconscious' level of mental activity, since it is here – rather than burrowing down to some notional 'unconscious' depths – that we are likeliest to get useful results; and (3) that any insights thus produced will involve not only a *semantics* of multiple meaning but also a *grammar* (or a logico-grammatical component) capable of fitting that semantics into a larger context of interpretive theory. Such was indeed the project that Empson had already undertaken in the work that occupied much of his time during the late 1940s, that is to say, the various essays that were eventually collected in his finest (but as yet little understood) book, *The Structure of Complex Words*. What I want to do now is give some idea of how that work developed out of his earlier interests, and then place it in relation to other, more *au courant* forms of literary theory. For if poststructuralists (among others) have much to learn from Empson – especially on questions of logic, language and truth – it will also mean unlearning some cardinal tenets of the latest theoretical wisdom on such matters.

ROMANTIC IRONY AND THE LIMITS OF PASTORAL

I have suggested that Pastoral was one way forward from those vexing antinomies that Empson discovered when trying to make 'decently intelligible' sense of ambiguities of the Seventh Type. In fact one could read the whole sequence of chapters in *Some Versions* as a progress through stages of increasing psychological complexity, but a progress which at every point plays off 'deep' (often Freudian) conflicts of motive and meaning against a sense of the mind's remarkable capacity for turning such conflicts to creative account by reading them as topics for speculative thought. Thus 'there is too much self-knowledge here [in Lewis Carroll's *Alice* books] to make the game of psycho-analysis seem merely good fun' (*SVP*, p. 218). Empson's point is much akin to the argument of Paul Ricœur in his book *Freud and Philosophy*: that depth interpretation (the 'archaeological' approach) can only produce worthwhile results if it is joined to a 'teleological' account of how language opens up new possibilities of meaning through the exercise of imaginative powers vested in the nature of all symbolic understanding. There are, in short, 'two hermeneutics', two interpretations of interpretation, 'one turned toward the revival of archaic meanings, . . . the other toward the emergence of figures that anticipate our spiritual adventures'.[30] To concentrate on the first of these dimensions alone – as in the more reductive applications of psychoanalytic method – is to close one's mind to the signifying potential (or the scope for reflective self-understanding) that enables language to transcend the condition of enslavement to deep-laid irrational meanings and desires. As with Empson's reading of 'The Garden', the aim of such a critical hermeneutics would be to occupy the zone of linguistic creativity where symbols can mediate between the two realms of prereflective, instinctual desire and knowledge arrived at through the exercise of reason in its 'complex' or speculative mode. 'This [i.e.. Marvell's handling of the theme] combines the idea of the conscious mind, including everything because understanding it, and that of the unconscious animal nature, including everything because in harmony with it' (*SVP*, p. 99). Both dimensions are necessary – Empson (like Ricœur) sets out to show – since between them they comprise a dialectics of interpretive thought in the absence of which there could be no accounting for language in its everyday, let alone its more creative, aspects.

In this sense, Pastoral on Empson's understanding of the term is not so much a genre – a literary 'form' with clearly marked stylistic attributes – as a kind of subjective correlative for feelings that would otherwise elude the best efforts of critical commentary. As Empson puts it in his chapter on 'Double plots': 'the value of the state of mind which finds double irony natural is that it combines breadth of sympathy with energy of judgement; it can keep its balance among all the materials for judging' (*SVP*, p. 57). Or again: 'he [the ironist] gives the same pleasure to his audience, [since] the process brings to mind the whole body of their difficulty with so much sharpness and freshness that it may give the strength to escape from it' (p. 56). What characterizes all Empson's versions of Pastoral – and marks the shift of emphasis from *Seven Types* – is this way of translating private or self-locked conflicts into a register of socialized interests and values which can then find expression through various forms of complex ironic displacement. Thus literature is essentially 'a social process . . . an attempt to reconcile the conflicts of an individual in whom

26

those of society will be mirrored' (p. 22). And this process works pretty well, Empson thinks, in so far as it helps to handle the various communicative problems that are sure to arise in any society where conflicting class interests (or the specialized division of labour) make it difficult to know just whom they are addressing, or at what precise level of 'conscious' or 'unconscious' reader-response.

This is why *Some Versions* often appeals to a certain idea of the theatre audience – especially in the Elizabethan period – as a useful analogue for what goes on when the reader confronts some problematic passage.

> Once you break into the godlike unity of the appreciator you find a microcosm of which the theatre is the macrocosm; the mind is complex and ill-connected like an audience, and it is as surprising in the one case as the other that a sort of unity can be produced by a play.
>
> (p. 60)

The main advantage of thinking in these terms is that it takes some of the strain off depth interpretation – or avoids the more dubious forms of 'psychological' criticism – by opening literature up to all the crosswinds of social and cultural difference. And to this extent it gives the interpreter a handle for understanding nuances or shades of implication that would fail to strike any critic too preoccupied with matters of profound psychological import. Empson makes the point with particular reference to Ernest Jones's essay on *Hamlet*, a reading whose chief fault (as he sees it) is the habit of assuming too readily that 'the only ideas with which an audience can be infected unconsciously are the fundamental Freudian ones' (p. 59). The effect is to narrow one's focus of interest to a point where the only 'explanations' that count are those that invoke some well-worn theme (like the Oedipus Complex) which offers little more than a catch-all interpretive slogan. But really the activity of audience-response is a lot more complex and therefore less subject to irrational drives and compulsions below the (presumed) threshold of conscious awareness. As Empson puts it:

> probably an audience does to some extent let loose the hidden traditional ideas common to its members, which may be a valuable process, but it also forms a small 'public

opinion'; the mutual influence of its members' judgements, even though expressed by the most obscure means or only imagined from their presence, is so strong as to produce a sort of sensibility held in common, and from their variety it may be wider, more sensible, than that of any of its members.

(*SVP*, p. 59)

And one can generalize this argument beyond the special case of plays that involve a 'pastoral' double-plot structure, or indeed beyond the confines of theatrical performance or stage drama as such. For it is Empson's idea that the same approach would work for any text – lyric poems and novels included – that possessed a sufficient degree of attitudinal complexity, or a tendency to call out varying responses from different readers, social interest groups, or (in Stanley Fish's phrase) 'interpretive communities'.[31] But he would also want to argue – as against Fish – that this diversity of actual or potential reader-response is enough to prevent such a theory from appealing to any one set of in-place consensus values conceived as placing limits on what counts as a good-faith or competent judgement at any given time. For it is precisely the virtue of this Pastoral attitude – indeed more an *attitude* than a genre, technique or regular structural device – that it doesn't force the critic to peer too fixedly into the 'very cauldron of the inner depths', and instead offers a reassuring sense that 'the appeal to a circle of a man's equals is the fundamental escape into the fresh air of the mind' (*SVP*, p. 59).

All the same there is a sense in which Pastoral could offer only a tentative and short-term solution to the problems that Empson encountered in his dealing with ambiguities of the Seventh Type. For the Pastoral ironist is a figure set about by all manner of conflicting pressures and demands, among them the claim of political commitment as against the more 'complex', self-occupied pleasures of a rich imaginative life. This dilemma is presented most explicitly in the book's opening chapter ('Proletarian literature'), where Empson contrasts the various forms or modalities of Pastoral with the line of communist Agit-prop thinking espoused by Soviet artist-intellectuals like Maxim Gorki. His main problem with work of this sort – despite Empson's plainly left-wing political sympathies – is that 'when it comes off I find I am taking it as pastoral literature; I read into

28

it, or find that the author has secretly put into it, these more subtle, more far-reaching, and I think more permanent, ideas' (p. 23). That is to say, Pastoral has a breadth of appeal – a capacity for handling complex states of psychological and social (class-based) feeling – which Empson misses in the products of party-line Soviet propaganda. All the same he has to admit that there may be good reason for socialists to reject the whole Pastoral bag of tricks, relying as it does on a root metaphor (that of 'putting the complex into the simple') which can easily be used to insinuate some form of covert 'bourgeois' ideology. For there is often more than a hint of the idea – one that Empson finds pervasively at work in Gray's 'Elegy in a Country Churchyard' – that no amount of social or political reform could ever significantly change the basic facts of human injustice, waste and inequality; that 'gifted' individuals somehow have a natural right to their class privileges, since after all they are the ones best fitted (whether by talent or breeding) to make good use of them; and therefore that such individuals should acknowledge the existing order – despite all its manifest imperfections – in a spirit of tragic pathos mixed with a certain melancholy irony. In other words, there is no prospect of large-scale social improvement – or of lessening the number of mute, inglorious Miltons – so one had better just accept that this is the case and perhaps turn it to creative account through one or another complex variation on the pastoral theme.

Empson is very far from endorsing this sentiment, and indeed expresses sympathy with those readers who, 'without being communists, have been irritated by the complacence in the massive calm of the poem' (*SVP*, p. 12). For there is, he acknowledges, a 'cheat in the implied politics', a naturalizing gambit that enables the author to carry off this piece of class propaganda by exploiting the pastoral convention in a way that cuts out alternative arguments. Thus

> the tone of melancholy claims that the poet understands the considerations opposed to aristocracy, though he judges against them; the truism of the reflections in the churchyard, the universality and impersonality this gives to the style, claim as if by comparison that we ought to accept the injustice of society as we do the inevitability of death.
>
> (p. 12)

On the strength of such passages one might well suppose that Empson shared the feeling expressed by many left-wing critics of pastoral, Raymond Williams among them: that this is a genre so riddled with attitudes of hypocrisy, class prejudice and patronage that any good-willed effort to redeem its fortunes is liable to fall into the same posture.[32] But in fact Empson goes on directly to claim that Gray's poem expresses one of the 'permanent truths' of human existence; namely, that 'it is only in degree that any improvement in society could prevent wastage of human powers', since 'the waste even in a fortunate life, the isolation even of a life rich in intimacy, cannot but be felt deeply, and is the central feeling of tragedy' (p. 12). As so often with *Some Versions*, it is difficult to know where paraphrase shades off into generalizing comment on Empson's part, or where the attempt to view all sides of a problem – one of the main virtues of Pastoral, as Empson conceives it – leans over into something more like an outlook of generous, all-accepting irony. At any rate one could hazard that sentiments of this sort would find little favour with Gorki, or indeed with Raymond Williams at those points in his work where Pastoral figures as a powerful (if oblique) expression of ruling-class interests.

Nor would these critics be at all mollified by Empson's subsequent efforts in this chapter to work out the basis of a reasonable compromise between the claims of Pastoral sentiment and those of straightforward social justice.

> Now all these ideas are very well suited to a socialist society, and have been made to fit in very well with the dogma of the equality of man, but I do not see that they would fit in with a rigid proletarian aesthetic. . . . They assume that some people are more delicate and complex than others, and that if these people can be kept from doing harm it is a good thing, though a small thing by comparison with our common humanity.
>
> (p. 23)

This theme is one that Empson takes up at greater length in his discussion of Shakespeare's Sonnet 94 ('They that have power to hurt and will do none'). But it is present throughout *Some Versions* as a running subtext, a kind of oblique confessional burden that regularly implicates 'the critic' – or the theorist of Pastoral – on terms that create an uneasy sense of the structural injustice, the exploitative order of social relations whereby such figures can assume their privileged mediating role. I cannot begin to summarize the extraordinary twists and contortions of imputed motive that Empson manages to tease out in his reading of Shakespeare's savagely double-edged 'tribute' to the shadowy patron. Indeed it is one of the great ironies of this book that it breezily flouts the New Critical veto on paraphrasing poems – most often by offering multiple pot-shots at a plain-prose summary – while its own interpretations are so complex (or so hedged about with qualifying ironies) that no paraphrase could possibly do them justice.

But if one thing is clear it is the fact that Shakespeare's sonnet is here taking on a surrogate burden of anxieties and obscure guilt feelings that have to do mainly with Empson's sense of the strong counter-arguments, ethical and political, that rise up against the whole complex of Pastoral ideas. Thus for instance:

> I must praise in you [i.e., the patron] your very faults, especially your selfishness, because you can only now be safe by cultivating them further; yet this is the most dangerous of necessities; people are greedy for your fall as for that of any of the great; indeed no one can rise above common life, as you have done so fully, without in the same degree sinking below it; you have made this advice real to me because I cannot despise it for your sake; I am only sure that you are valuable and in danger.
>
> (p. 85)

It is a remarkable passage for various reasons, not least the degree of self-implicating irony – or the hint of a readiness to view his own efforts in a similar, none too flattering light – that comes across in Empson's speculative treatment of the background situation in the Sonnets. At any rate it seems only 'sensible' (as Empson might say) to suppose that such otherwise very curious pieces of commentary will turn out to bear some tangible relation to the ironies that characterize the Pastoral stance in its literary-critical guise. And that relation is best understood, I think, in terms of the conflicting values or priorities that emerge so often when Empson touches on matters of ethical or socio-political concern. For it is here that Pastoral once again comes up against the problem he had addressed in the reply to Sparrow and the closing (mainly theoretical) chapter of *Seven Types*: that is to say, the issue of 'analytical' versus 'appreciative' criticism, or the

31

question how best to reconcile these seemingly divergent lines of approach.

At that time – we may recall – Empson had come out strongly in favour of a rationalist philosophy of mind and language, an attitude that effectively minimized the difference between poetry and other (prosaic or 'everyday') kinds of discourse. After all, as he remarks, 'analytical is more cheerful than appreciative criticism (both, of course, must be present) precisely because there is less need to agonize over these questions of tone' (*ST*, p. 251). But one doesn't have to read very far into *Some Versions* to see how these 'questions of tone' are still an issue, not only as regards the mode of address best suited to literary criticism, but also in relation to the intellectual's role *vis-à-vis* questions of social and political justice. It is only with *The Structure of Complex Words* – his most ambitious and philosophically far-reaching work – that Empson manages to articulate the interests of critical theory with those of a broad-based humanist ethic which no longer runs the risk – ever present for the Pastoral critic – of finding itself 'forced into tragic isolation by sheer strength of mind'. What seems to have brought this change about (at much the same time, incidentally, as Empson officially 'gave up' writing poetry) was the shift from a mode of verbal exegesis trained up on the depth-psychological approach to a socialized account of meaning and context that enabled an escape into the 'larger air' of open public debate. Towards the end of *Seven Types* he had rather fretfully noted that 'I am treating the act of communication as something very extraordinary, so that the next step would be to lose faith in it altogether' (p. 243). And the best alternative at that stage seemed to be an attitude of sturdy (if 'prosaic') rationalism which at least had the virtue of making poems more accessible to our ordinary waking habits of thought. Besides, 'it often happens that, for historical reasons or what not, one can no longer appreciate a thing directly by poetical knowledge, and yet can rediscover it in a more controlled form by prosaic knowledge' (p. 243). But again this gives rise to all the troublesome antinomies – intuitive/analytic, creative/critical, poetry/prose and so forth – which Empson was to pursue (though never resolve) through the various generic displacements of Pastoral irony. In *Seven Types* he can offer little more than the general observation that 'a poetical word is a thing conceived in itself and contains all its meanings', whereas 'a prosaic word is flat and useful and might have been used differently' (p. 252). In which case the relation between poetry and criticism would remain a highly puzzling, paradoxical affair, best handled – as Empson pragmatically concludes – by 'trying to understand as many things as possible', and not getting too hung up on philosophical problems.

In *Some Versions* those problems re-emerge in the form of a deepening reflective irony which at times takes on a distinctly Hegelian character. In fact Empson mentions Hegel only in passing – p. 24 – but the book has numerous passages that suggest at least some measure of familiarity with his thought. Thus the Pastoral progress through stages of increasing ironic detachment finds a parallel in Hegel's phenomenology of Mind on its journey from the first stirrings of reflective thought to the highest, most developed forms of speculative reason.[33] And this parallel is closest when Empson (like Hegel) stresses the element of 'unhappy consciousness', or the internal conflicts and divisions that Mind encounters in the course of its spiritual odyssey. It may be wise not to push these analogies too hard since Empson didn't take kindly to critics who hunted out obscure 'philosophical' ideas in his work. All the same there are passages in *Some Versions* – and indeed whole aspects of the Pastoral genre as Empson conceives it – which can best be understood in the light of such ideas. (Besides, he had reviewed a good number of books that reflected the lingering influence of German idealist philosophy on British thinkers, even after the famous 'revolution' brought about by Russell, Moore and their contemporaries.) Anyway, it would seem at least plausible to argue that these interests are somewhere in the background when Empson writes (in his chapter on the *Alice* books) that Pastoral may well involve reflection on 'the mysteries of self-knowledge, the self-contradictions of the will, the antinomies of philosophy, the very Looking Glass itself' (*SVP*, p. 232). Such a passage carries overtones not only of Hegel but of the whole post-Kantian development of thought which explored these speculative (mirror-like) abysses encountered by consciousness in its quest for self-knowledge. One could even suggest that Pastoral – on its widest definition – performs the same role as Romantic irony in the thinking of those German critic-philosophers (the Schlegel brothers chief among them) who raised it to a high point and principle of all modern art.[34] At any rate there is a clearly marked kinship – especially so towards the end of *Some Versions* – between the Romantic Ironist and the Pastoral 'critic-as-hero', that figure set about by all the vexing contradictions which philosophy is finally unable to resolve, and which literature can only express through forms of increasingly complex ironic displacement. '*Wonderland* is a dream, but the *Looking-Glass* is self-consciousness'; at which point Pastoral undergoes something like a qualitative change, an extreme dissociation of 'conscious' and 'unconscious' realms, such that there exist no social or generic conventions – no forms of communal understanding – capable of bridging the distance between them.

Neil Hertz is not the only reader to suggest a certain unacknowledged kinship (or elective affinity) between Empson and the avatars of German nineteenth-century idealist and speculative thought. There is some interesting commentary to much this effect in an early essay by Paul de Man ('The dead-end of Formalist criticism')[35] where he praises Empson as the one figure in recent Anglo-American debate who had perceived how 'true poetic ambiguity' takes rise from a 'deep division of Being', an ontological difference – to adopt the Heideggerian idiom – that cannot be reconciled by any degree of interpretive or hermeneutic tact. 'What is the Pastoral convention,' de Man asks,

> if not the eternal separation between the mind that distinguishes, negates, legislates, and the originary simplicity of the natural? A separation that may be lived, as in Homer's poetry (evoked by Empson as an example of the universality of its definition), or may be thought in full consciousness of itself as in Marvell's poem. There is no doubt that the pastoral theme is, in fact, the only poetic theme, that it is poetry itself. Under the deceitful title of a genre study, Empson has actually written an ontology of the poetic, but wrapped it, as is his wont, in some extraneous matter that may well conceal the essential.
>
> (*BI*, p. 239)

His comments are fully justified as regards that aspect of Empsonian Pastoral irony that becomes more complex and elusive – more susceptible to depth interpretation – as the genre approaches its limit point in Carroll's curious variations on the theme. In short, de Man fastens unerringly on those elements in the Pastoral complex of ideas which enable him to make the looked-for connection with German Romanticism, Hegel's 'unhappy consciousness', and Heidegger's late meditations on language, poetry and ontological difference.[36] These affinities are, as I have said, well worth noting, and certainly they offer an 'angle' on Pastoral – a philosophic and historical point of entry – which seems to have escaped most of Empson's Anglo-American commentators.

But de Man is less perceptive (indeed quite uncomprehending) when it comes to that other, social and political dimension which plays an equally important role in the various generic transformations that Empson traces down through the history of Pastoral thought. In fact it is a chief claim of de Man's essay that sociological (especially Marxist) approaches are sure to go wrong at a certain point when they allow such short-term political concerns to substitute for the 'deep division of Being' that characterizes all authentic thinking on the nature of poetic language. Thus 'Marxism is, ultimately, a poetic thought that lacks the patience to pursue its own conclusions to their end'. And again, more explicitly:

> having started out from the premises of the strictest aesthetic formalism, Empson winds up facing the ontological question. It is by virtue of this question that he stands as a warning against certain Marxist illusions. The problem of separation inheres in Being, which means that social forms of separation derive from ontological and meta-social attitudes. For poetry, the divide exists forever.
>
> (*BI*, p. 240)

This all follows directly from de Man's Heideggerian conviction that history and politics belong to a merely 'factical' domain, a level of thought unconcerned with questions of a deeper (authentic or primordial) import. But if there is, undeniably, an aspect of Pastoral that answers to this depth-hermeneutical approach, there is still a great deal that de Man has to leave out of account in order to make his interpretation stick. For one thing, he ignores the Empsonian stress on those countervailing values of wit, self-critical irony and social 'poise' which most often make possible the Pastoral escape into a wider dimension of meaningful exchange between various classes, interest groups, or interpretive communities. Where this dimension is lacking – or when the writer retreats, like Lewis Carroll, into a near-private world of obsessional motifs where his sanity is barely saved by the shift towards a different, narrower range of reader-response –

then Empson sees it as a basically pathological variant of the Pastoral theme, and not (like de Man) as conveying a fundamental truth about poetry and language.

This difference comes out most strikingly at those points where Empson's commentary seems within reach of a generalized 'existential' brooding on the facts of human isolation, mortality and finitude. 'Once at least in each book,' he remarks,

> a cry of loneliness goes up from Alice at the oddity beyond sympathy or communication of the world she has entered – whether that in which the child is shut by weakness, or the adult by the renunciations necessary both for the ideal and the worldly way of life (the strength of the snobbery is to imply that these are the same).
>
> (*SVP*, p. 230)

It is an extraordinary passage, to be sure, and one that goes so far beyond a straightforward response to the 'words on the page' that it must suggest some similar burden of anxiety on Empson's part, or at any rate a strongly marked predisposition to find such meanings at work. But again, there is a crucial difference between the sombre pathos of de Man's Heideggerian rhetoric – according to which this 'division of Being' is inherent in the very nature of 'authentic' language, poetry and thought – and Empson's idea that it only comes about at moments of extreme psychological stress when the normal machinery of communication has somehow broken down. Hence the tone of sturdy rationalism that comes across even when Empson is commenting on the strangest episodes in the *Alice* books.

> One must be struck by the depth at which the satire is hidden; the queerness of the incident and the characters takes on a Wordsworthian grandeur and aridity, and the landscape defined by the tricks of facetiousness has the remote and staring beauty of the ideas of the insane.
>
> (p. 232)

Nothing could be further from de Man's in the end rather placid and self-supporting strain of 'ontological' pathos, his assumption (following Heidegger) that language must *always and everywhere* enact that dehiscence or cleft within the thought of Being whose history is that of 'Western metaphysics' at large. For de Man, once more,

[t]he ambiguity poetry speaks of is the fundamental one
that prevails between the world of the spirit and the world
of sentient substance: to ground itself, the spirit must turn
itself into sentient substance, but the latter is knowable only
in its dissolution into non-being. The spirit cannot coincide
with its object and this separation is infinitely sorrowful.

(*BI*, p. 237)

Again, I wouldn't wish to deny that this commentary responds to
something genuinely 'there' in Empson's criticism, a sense of the
alarming depths that may always be revealed when Pastoral irony
fails to discover any adequate (social or communicative) means
to externalize these deep-rooted conflicts. But to turn this into a
profound truth about literature, criticism and language *in general*
is to misread Empson in pursuit of a thesis which he would surely
and emphatically reject. For it assumes – against all the evidence
of *Some Versions* – that the most typical or representative
instances of Pastoral are those which stand, like the *Alice* books,
on the verge of self-locked neurotic inhibition or a breakdown
in the circuits of communal exchange between 'complex' and
'simple' modes of understanding. And this gets the message of
the book completely upside-down. What has changed since Marvell so adroitly conjured his witty variations on this theme is the
fact that Lewis Carroll must now resort to 'child-cult' – a belated,
neurotic, self-isolating variant of Pastoral – in order to articulate
feelings that can find no alternative mode of expression, no
escape into the 'larger air' of socialized values and conventions.
As Empson remarks of this curious development, 'the pathos of
its futility is that it is an attempt for reason to do the work
of emotion and escape the dangers of the emotional approach
to life' (p. 231). In short, we shouldn't take such limiting cases
of the Pastoral genre – instances that mark a near-crisis or collapse of all its working values and assumptions – as in any sense
conveying some ultimate truth at the end of critical enquiry.

Empson makes this point most explicitly when discussing 'The
Garden' and Marvell's deft way with the antinomies of mind and
nature, subject and object, or conscious and unconscious modes
of knowledge. Later on – with the advent of Romanticism and a
mystical-intuitive (Wordsworthian) approach to such themes – it
would appear that by far the most valuable moments in poetry
were those when the mind transcended such bad antinomies and

achieved a kind of hypostatic union, a condition of unmediated inwardness with the forms and appearances of nature. In Marvell, however, the emphasis falls rather differently, and Empson makes no secret of his preference for the earlier Pastoral style.

> The value of these moments made it fitting to pretend they were eternal; and yet the lightness of his expression of their sense of power is more intelligent, and so more convincing, than Wordsworth's solemnity on the same theme, because it does not forget the opposing forces.
>
> (*SVP*, p. 108)

De Man is just as sceptical as Empson about the visionary claims of 'high romantic argument', the idea – taken over by mainstream scholars of Romanticism like M. H. Abrams – that poetry can actually attain to this wished-for condition of organic communion with nature or pure, self-present, unmediated access to the processes of natural development and growth. In fact it is a notion that he regards as having produced all manner of mischievous effects, among them that potent 'aesthetic ideology' whose avatars range (improbably enough) from idealist poet-philosophers like Schiller to Nazi propagandists like Goebbels. By far the greater part of de Man's critical work from the mid-1960s on – including his classic essay 'The rhetoric of temporality' – was devoted to the business of deconstructing this mystified organicist creed.[37] But he always took it for granted – unlike Empson – that the only kind of criticism adequate to this task was one that engaged texts at a level where conscious meanings or motives played little part, and where language itself could be shown to enact the endless dialectical interplay between 'blindness' and 'insight'. This presumption remains constant in de Man across some otherwise very marked shifts of emphasis, including his abandonment of the Heideggerian jargon of authenticity in favour of a more technical, analytic idiom which eschews such potentially coercive sources of rhetorical pathos and instead examines texts in the light of the distinction – revived from the classical *trivium* – between logic, grammar and rhetoric.[38] Still there is no question, for de Man, of criticism concerning itself with 'witty' tricks of style – or 'preconscious' subtleties of thought and technique, as in the Marvell poem – that would enable an escape into what Empson breezily calls the 'fresh air of the mind'.

Impossible to imagine de Man coming up with those passages

of joky paraphrase, offhand commentary and sidelong reflection which characterize Empson's chapter on 'The Garden'. But this is very much the point of his essay: that one may do better not to stand on one's dignity – like Wordsworth (or de Man) when confronted with these 'deep' ontological questions – since there is perhaps more wisdom to be had by following Marvell's good-humoured example and allowing the mind full scope for its exercise of 'conscious' and 'unconscious' powers. 'Only a meta-physical poet with so perfect a sense of form and so complete a control over the tricks of the style, at the end of its development, could actually dramatize these hints as he gave them' (*SVP*, p. 119). Again, nothing could be further from de Man's dark-toned meditations on Pastoral, his talk of 'ontological difference' and other such portentous themes. And this is at least partly a matter of *tone*, of de Man's being deaf to those inflections in Empson's writing that don't, as he puts it, 'forget the opposing forces', or the claims of a witty, self-conscious, speculative reason, as against the claims of a depth hermeneutic that finds no room for such qualities. For it is, according to Empson, one great virtue of the Pastoral complex of feelings that it points a way beyond these deadlocked antinomies, allowing us to glimpse – momen-tarily at least – a happier state of mind where they would no longer seem anything like so urgent or compelling.

It is the mood well captured by Empson's gloss on some lines from 'The Garden' which – as he reads them – have to do precisely with this wise passivity or state of reflective equilibrium.

> Self-knowledge is possible in such a state so far as the unruly impulses are digested, ordered, made transparent, not by their being known, at the time, as unruly. Consciousness no longer makes an important distinction; the impulses, since they must be balanced already, neither need it to put them right nor are put wrong by the way it forces across their boundaries. They let themselves be known because they are not altered by being known, because their principle of indeterminacy no longer acts. This idea is important for all the versions of pastoral, for the pastoral figure is always ready to be the critic; he not only includes everything but may in some unexpected way know it.
>
> (*SVP*, p. 103)

One could plausibly say of this passage – as indeed of many others

in *Some Versions* – that it moves within the ambit of Romantic irony
and of all those self-reflexive puzzles and paradoxes that occupy
a critic like de Man. But in that case one would have to go on
and specify just why this comparison ultimately misses the mark,
or how it is that Empson's treatment of the Pastoral theme opens
up such strikingly different possibilities of feeling and thought.
For it does seem somewhat off the point – as Empson might say
– to compare this sequence of deftly handled paradoxes with
the notion of specular regress or textual *mise-en-abîme* that links
deconstruction to its intellectual sources in the German Romantic
tradition. And here it might be useful to recall his gloss on a
single word from 'The Garden' which strikes Empson as somehow
condensing this entire range of implications.

> *Happiness*, again, names a conscious state, and yet involves
> the idea of things falling right, happening so, not being
> ordered by an anxiety of the conscious reason. (So that as
> a rule it is a weak word; it is by seeming to look at it hard
> and bring out its implications that the verse here makes it
> act as a strong one.)
>
> (*SVP*, p. 104)

From de Man's viewpoint – as presented in that early, admiring
essay on Empson – this could only figure as a momentary lapse,
a retreat from his otherwise exemplary insistence that Pastoral
offers no false promise of reconciliation, no means of overcoming
the 'ontological difference' (or the deep 'division of Being') that
inhabits all forms of authentic reflection on language, poetry and
criticism. For it is a truth beyond question, at this stage in de
Man's thinking, that any hint of 'reconciliation' between mind
and nature, subject and object or conscious and unconscious
thought-processes will always turn out to involve a certain motivated 'blindness' – or strategy of self-willed evasion – on the
critic's part.

In fact the essay tells us much more about de Man and his
distinctive (not to say obsessive) concerns than it does about
Empsonian ambiguity and Pastoral. So determined is he to find
in Empson a strong precursor of his own kind of criticism that he
misreads the chapter on Marvell as an exercise in the 'essentially
negative activity of thought', one in which the poem's climactic
lines ('Annihilating all that's made / To a green thought in a
green shade') are glossed as reflecting on the *destruction* of nature

through the mind's relentless powers of self-ironizing inwardness or negation. Thus 'it [the word "green"] is reintroduced at the very moment when this world had been annihilated. It is the freshness, the greenness of budding thought that can evoke itself only through the memory of what it destroys on its way' (*BI*, p. 239). One can see very well why de Man wanted to read both the poem and Empson's essay this way. It is a reading that perfectly endorses his idea of how criticism can work to deconstruct the fallacious organicist or naturalizing drive that subtends all versions of 'aesthetic ideology', all attempts to treat poetry as somehow sharing in the life-world of natural processes and forms. But this doesn't make it any more convincing as an account of what Empson *actually says* in the course of his essay on 'The Garden'. What de Man has to ignore – or consistently play down in keeping with his whole Heideggerian line of approach – is the extraordinary sense of intellectual uplift, the excitement and feeling of new-found creative possibilities, that Empson sees everywhere implicit in Marvell's handling of the Pastoral theme. Thus

> the personalized Nature is treated both as external to man and as created by an instinct of the mind, and by tricks of language these are made to seem the same. But if they were simply called the same we would not be so easily satisfied by the tricks. What we feel is that though they are essentially unlike they are practically unlike in different degrees at different times; a supreme condition can therefore be imagined, though not attained, in which they are essentially alike. (To put it like this is no doubt to evade a philosophic issue.) A hint of the supreme condition is thus found in the actual one (this makes the actual one include everything in itself), but this exalted claim is essentially joined to humility; it is effective only through the admission that it is only a hint.
>
> (*SVP*, p. 112)

Of course it might be said – and any follower of de Man would be likely to make this point – that the crucial sentence here is the throwaway parenthesis; that Empson has indeed managed to evade the chief 'philosophic issue', namely the insuperable distance that exists between beings and Being, or the sheer *impossibility* that mind should achieve such an easygoing commerce with

41

the realm of physical nature. But this is to assume that 'philosophy' (or real, authentic philosophy) can only be construed in Heideggerian terms as a thinking of the 'ontological difference' which will always be found unavoidably installed at the heart of philosophical reflection. And it is precisely this idea that Empson challenges by stressing the mind's capacity – at least on rare occasions – to think its way creatively *through and beyond* the subject/object or conscious/unconscious dualisms.

His point is not at all to reject 'philosophy' (since *Some Versions* is a deeply 'philosophical' book on almost any definition of the term), but to show what possible alternatives exist for the kind of intelligence that can treat these problems at full imaginative stretch. Moreover, the condition for attaining such insight is that the mind should not become too preoccupied with these and kindred ontological questions, but instead take account of the social dimension – the multiplicity of human interests and values – that Pastoral brings into play. This is why the 'apparently exalted claim' is 'essentially joined to humility'; it can only work at all in so far as it acknowledges the complex nature of its own satisfactions and the force of opposing arguments. In short, 'something of the tone of pastoral is inherent in the claim; the fault of the Wordsworthian method seems to be that it does not show this' (*SVP*, p. 112). And the same might be said of de Man's criticism in so far as it makes a programmatic point of ignoring (or suppressing) the social aspects of Pastoral, along with that closely related dimension where 'deep' anxieties discover an escape-route into the 'larger air of speculative reason'.

To say that all this drops out of the picture on de Man's reading of Empson is to point up the shift of priorities that has occurred in recent literary theory. *Some Versions* offers at least the common ground of an interest in Romantic irony – though Empson never uses that term – and a readiness to pursue this topic into regions where criticism (in de Man's words) opens up 'unexpected perspectives on human complexity' (*BI*, p. 238). But that is about as far as the resemblance goes, since Empson – as we have seen – wants to keep these puzzles firmly on the side of reflective self-knowledge, rather than raise 'fundamental' questions beyond hope of enlightened rational debate. And in *The Structure of Complex Words* he develops a line of argument that goes clean against the working assumptions of just about every modern school of literary-critical thought, from the 'old' New Criticism to deconstruction. All that I can reasonably hope to do, in the limited space available here, is outline some of the book's major claims and suggest what kind of alternative they offer to these taken-for-granted values and beliefs. This will serve some purpose if at least a few readers are thereby persuaded to investigate the book which Empson considered his most important work, but which commentators have often treated with reactions ranging from indifference to bafflement or downright uninformed hostility.

Nor are these responses hard to understand, given the extent of Empson's disagreement with various present-day orthodoxies. For *Complex Words* is a book dedicated to several quite explicit propositions. These include (1) the defence of liberal humanism, or of an ethics of interpretation that builds on liberal-humanist values and assumptions; (2) the indispensability of truth – or of a truth-functional approach to questions of literary meaning – which comes out squarely against all forms of cultural-relativist doctrine; (3) the idea that literary texts *make statements* (or possess an assertoric force) unaccounted for by any theory that treats multiple meaning in purely rhetorical terms, whether of 'irony', 'ambiguity', 'paradox', 'intertextuality', or whatever; and (4) the argument that criticism therefore needs some grounding in the kind of semantic theory (or analytic philosophy of language) that might hope to provide at least a working basis for the conduct of interpretive debate. To which might be added the 'commonsense' belief – so strong in Empson's writing at every stage – that poetry (and literary criticism likewise) were continuous with the interests of commonplace (social and moral) human well-being, and were therefore ill served by any theory, no matter how sophisticated, which made that continuity more difficult to sustain.

Such was his response to the American New Criticism, a movement that Empson increasingly came to see as given over to a species of irrationalist rhetoric (witness the privilege accorded to figures like paradox), joined to a strongly marked 'neo-Christian' strain of orthodox religious values. Thus 'any poet who tells his readers what he thinks about the world is getting mixed up with Truth, which [Cleanth] Brooks wants to keep out of poetry'.[39] In fact one can see him getting more and more suspicious of 'theory' as the books come in for review, to the point where almost anything with a tinge of philosophical reflection strikes Empson as most likely just a pretext for some kind of 'bother-headed' abstract talk. But he is also very aware that the appeal to unexamined commonsense values is one that can easily slide over into mere prejudice or inert conformist thinking. Thus 'the English like to assume that they are sensible, therefore don't require abstruse theory, but there is no guarantee of that'.[40] What Empson really found most objectionable in the works of 'theory' that came his way from the early 1950s on was the specialization of lit.-crit. method as a means of isolating poetry (or fiction) from language in its everyday constative or truth-telling mode. Indeed, as we have seen, it is an issue that goes back to his quarrel with Richards over the latter's idea that poetry belonged to a realm of 'emotive' pseudo-statement, a domain where values of truth and falsehood simply didn't apply. Later on he was to find the same principle at work – despite the large shift in ontological priorities – in the New Critics' thoroughly 'perverse' refusal to entertain questions of authorial intention or relevant background knowledge. For this was just the end result, as Empson put it, of 'imitating the Logical Positivist in a different field of study', or allowing a narrowly prescriptive idea of what counted as veridical knowledge to dictate in matters far beyond its legitimate scope. The trouble with such self-denying ordinances – no matter how strongly backed up 'in theory' – was that they cut out so much of the rational sense-making activity which, in the end, was the critic's only claim on the reader's interest or attention.

The same kind of prejudice was still much in evidence – or so Empson thought – in those varieties of structuralist or poststructuralist criticism that began to emerge on the Anglo-American scene in the mid-1970s. Thus, of Frank Kermode's *The Genesis of Secrecy*:

> he looks at a landscape with half-closed eyes through a mist, or in a Claude-glass, or upside down from between his legs; and this is not a good way to read a novel, which is usually better read as if it were a history.[41]

What Empson caught more than a hint of in Kermode's book was the idea – nowadays a staple of postmodernist thought – that ultimately all kinds of discourse (history and theory included) come down to a fictive or tropological dimension, a level where the explanations run out and 'truth' can only be a matter of choice between various competing narratives, discourses or paradigms.[42] This struck him – predictably – as just another instance

44

of the way that 'sophisticated' textualist theories could produce all manner of perverse misjudgement or dead-end sceptical doctrine. In *Complex Words* he had set out to produce nothing less than a full-scale rejoinder to these and other versions of the widespread irrationalist or counter-Enlightenment drift which Empson considered such a harmful influence on present-day literary studies. Small wonder, therefore, that he saw little virtue in those forms of 'advanced' poststructuralist theory that not only ignored his book but seemed bent upon denying any relation between literature, criticism and the interests of truth-seeking rational enquiry.[43]

He strikes the same note in a 1977 review of Raymond Williams's *Keywords*, a book which one might have expected Empson to admire – or at any rate treat sympathetically – since it adopts something very like his own procedure, in *Complex Words*, of analysing the verbal 'equations' (or structures of compacted propositional meaning) contained in certain crucial or ideologically loaded terms.[44] On the contrary: Williams (as Empson reads him) has greatly exaggerated the power of such words to influence our thinking in ways that put language beyond all reach of self-critical or reasoned thought. Thus 'part of the gloom, I think, comes from a theory which makes our minds feebler than they are – than they have to be, if they are to go through their usual performance with language'. And the review ends up with a baleful glance in the direction of other recent movements in criticism:

> The longest entry in the book . . . is for *structural,* and here my sympathy breaks down altogether; the theories he is describing seem to me terrible waffle. What he needs to consider is the structure relating two meanings in any one of his chosen words, so that they imply or insinuate a sentence: 'A is B'. Under what conditions are they able to impose a belief that the speaker would otherwise resist? As he never considers that, he is free to choose any interpretation that suits his own line of propaganda.[45]

Of course this amounts to a summary description of exactly the project that Empson had undertaken in *The Structure of Complex Words*. And it also suggests why he took exception to that other kind of 'structuralist' thinking – the kind represented by Williams's *Keywords* entry – which derived mainly from French developments in the wake of Saussure's linguistic revolution. For this theory took it as axiomatic that language was a network of signifying features 'without positive terms'; that meaning was constituted through the play of differential elements (i.e., the contrastive structures of sound and sense), rather than forms of logico-semantic entailment; and therefore that questions of truth and reference were strictly off limits for any account of language – or any literary theory – that sought to describe these characteristics in a properly *structural* mode.[46] One could argue (as I have elsewhere) that this whole development took rise from a basic misunderstanding of Saussure, a desire on the part of literary theorists to extend his various heuristic formulations (e.g., the 'arbitrary' nature of the sign) from the specialized field of synchronic language-study to the entire domain of cultural and textual representation.[47] Hence – among other things – the reflex poststructuralist aversion to that typecast mythical entity, the 'classic realist text', along with the high valuation attached to its equally mythical counterpart, the text that multiplies meanings to infinity and slips all the bonds of naturalized reference or 'bourgeois' realism.[48] In any case it is clear that, to this way of thinking, criticism achieves its best, most 'radical' or liberating insights when it ceases to concern itself with truth, valid argument or other such (supposedly) ideological values.

So one can understand why Empson should have viewed these developments as a mere continuation of the 'old' New Criticism by different rhetorical means. In *Complex Words* he sets out the alternative case for a rationalist semantics – or a truth-functional theory of literature and criticism – which would point the way beyond these various kinds of out-and-out sceptical doctrine. Although the book was written some two decades before French structuralism made its appearance on the Anglo-American scene, it does have an Appendix on Leonard Bloomfield's *Language* – one of the major works of structural linguistics in its other, US-domesticated form – which anticipates some of the same basic issues.[49] What Empson chiefly objects to in Bloomfield's approach is the behaviourist assumption that one can only have a 'scientific' theory of language in so far as one suspends all consideration of how the mind actually works in producing or interpreting words in context.

This whole notion of the scientist viewing language from

outside and above is a fallacy; we would have no hope of dealing with the subject if we had not a rich obscure practical knowledge from which to extract the theoretical.

(*CW*, p. 438)

And again:

till you have decided what a piece of language conveys, like any other literary critic, you cannot look round to see what 'formal features' convey it; you will then find that some features are of great subtlety, and perhaps fail to trace some at all.

(p. 437)

The main problem with Bloomfield's approach is that he wants to exclude all 'mentalist' criteria – all reference to the powers of cognitive grasp or interpretive 'competence' possessed by individual language-users – while claiming to provide a full-scale structural analysis of language not only at the level of phonetics (where his approach might work at least up to a point), but also when dealing with metaphor, ambiguity, semantic change and other such features that would remain wholly unintelligible if one applied the rule strictly. In fact – as Empson is relieved to point out – the book is much 'larger than its theory', and Bloomfield often comes up with hypotheses that do take account of utterer's intention, interpretive strategies, motivated choice between variant meanings and so forth. But on the strict (antimentalist) reading of his book it would appear that Bloomfield could have no time for the sorts of logico-semantic investigation that Empson has been pursuing in *Complex Words*. For 'if you take at their face value these remarks that he lets drop, he is saying that such work would be beyond the pale of the exact sciences, impossible to understand, impossible to criticize' (*CW*, p. 443). And this clearly strikes Empson as yet another instance of the way that theorists in the humanistic disciplines – especially linguistics and literary criticism – are liable to pick up scientific or positivist notions and apply them far outside their legitimate domain.

This quarrel with Bloomfield might seem pretty remote from Empson's differences with the New Criticism and later (post-Saussurean) variants of structuralist theory. But there is – as I have suggested – a linking factor in his argument that each of these doctrines goes wrong through its refusal to credit the human mind with sufficient powers of self-understanding or rational grasp. And the best way to counter this unfortunate trend, so he thinks, is to show what resources – what interpretive 'machinery' – we do in fact possess for making sense of language in its more challenging or semantically complex forms. At its highest level of generality – that is to say, as a matter of principled rationalist or liberal-humanist conviction – this amounts to a belief that 'the human mind... , the public human mind, as expressed in language, is not irredeemably lunatic and cannot be made so' (*CW*, p. 83n). This remark occurs in a footnote reference to Orwell's *Nineteen Eighty-Four*, a book which poses real problems for Empson's theory since it appears to show how language can insinuate all manner of ghastly paradox ('War is Peace', 'Ignorance is Knowledge', etc.), and how little resistance the mind can put up to such forms of perverse or irrational belief. Thus

> what he [Orwell] calls 'double-think', a process of intentional but genuine self-deception, . . . really does seem a positive capacity of the human mind, so curious and so important in its effects that any theory in this field needs to reckon with it.
>
> (p. 83n)

But it is a main point of Empson's argument throughout *Complex Words* that although language can sometimes be made to behave this way – as for instance in the paradoxes of Christian religion ('God is Love'), or other such varieties of potent irrationalist doctrine – nevertheless one can best get a grip on these problematic items by looking more closely at the structures of semantic entailment that mark them out as clearly deviant cases. And this applies just as much when a poet like Wordsworth manages to communicate his pantheist 'philosophy' of interfused mind and nature through the use of vague but powerful rhetorical devices which effectively short-circuit the normal requirements of sense-making logic or reason. Thus

> it does not seem unfair to say that he induced people to believe he had expounded a consistent philosophy through the firmness and assurance with which he used equations

of Type IV; equations whose claim was false, because they did not really erect a third concept as they pretended to.

(*CW*, p. 305)

And this despite the fact, as Empson goes straight on to say, that 'the result makes good poetry, and probably suggests important truths'.

The problem with Wordsworth was one that Empson had worked at for several 'niggling' pages in *Seven Types*. There he had fastened on the logical grammar – more specifically, the subtle confusions of grammar and logic – in those lines from 'Tintern Abbey' where Wordsworth achieved what is often regarded as the finest expression of his mystical nature-doctrine. Empson doesn't deny that the lines have great poetic force; even that they may communicate some genuine wisdom at the level of depth psychology or emotional need. All the same he insists that this is no reason to suspend one's critical faculties, ignore the logico-grammatical confusions, and simply go along with the poem's mood of mystical-pantheistic uplift. Empson's commentary is far too complex and detailed to allow for any adequate summary here. The most important points for our present discussion are (1) his claim that the pantheist doctrine involves not so much a transcendence as a collapse of the normal order of predicative (subject-object) relations, an effect that can only be achieved *by rhetorical means*, and at the cost of some highly dubious grammar; (2) his argument, following from this, that the difficulty of grasping Wordsworth's 'philosophy' is really a problem for the poet, not his exegete, since it reflects deep confusions of language and thought; and (3) Empson's principle – taken up and developed in *Complex Words* – that these confusions had best be treated as such, and not declared exempt from rational critique on grounds of their supposedly higher ('paradoxical') truth. After all, as he remarks, Wordsworth appears to have taken these doctrines very seriously indeed, so that it is only reasonable for us, his readers, to 'try to extract from this passage definite opinions on the relations of God, man and nature, and on the means by which such relations can be known' (*ST*, p. 152). And if it turns out on a close reading that those relations are strictly unintelligible – that the grammar and the logic of Wordworth's poem just don't hang together in the way that his rhetoric requires – then

49

this fact had better count in any critical assessment of the poetry's undoubted persuasive or emotional force.

All the same it is clear from the last few sentences of Empson's commentary that he finds it increasingly hard to reconcile these two divergent lines of response. On the one hand 'I must protest again that I enjoy these lines very much. . . . probably it was necessary for Wordsworth to shuffle, if he was to maintain his peculiar poetical attitude'. On the other:

> the reason why one grudges Wordsworth this source of strength is that he talks as if he owned a creed by which his half-statements might be reconciled, whereas, in so far as his creed was definite, he found these half-statements necessary to keep it at bay.

(p. 154)

In *Seven Types*, working with the admittedly rather catch-all notion of poetic 'ambiguity', Empson had as yet no adequate means of explaining how emotions – or intuitive responses – could get so completely out of touch with the 'machinery' of a reasoned analytical approach, a criticism that didn't rest content with such vague sources of poetic satisfaction. In *Complex Words* this problem becomes a main topic of the book's 'theoretical' chapters and one that Empson frequently reverts to in the reading of particular texts. But it is no longer a question – as it was with Pastoral – of pursuing the various 'inward' complications, the reflective ironies and paradoxes of self-conscious thought, that marked out the stages of a history conceived in broadly Hegelian terms. This was Empson's 'phenomenology of spirit' rewritten in the mode of a speculative genre-study with the Pastoral figure – especially the 'critic-as-hero' – occupying the roles of protagonist and commentator at each new vantage-point along the way. But it was also, as we have seen, a problematical book, not least on account of its implied message – more explicit in the later chapters – that Pastoral irony required an increasingly difficult balancing-act between the specialized pleasures of a rich and complex intellectual life and the demands of commonplace human sympathy or straightforward social justice. This becomes most evident in his commentary on the *Alice* books, a chapter where one feels that Empson (like Carroll) is juggling with a range of painful antimonies that might at any moment precipitate the collapse into neurosis or total, psychotic isolation. 'It is the ground-bass of this kinship with madness, I think, that makes it so clear that the books are not trifling, and the cool courage with which Alice accepts madmen that gives them their strength' (*SVP*, p. 233). At this point the Pastoral conventions are manifestly falling apart under the strain of an increasingly drastic split between consciousness and unconsciousness, 'complex' and 'simple' (or hyperintellectual and quasi-primitivist) modes of self-understanding.

COMPLEX WORDS AND THE GRAMMAR OF ASSENT

In short, Empson had travelled about as far as possible along that path of phenomenological reflection – allied to a strain of Romantic irony – which opened up such alarming prospects of terminal non-communication. *Complex Words* can then be seen as his consequent attempt to provide an alternative, more helpful (or theoretically adequate) account of the ways in which language can put up resistance to our normal powers of intellectual grasp. And it does so by shifting the focus of interest from conjectural states of mind in the author or reader to complexities of logico-semantic 'grammar' which are understood precisely as specific *deviations* from a shared basis of rational intelligibility. The 'bits of machinery' that Empson proposes in the book's opening chapters are basically those of two-place predicate logic ('A = B'), eked out with a range of fairly homespun ancillary notions to cover those cases where the structure of semantic entailment cannot be coaxed into a clear-cut pattern of compacted logical grammar. W. V. Quine offers a useful brief statement of why this procedure is so important for logicians and how it serves to clear up various sources of confusion in 'natural' language.

> What follows from what is largely a question of the patterns formed within a text by various grammatical connectives and operators, and of the patterns in which the verbs, nouns, adjectives and pronouns recur and interweave. Predicate logic abstracts those patterns from the embedding texts by substituting neutral letters for the *predicates* – that is, for the verbs, nouns and adjectives that bear all the burden of subject matter. Just one of the predicates is retained intact, the two-place predicate '=' of Identity, as a distinctly logical predicate.[50]

For Quine – as indeed for Frege, Russell and other philosophers who have written on the topic – such techniques can only operate at a high level of abstract logical regimentation where semantics gives way to syntax, or where the vagaries of meaning that accrue to individual words in context are bracketed out with the object of revealing some crystalline logical structure. In this way, so it is hoped, language can be purged of its rich though messy 'natural' condition and reconstituted in a form more amenable to the purposes of logical analysis and critique. Thus, as Quine puts it,

> paraphrasing and trimming, we can coax vast reaches of language into this skimpy structure. A celebrated example of paraphrase is that of 'if p then q' into 'not (p and not q)', which is faithful enough for most purposes. Our identity predicate '=' comes to the fore in paraphrasing 'else', 'except', and the singular 'the'. A complex segment of discourse may, on the other hand, be swept into the framework of predicate logic as a seamless whole and not be treated as atomic when its internal structure offers nothing to the logical argument at hand.[51]

In other words the precondition for attaining this degree of analytical clarity and rigour is that complexity of meaning be treated as a function of the logico-syntactic relationship between terms (or stretches of discourse conceived for this purpose as 'atomic' elements), and that semantic questions be as far as possible ruled out of court. Thus the usefulness of the method varies inversely with the scope it provides for interpreting such natural-language features such as ambiguity, metaphor, connotative meaning, rhetorical complexity and so forth. Precision comes only at the price of excluding any semantic functions that cannot be 'coaxed' into this kind of minimalist framework.

Empson's most striking innovation in *Complex Words* is to take this approach and see how it works when applied not so much to the logical grammar (or order of predicative relations) *between* various terms, propositional functions, etc., but rather to the structure of implicit semantic 'equations' that operate *within* certainly highly charged or ambivalent words, and which thus make it possible for such words to carry a force of implied argument in and of themselves. As I have said, his basic term of analysis is the identity relation ('='), although compared with Quine he allows much greater scope for the varieties of logical entailment brought about by differing contexts of usage or structures of semantic implication. The following, highly schematic table of functions (reproduced from *Complex Words*, p. 54) will give some idea of Empson's analytical approach:

	Subject	Predicate
The major sense of the word is the . . .		
The sense demanded by the most		
immediate context is the . . . **Subject**	II	I
. . . **Predicate**	III	V
The order of the senses is indifferent:	IV	

The roman numerals denote the various classes of semantic equation which – according to Empson – provide the most useful 'machinery' for coping with the otherwise unmanageable range of possible meanings or implicative structures in context. Type IV is the most problematic class since it has to include all those dubious instances where there exists no clear-cut order of logical priority, that is to say, no means of deciding between 'A = B' and 'B = A'. Such cases range from the paradoxes of religion ('God is Love') to political slogans, propaganda techniques, so-called 'primitive' uses of language, and expressions like Keats's 'Beauty is truth, truth beauty', whose sense of profound psychological conviction goes along with a certain ambiguity or vagueness of philosophic import. Nevertheless – Empson argues – it is important to see just how these rhetorical devices take effect and at what point precisely they offer resistance to the efforts of logico-semantic paraphrase. After all, 'if he [Keats] leads up with clear marks of solemnity to saying that Beauty is Truth he doesn't want to be told, any more than anyone else, that "of course" he meant nothing at all except to excite Emotion' (*CW*, p. 7).

This is the main ground for Empson's quarrel with the emotivist theory of poetic meaning proposed by I. A. Richards. It is also his reason for rejecting the idea – as argued by Cleanth Brooks and the American New Critics – that poetry embodies an order of 'paradoxical' wisdom above or beyond the requirements of rational prose sense. For this doctrine can just as easily be used to defend any kind of irrationalist or muddle-headed sentiment, any use of language that evades the protocols of sense-making logic and consistency in order to insinuate some 'profound' pseudo-truth under cover of its special dispensation. At least critics shouldn't raise paradox into a high point of principle or a kind of self-promoting aesthetic ideology that effectively lumps poetry together with the worst, most actively misleading forms of religious or political dogma. Thus when Empson comes back to the lines from Keats later in his book it is by way of taking issue with Brooks's reading and the idea that this poetry is somehow all the better – more authentically poetic – for not making sense in logically accountable terms. In fact it now strikes him as a Type IV equation, one in which 'the assertion goes both ways round', so that 'either each entails the other, or both are examples of some third notion in which they are included' (p. 372). This is not to say that since the lines establish their own particular 'logic' of meaning – what Empson calls a structure of 'mutual metaphor' – they must therefore be regarded as enouncing a truth beyond reach of commonplace rational grasp. On the contrary: his response, here as with the passage from Wordsworth in *Seven Types*, is to press as far as possible towards analysing their effect and then admit frankly that the lines *don't work* – or that they fail to make good their high Romantic argument – if read with a view to their implicit structures of logico-semantic entailment. The main problem is that Keats seems to exploit his Type IV equation (i.e., the reversible order of priorities between 'A = B' and 'B = A') in order to suggest that Beauty and Truth are so perfectly interchangeable that 'there are no ugly truths', so that 'all truths are to be included in some kind of beauty' (p. 372). And such devices are always suspect – so Empson believes – when they fall back on vague intimations of a visionary insight or reconciling power inaccessible to plain-prose reason. Thus

> here the identity becomes a full case of Mutual Metaphor, or a full parallel to an equation of Type IV, because the third notion which is supposed to be brought forward has not much likeness to either of the two things identified.
>
> (p. 373)

Empson is not alone among critics of Keats in entertaining the suspicion that this sentiment is both morally dubious – since based on a form of aesthetic ideology indifferent to the harsher realities of human experience – and overly (even offensively) 'rhetorical' in so far as it lacks any adequate structure of argument by which to back up its claim. Thus one might come to feel – and here he cites Robert Bridges – that 'the last lines with their brash attempt to end with a smart bit of philosophy have not got enough knowledge behind them' (p. 374). But such a negative judgement would carry weight only if one had tried out various possible ways of fitting the lines into some kind of rational sense-making structure, and not simply read them (on Richards's terms) as appealing to a complex of emotional 'attitudes' in the reader, or again – following Brooks – as belonging to a realm of supra-rational poetic 'paradox' where standards of truth or valid argument simply don't apply. Empson does his best to give the lines a 'sensible' interpretation, and in fact comes up with some plausible ideas of how the poem's crowning statement might be found to follow with a measure of supporting 'philosophical' conviction. All the same he concedes that 'there is perhaps a puzzle about how far we ought to make this kind of effort, and at what point the size of the effort required simply proves the poem to be bad' (p. 374).

His main point, here and elsewhere, is that we won't do justice to poetry or to ourselves as intelligent readers if we give up this effort at an early stage and resort to some saving irrationalist formula (or handy emotivist escape route) which consigns poetry to a realm of 'pseudo-statements' devoid of argumentative or truth-telling warrant. 'Emotions well handled in art are somehow absorbed into the structure; their expression is made also to express where and why they are valid' (p. 372). This sounds like a version of Eliot's 'objective correlative', with the difference – the crucial difference for Empson – that the kind of adequacy involved has to do with matters of truth-functional or logico-semantic grasp, and not (as in Eliot) with an imagist appeal to sensuous intuitions supposedly captured in a language of immediate visual or tactile apprehension. In fact Empson has little time for this idea that poetry's proper business is to 'hand across sensations bodily', a quasi-phenomenalist confusion of language with the realm of natural or organic processes which he – like Paul de Man – finds responsible for manifold errors in the discourse of modern (post-Romantic) literary criticism.[52] What Empson means when he says that emotions well handled are somehow 'absorbed into the structure' is that good poetry stands up better to the kind of analytical commentary – the seeking out of semantic 'equations' or intelligible structures of compacted argument – which enables the critic to avoid such forms of premature phenomenalist appeal. None the less, 'it often happens that a poet has built his machine, putting all the parts into it and so on very genuinely, and the machine does not go' (*CW*, p. 374). And there is still some doubt in Empson's mind – despite all his valiant sense-making efforts on Keats's behalf – as to whether the poem actually succeeds in giving substance to its visionary claims. Hence what many readers have found vaguely offensive in the last two lines; 'there is a flavour of Christian Science; they fear to wake up in Fairyland, and probably the country of Uplift' (p. 373). Empson goes various ways around to contest this view but in the end – as with Wordsworth's 'Tintern Abbey' – he has to admit that this rhetorical 'uplift' is doing much of the work and continues to resist the best efforts of analysis along logico-semantic lines.

It is important to grasp that there is more at stake here than a technical dispute about 'emotive' versus 'cognitive' approaches to the language of poetry, or perhaps just a perverse rearguard attempt, on Empson's part, to translate the programme of logical positivism into a method for literary criticism. Certainly *Complex Words* is very much a part of that Cambridge ethos that produced Bertrand Russell's celebrated 'theory of descriptions' and his analysis of referring expressions in terms of their 'logical grammar' and structures of compacted propositional sense.[53] (Whether Empson had also read Frege at this stage, especially his cardinal essay on 'Sense and Reference',[54] can only be a matter for conjecture.) But there is a larger, moral or ethical dimension which joins on directly to these specialized researches and which Empson thinks indispensable for any self-respecting practice of literary-critical judgement. He takes A. E. Housman as a test-case here since on the one hand Housman's poems undoubtedly 'work' (i.e., succeed remarkably in putting across their peculiar mixture of fatalist gloom, contempt for all 'merely' human values and activities, and attitude of moral indifferentism in the face of Nature's destructive forces) while on the other their 'philosophy' is one that most readers would reject outright – and quite properly so, Empson thinks – if asked to accept it as a matter of plain-prose argument or practical belief. Thus 'Housman is about as pure a case as you can get of a poet using untruths to excite attitudes' (p.13). But this doesn't mean – far from it – that one had better fall back on the Richards line, discount any truth-claims that the poetry might seem to assert, and allow those 'attitudes' to carry one along for the sake of some odd (if intense) emotional experience. In short, 'even here I think it would be a tedious flippancy to say that the truth or untruth of the assertions is simply irrelevant to the poem' (p. 13).

This is why Empson's arguments in *Complex Words* are aimed just as much against pragmatist accounts of meaning and truth as against I. A. Richards and other proponents of the emotivist doctrine. (See for instance his three Appendices on 'Theories of value', pp. 414–43.) Thus on Richards's view 'the acceptance which a pseudo-statement receives is entirely governed by its effect upon our feelings and attitudes. . . . a pseudo-statement is "true" if it suits or serves some attitude or links together attitudes which on other grounds are desirable' (cited in *CW*, p. 13). But of course this leaves wide open the question as to just what 'desirable' means in various contexts of evaluative usage; whether attitudes of a plainly irrational or (in Housman's case) a regress-ive and well-nigh paranoid character might be 'desirable' for readers in search of some vicarious emotional release; or indeed whether poetry has anything to do with questions of truth, right reason or ethical judgement as applied in areas outside this charmed aesthetic domain. Empson puts the case as forcefully as possible when he remarks on the obvious *undesirability* of Hous-man's poetic creed when considered not only in terms of rational self-interest, narrowly conceived, but also from the wider (other-regarding) standpoint of a shared human interest in the commu-nal good. This outlook – roughly speaking, a Benthamite ethic of 'the greatest happiness for the greatest number', tempered by a sense that such values must include some measure of enlight-ened altruism – is a constant point of reference in Empson's criticism, especially his later attacks on 'neo-Christian' interpreters who raised their contempt for all merely human pleasures and enjoyments into a form of perverse self-denying ordinance or high-priestly mystification. (There is a nice example in *Milton's God* where he takes T. S. Eliot to task for suggesting that Milton's Hell is a lot more convincing than his vaguely visualized scenes in the Garden of Eden. 'So long as you gave Mr Eliot images of someone being tortured his nerves were at peace, but if you gave him an image of two people making each other happy he screamed.')[55]

What needs to be understood here is the close relation that Empson perceives between a rationalist approach to questions of poetic meaning and a theory of value (or enlightened mutual self-interest) that likewise avoids the dangerous appeal to modes of 'satisfaction' supposedly exempt from any such normative stan-dards of judgement. His simplest statement of the ethical position occurs in Appendix I of *Complex Words*, where Empson sets it down as a matter of logical inference that

> [t]he creature must think 'It is good, in general, to act so as to produce good effects. Good effects are the same when I am there as when I am not, like the rest of the external world, hence they are good in you as well as in me. Hence, it is good for me to produce good effects in you.' Surely this simply follows from the intellectuality of the creature; it does not depend on exciting emotions of fraternal love or what not, though no doubt they are needed if he is to act in the belief when under strain. It is part of the process of believing that there is a real world outside you, an idea which is built up by generalization and analogy.
>
> (p. 427)

Going back to the Housman example we can now perhaps see more clearly why it struck Empson both as an extreme case (i.e., of 'emotions' getting out of touch with cognitive interests or veridical truth-claims), and also as a case that his theory would need to confront if it wanted to offer anything more than a vague sense of rational reassurance. For if Wordsworth and Keats put problems in the way of Empson's analytical approach – problems having to do with the disjunctive relation between logic, grammar and rhetoric – then Housman is a poet whose undoubted power of lyrical utterance goes along with a massive and perverse indifference to the claims of reason, morality and mere good sense. In Empson's words,

> there is a sullen conviction that no effort is worth making, a philosophy for the village idiot; and the illogicality which we are told to admire (as being typical of poetical language) is not any 'freedom' from logic but the active false logic of persecution mania.
>
> (p. 13)

On the other hand he is also compelled to admit that Housman's poems have a genuine power and intensity of lyric feeling which cannot be ignored whatever their deficiencies at the level of argument or 'philosophic' import. Hence the great problem for Empson's approach in *Complex Words*: that 'on this theory the poetry is very bad, whereas it seems clear that an adequate theory would be able to admit its merits' (p. 13). That is to say, the 'machinery' of verbal exegesis is always liable to encounter cases where the meaning is resistant to further explication, or where the structures of logico-semantic entailment produce some plainly absurd set of attitudes, meanings, or beliefs. Even so, Empson argues, one is justified in sticking to the machinery despite these problems that rise up against it when applied to such anomalous or recalcitrant material. After all, 'what is done in other fields of study . . . is to give symbols to a few elements that seem essential, avoid refining on the definitions till the examples make it necessary, and try how far the symbols will go' (p. 2). This is pretty much Empson's manner of approach in *Complex Words*, and it is one whose occasional (and readily admitted) failures shouldn't be allowed to obscure the book's extraordinary range of speculative insight.

It is worth saying something more about the Housman case since it brings out the extent to which, in Empson's criticism, questions of method (or interpretive theory) always go along with issues in the realm of moral and socio-political concern. The following is typical of many passages in his later work which readers – especially academic critics – have tended to regard as mere 'anecdotal' detail, no doubt of some interest from a life-and-times viewpoint but otherwise somewhat beside the point.

> I remember a Japanese class of mine reading Housman in 1931, when they were liable to be conscripted to fight in Manchuria, indeed a man had already been drafted from the class and killed in Shanghai, and they wrote down pretty consistently, 'We think Housman is quite right. We will do no good to anyone being killed as soldiers, but we will be admired, and we all want to be admired, and anyway we are better dead.' To do the old gentleman [Housman] justice, I think he would have been shocked by these bits of schoolwork.
>
> (*CW*, p. 13)

His central point here – as throughout *Complex Words* – is that criticism is simply not doing its job if it fails to make a bridge between 'technical' interests (like the status of poetic truth-claims or modes of semantic implication) and issues of a real-world moral and practical kind. Such is indeed his main argument against the 'emotive' theory of poetic language and its various non-cognitivist offshoots: namely that these doctrines work out in practice as a pretext for critics to focus their attention exclusively on 'the words on the page', and thus to discount all the problems that arise when literature is read and taught in differing socio-historical contexts. Hence Empson's attitude of sturdy contempt for any theory – like the 'old' New Critical veto on talk about intentions, biography, historical background, and so forth – which invents 'bother-headed' philosophical reasons for treating poetry as a special kind of language, a self-enclosed domain of purely rhetorical structures and devices. For the effect of such (in his view) mind-warping preconceptions is to persuade critics first that they must suspend all their normal waking habits of judgement when interpreting poetry, and second that it is some kind of vulgar mistake – or at any rate a breach of critical etiquette – to ask the plain question whether poems *make sense* in terms of propositional content or valid argument.

This is why Empson says (in a footnote to *Complex Words*) that

the term Ambiguity, which I used in a book title and as a kind of slogan, implying the reader is left in doubt between two meanings, is more or less superseded by the idea of a double meaning which is intended to be fitted into a definite structure.

(p. 103n)

The virtue of this approach is that it gives a hold for discussing truth-claims, beliefs and propositional attitudes, rather than talking more vaguely – as in *Seven Types* – about the various possible senses of a word, line or stanza conceived as so many loosely articulated units or atoms of meaning. And it is Empson's argument – one that he shares with some current analytical philosophers of language, Donald Davidson among them[56] – that one can best take account of the real variety of values, world-views, ethical belief-systems, etc., *not* by espousing a wholesale relativist creed but by imputing a large measure of shared rationality to all language-users and then making sense of problematical cases as and when they come up. For Davidson this has to do with the much-discussed problem of 'radical translation', the question whether – in principle – one could ever make a start in understanding or translating some alien language, given the fact of 'ontological relativity' (i.e., the scope for a large-scale mismatch between referring expressions, logical constants, modes of ostensive definition, etc.), and the consequent lack of any firm assurance that one has got the 'native informant' right on even the most basic details.[57] Empson – needless to say – doesn't have much time for such extravagant varieties of sceptical doubt. But it is clear that *Complex Words* is intended in part as a rejoinder to those various forms of non-cognitivist doctrine which imply a similar breakdown of rational confidence in the power of language to communicate meanings – or articulate truth-claims – across different contexts of informing value and belief. Moreover, he is at one with Davidson in thinking that relativism, at least in its more sweeping or doctrinaire versions, most often takes rise from a single basic error: that of starting out from a theory of language which relativizes words to their whole background of meanings, assumptions, language-games, cultural 'forms of life' and so forth, rather than looking to the truth-conditions (or the structures of logico-semantic entailment) which then give a hold for interpreting the word in this or that specific context of utterance. Where Empson differs from Davidson and other like-minded analytical philosophers is in locating those structures *within* single words whose range of co-implicated senses and logical relations can thus provide the basis for a worked-out 'grammar' of the various orders of semantic equation.

This argument takes a reflexive turn when Empson considers the key-word 'grammar' itself, a term that is used in two very different (indeed flatly opposite) senses, and whose semantic structure – or force of 'compacted doctrine' – is seen to vary according to which takes precedence in any given instance. One idea of 'grammar' (the descriptivist attitude) can best be summarized in Empson's words: 'grammar is merely a codification of usage, and therefore must not attempt anything else' (*CW*, p. 311). The other (prescriptivist) account takes an altogether more elevated view of the grammarian's role since it allows him or her to define good usage – or to lay down standards of linguistic competence – according to precedent, rule, or normative criteria. Empson is not so much interested in this old conundrum (though he does have some relevant things to say on the topic) as in the way that the word 'grammar', as used by both parties, effectively encodes a whole set of attitudes compacted into a single key-term which carries the entire weight of implied argument.

Here again it is Richards who sets his thinking off in this direction by adopting a broadly contextualist definition of 'grammar' according to which the word – like the discipline – takes its sense (or its methodological bearings) from the whole surrounding context of argument.[58] For Empson, on the contrary, 'grammar' (the word and the practice) involves a lot more in the way of directive intelligence or power to influence language and thought through structures of meaning that cannot be explained on a straightforward contextualist account. Thus Richard's theory

> makes the prelogical (or usual) thinking a matter of whole sentences or paragraphs. . . . it is only in logical thinking, which recognises that the definition of a term is different from statements about an already defined term, that the analyst can usefully attend to the meanings of single words. . . . In [this] fluid state the words 'cannot be said to have any meaning'; no doubt the single words have functions, but such a word is hardly more than an aggregate of potentialities, like what you feel for a syllable used for many words. . . . No doubt this process actually occurs. But in general the language performance is about a topic which can be given in a single word. . . . And, precisely because of the fluidity of words in general, the word recognised as the topic is likely to grow a more inclusive structure in the process. . . . Precisely because they have not got single meanings, they can be made to sum up the process of thought.
>
> (*CW*, pp. 312–13)

This passage carries echoes of a long line of philosophico-linguistic speculative thought, running all the way from Plato's *Theaetetus* to Gilbert Ryle's essay 'Letters and syllables in Plato'.[59] That is to say, it raises the question of precisely what constitutes the minimal distinctive unit of sense or intelligibility in language, given that words only signify by virtue of their role in some larger context of articulated meanings or truth-values. Like Plato, Empson sees a useful analogy with the various levels of constituent analysis applied in morphological studies, i.e., the ascending series of integrative functions that starts out from letters, combines them into syllables, and then arrives at the word boundaries beyond which lexical units enter into larger (syntactic or discursive) chains of utterance. As developed by Ryle, this analogy points to the fact that no single word possesses meaning in and of itself; that it is only through a process of higher-level integration – by grasping the word in its 'syncategorematic' role – that we are able to assign the operative truth-conditions and hence the word's meaning in any given context. All this Empson accepts, though with the further (and highly significant) proviso: that such structures of logico-semantic implication may sometimes operate *within single words* so as to give them a certain propositional force – or a capacity for bearing various kinds of 'compacted' doctrine – that could not be explained on any purely contextualist account.

This is why 'grammar' is such an interesting case: because it divides theorists into two chief camps (the prescriptive and descriptive grammarians), both of whom make it a code-word for their sense of priorities *vis-à-vis* usage and correctness. But only from a qualified prescriptivist standpoint could one offer a generalized theory (like Empson's) designed to take adequate account of this 'machinery' and explain how the mind makes rational sense of the semantic operations involved. For there is a 'grammar' of complex words which raises all the same issues, in particular the question whether words take on meaning by absorption, so to speak, from associated contexts of utterance, or whether they can act as a focus and vehicle for structures of inbuilt semantic implication which in turn redefine the very sense of that operative context. Thus it may be the case – as Empson readily concedes – that

> when a man is talking straight ahead he cannot be supposed to give individual words a great deal of attention, and in arguing that one of them has a particular structure the theorist must be supposing he gives it that structure in his subconscious mind.
>
> (*CW*, p. 319)

But this is after all not so wildly improbable since 'the subconscious mind is patently doing a great deal of work anyhow; for one thing it is getting the grammar in order'. Or again: 'it [i.e., the putative "grammar"] would be wrong if it did not correspond to anything in the speaker's mind, but he cannot be supposed to string his sentences together without any mental operation at all' (p. 319). What this amounts to – in brief – is a rationalist philosophy of mind, language and interpretation which assumes that literary critics (like grammarians) can best start out from the relevant facts about our competence or powers of intuitive grasp as language-users, and then go on to derive a more elaborately formalized account of the processes involved.

Indeed one could draw an interesting parallel with Chomsky's theory of generative grammar, especially those later (modified) versions of it that take more account of semantic factors in constructing their models of grammatical intelligibility.[60] But my main purpose in conducting this excursion through the thickets of linguistic philosophy is to place Empson's book in the wider context of modern ideas about language, logic and truth. For it then becomes clear that *Complex Words* takes its place in a tradition of thought whose major representatives are Frege, Russell, Davidson, and other such proponents of a logico-semantic analytical approach which goes clean against the dominant drift of recent poststructuralist literary theory. Thus Empson's objections to a radically contextualist account of meaning and interpretation would also apply to those modish versions of poststructuralist thinking which take it pretty much for granted (following Saussure) that language is a network of signifying relations 'without positive terms'; that all our operative notions of truth, reference, logical entailment, etc., are contingent upon the various codes, conventions or 'discourses' in circulation at any given time; and therefore – what appears the inevitable upshot – that critics are deluded if they think to offer any workable *theory* of language, logic and interpretive truth which doesn't concede the utter relativity of all such notions. Empson's book appeared long before the poststructuralist vogue but it does engage with quite a range of adversary positions, among them (as we have seen) several that anticipate these current ways of thinking.

Complex Words comes up with the following counter-arguments, some of them explicit, others requiring a degree of extrapolative licence, or what philosophers politely call 'rational reconstruction'. (1) There is no reason, aside from various kinds of deep-grained cultural-relativist prejudice, to suppose that language must exhibit such a range of possible meanings, conventions, or signifying structures that any generalized theory – any 'grammar' of complex words – must be a vain hope and chimerical delusion. (2) The chief point of convergence between Empson and Davidson: understanding the sense of a given expression is a matter of grasping its truth-conditions, rather than the other way around. (3) Following Russell, whom Empson had clearly read with some care, as well as Frege, whose argument he is perhaps reinventing: one cannot (like the poststructuralists) erect Saussure's specialized requirements for the project of synchronic linguistics into a

64

wholesale anti-realist ontology, allowing all questions of referential truth to drop clean out of the picture, and treating language as a strictly two-term relation between signifier and signified. For if indeed it is the case – as Frege says – that 'sense determines reference' in all instances save those of straightforward ostensive definition, still one couldn't even make a start in learning, using, interpreting or translating any utterance unless one had grasped the relevant conditions for what qualified as a veridical speech-act or a paradigm case of referential discourse.[61] (4) There is no accounting for our normal capacity as language-using creatures – let alone our ability to interpret metaphors, deviant 'equations', paradoxical utterances and other such 'extraordinary' forms of expression – without imputing a large measure of shared interpretive competence which goes far beyond anything envisaged on the structuralist or cultural-relativist model. (5) This is also an argument against any premature retreat into 'emotive' theories of poetic or literary language, theories which tend to underestimate the extent to which 'feelings' in words (or matters of emotional 'tone') can be analysed in cognitive or truth-functional terms. Thus: 'much of what appears to us as a "feeling" (as is obvious in the case of a complex metaphor) will in fact be quite an elaborate structure of related meanings' (*CW*, pp. 56–7).

From all of which it follows (6) that literary theory cannot get along without at least some grounding in logic, semantics and analytical philosophy of language, even if it mostly takes them on board by a kind of 'commonsense' intuitive osmosis, without much need for explicit clarification of the formal principles involved. Of course there is a problem about claiming Empson as an ally for 'theory' in the current, highly charged polemical climate since he later came to feel such a strong aversion towards the various developments – from New Criticism to deconstruction – bearing that name. But what he found most objectionable in these movements was the mixture of geared-up professional expertise – pseudo-expertise, as he thought it – and extreme remoteness from the practical business of interpreting literary texts. His 'Comment for the second edition' of *Complex Words* puts the case with regard to ethical theory, but could also serve as a general statement of Empson's approach to such questions.

> Someone said that my Appendix on Theories of Value confuses the necessary distinction between meta-ethics and

ethics, because it assumes that theories about the meaning of ethical terms also make ethical recommendations; he felt this enough to sweep aside my amateur [arguments]. But I think that they obviously do. A man can generally see that other people's do, though he tends to feel that his own are universal common sense. The idea that the theorist is not a part of the world he examines is one of the deepest sources of error, and crops up all over the place.

(p. 445)

His point – taken up in a variety of ways throughout *Complex Words* – is that 'theories', even those of a technical or specialized character, can still have substantive implications beyond their particular expert domain. Thus, for instance, any linguist (or literary critic) who adopts something akin to Empson's view of the relation between thought, language and interpretation is likely to match it with a high general estimate of human rationality and purposive intelligence. What is more, such an attitude will tend to go along with certain condign ethical or socio-political beliefs, as in Chomsky's espousal of a left-libertarian stance which derives – or at any rate claims philosophical support – from his arguments for a rationalist philosophy of mind backed up by the evidence of linguistic universals vested in the nature of human understanding.[62] Thus for Chomsky, as for Empson, there is an obvious link between issues in the realm of linguistic theory (or the semantics of complex words) and questions of moral and political accountability.

In Empson's case this commitment takes the form of a preference for words which convey a certain humour of mutual or self-implicating irony, a 'pastoral' sense of the speaker's being somehow caught up in the same kinds of complex social predicament that he or she typically detects in other people. Hence his comment on the key-word 'dog' in its 'hearty' Restoration and eighteenth-century usage as a term of half-mocking, half-affectionate abuse: that 'when you call a man a dog with obscure praise, or treat a dog as half-human, you do not much believe in the Fall of Man, you assume a rationalist view of man as the most triumphant of the animals' (*CW*, p. 176). The point about such words is that they seem to involve both a generalized 'grammar' of semantic implication with strong universalist claims, and a normative aspect – or force of ethical recommendation – which inevi-

66

tably brings value-judgements into play. The same applies to 'sense', one of Empson's main exhibits, and a word whose extraordinary range of meanings – from 'sense-impression' via 'commonsense judgement' to Wordsworth's prophetic 'language of the sense' or mystical 'sense of something far more deeply interfused' – allows it to convey the most diverse kinds of compacted philosophical doctrine. All the same, Empson thinks, there is a middle-ground set of equations clustered around the basic idea of 'good sense' and tending to imply that this quality involves a healthy respect for the claims of sensuous experience and a 'sensible' degree of scepticism with regard to other, more mysterious or elevated forms of extra-sensory knowledge. In its simplest version this amounts to a kind of phenomenalist doctrine whereby 'good sense' equates with 'trusting to the senses' or getting along – like the 'dog' of popular repute – on a rock-bottom basis of reliable instinct coupled with the elementary social desires imposed by the need for survival. This usage has a distinctly 'period' feel and goes along with the notion, most pronounced in English writers of the early modern or Renaissance period, that 'a sensible man will be a bit of a sensualist, well rooted in the earth, and that his judgements will be based on the evidence of the senses supposed to be free from "theory" ' (p. 264). But it can also be extended – as Empson shows from various (mostly eighteenth-century) examples – so as to take in the idea that 'sense' and 'sensibility' are related through a structure of mutual entailment, so that having 'good sense' is a fair indication of possessing good feelings (or sufficiently refined moral sentiments).

Of course the two words can get into conflict, as when Jane Austen constructs a whole plot around the rival claims of 'sense' and 'sensibility', playing them off through a series of structural ironies which the reader – at any rate the fit reader – is expected to pick up on cue. And 'sense' can itself give rise to all manner of deviant (indeed pathological) equations, as in Shakespeare's 'problem play' *Measure for Measure*, where the commonsense or 'middle-range' meanings of the word tend to fade into the background, so that everything turns on a drastic confrontation between hedonist and puritan attitudes, both of which reduce to the stark proposition that 'sense = mere sensuality'. Not that one could find all of this 'in' the play without possessing at least some knowledge of the relevant historical 'background'. In Empson's words:

there was a strand of loathing for sexuality in any form,
partly no doubt as an intellectual agreement with the Puritans, but one that he [Shakespeare] recognised as a diseased
frame of mind; and contrasting with this a loathing for the
cruelty which this line of feeling produced in the Puritans,
above all for the claim that to indulge the cruelty satisfies
justice.

(*CW,* p. 272)

But it is Empson's claim that if one knows this much – a fairly
basic provision of readerly competence – then all the play's major
themes and conflicts of motive may be seen as carried by the
key-word 'sense' and its various structures of semantic implication. What makes *Measure for Measure* such a problematic case
is the way it cuts out a whole range of meanings normal to the
word and brings in a set of alternative equations – some of them
deriving (as Empson suggests) from darker passages in the sonnet
sequence – by way of exploring this nexus of ideas around puri-
tanism, sensuality, and repressed sexual drives. Thus

the subtle confusion of the word is used for a mood of
fretted and exhausting casuistry; the corruption of the best
makes it the worst; charity is good, but has strange and
shameful roots; the idea of a lawsuit about such matters is
itself shameful, and indeed more corrupt than natural evil.

(p. 273)

But it is still the case – so Empson believes – that the 'normal'
interpretive machinery must be working somewhere in the background, since otherwise we should have no comparative yardstick,
no handle by which to get a hold on these deviant equations.
Thus finally the play 'moves over, as the key-word does, from a
consideration of "sensuality" to a consideration of "sanity", and
then the action is forced round to a happy ending' (p. 287).

Even so, as Empson's comment suggests, this reversal is
achieved against large dramatic odds, and with no very plausible
show of motivational psychology. The most powerful and oddly
convincing passages are those where 'sense' undergoes such
extreme contortions of meaning that the play comes across as
'an examination of sanity itself, which is seen crumbling and
dissolving in the soliloquies of Angelo' (p. 270). And at this
point clearly it puts a great strain on Empson's rational-humanist

conviction that the best, most rewardingly complex instances of poetic language are those that involve some tacit background of argument, some structure of implied propositional attitudes, by which to make good their normative claim, as opposed to the kinds of irrationalist paradox that critics are often over-willing to praise. This is a real problem with *Complex Words*, and one that Empson confronts most directly in his Note on Orwell's *Nineteen Eighty-Four*. Thus,

> what he [Orwell] calls 'double-think', a process of intentional but genuine self-deception, really does seem a positive capacity of the human mind, so curious and so important in its effects that any theory in this field needs to reckon with it.
>
> (p. 83)

All the same – as with *Measure for Measure* – Empson thinks that we can best get a grip on such linguistic perversions by applying the more normal interpretive machinery and sticking to the basic rationalist principle, namely that 'the human mind, that is, the public human mind as expressed in a language, is not irredeemably lunatic and cannot be made so'. But the question remains as to whether this amounts to much more than a pious hope, a preference – as manifest in so much of Empson's criticism – for examples that happen to chime with his own strong rational-humanist beliefs.

Empson had worked during the war in the Far Eastern section of the BBC's foreign service, a job which he found both depressing and instructive. Such work, he wrote later in *Milton's God*, 'cannot narrow a man's understanding of other people's opinions', though it may in the end 'narrow his own opinions'.[63] Milton had done his own share of anti-royalist propaganda – some of it decidedly devious – and Empson found the experience useful as a way into Milton's tortuously complex psychology. But the real challenge to the rationalist semantics of *Complex Words* comes from Orwellian 'Newspeak', the idea of a language wholly given over to falsehood, paradox, and ideological brainwashing. As a specialist advisor to the Indian and Burmese service, Orwell had worked alongside Empson in the wartime BBC. Empson had derived some philosophical comfort from the fact that such work could be carried on without abandoning all respect for rational thought. Orwell drew the opposite conclusion: that language was open to a whole range of perverted rhetorical techniques which in the end might reach the point of erasing all distinctions between truth and falsehood, fact and fiction, logic and 'the active false logic of persecution mania'.[64] His novel struck Empson as a 'hideously special case' from which it was wrong to draw any generalized conclusions. Its effectiveness depended largely on its power to 'frighten the reader into believing the possibility of what he does not really think possible'. What this argument comes down to, in face of Orwell's 'nightmare' book, is a belief that there are limits to the powers of unreason or the psychopathology of language when placed in the service of this or that mendacious totalitarian creed. And this despite the fact – as Empson concedes – that the paradoxes of Newspeak are not so very different from the kinds of suasive rhetorical device that characterize the language of certain types of poetry. At any rate the rationalist would need to explain how such devices could carry real conviction if on the one hand their truth-claims were manifestly false, while on the other hand (*contra* Richards) they couldn't be treated as just a species of 'emotive' language, exempt from all the customary standards of veridical utterance or cognitive accountability.

Complex Words may be read as testing Empson's argument across a wide range of literary cases which put up varying degrees of resistance. More than once the method threatens to break down entirely, as in the somewhat baffled chapter on Milton's use of 'all', where the word takes on such a massively encompassing variety of senses that it feels to Empson like some kind of deep unconscious 'symbol', beyond reach of analysis on rational or logico-semantic lines. In this instance – perhaps the most extreme of its kind – the Richards doctrine may indeed be the only one that works, since 'so far from being able to chart a structure of related meanings in a key-word, you get an obviously important word for which an Emotive theory seems all that you can hold' (*CW*, p. 101). Nevertheless, Empson thinks it an untypical case and one that reflects not so much some ultimate truth about the nature of poetic language – i.e., its illogicality, resistance to paraphrase, paradoxical character or whatever – but the sheer psychological strain imposed by Milton's attempt to make decent (humanly intelligible) sense of a thoroughly pernicious and mind-bending creed.

That his feelings were crying out against his appalling theology in favour of freedom, happiness and the pursuit of truth was I think not obvious to him, and it is this part of the dramatic complex which is thrust upon us by the repeated *all.* . . . One could draw up equations for the effect of *all* in Milton, relating not so much senses of the word as whole contexts in which it has become habitual. But they would no longer be tracing a clear-cut, even if unconscious, mental operation, like those which let us talk straight ahead and get the grammar in order; they would be concerned with something more like a Freudian symbol.

(p. 104)

It was this line of argument that Empson took up in *Milton's God* (1961) and the other late essays attacking what he saw as the corrupting influence of 'neo-Christian' values and assumptions when applied to the reading of Renaissance and modern texts. One could argue that his failure to make much headway with the structural-semantic analysis of Milton's 'all' was a major reason for Empson's abandoning the abstruse researches of *Complex Words* and going over to a less 'theoretical' kind of criticism, one that on the whole abjured such speculative interests and stuck to matters of historical and psycho-biographical import. But in fact these two aspects of his work were closely related, since the main purpose of *Complex Words* was to provide a kind of broad-based theoretical support – a 'machinery' of interpretive procedures and ground-rules – for the liberal-humanist position adopted in his reading of individual texts. Here again it is Empson's great argument that one can in fact derive normative principles (or an ethics of interpretive practice) from a generalized theory of language and literature with strong universalist claims.

In *Milton's God* he found the Christian commentators divided into two main camps of opinion. On the one hand were those (C. S. Lewis among them)[65] who recognized the barbarous character of Milton's 'official' theology but saved their belief by arguing that the poet had got things wrong about Christianity in some crucial respect. On the other were those who rejected this easygoing 'liberal' option, declaring that Milton had got things more or less right and that faith – not reason – was required to make sense of God's mysterious (not to say brutally arbitrary) ways. The one interpretation, as Empson saw it, tried to make

71

something tolerably decent of the Christian religion by treating Milton as a muddle-headed poet scarcely in command of his material. The other praised Milton for all the wrong reasons: for lending full credence to a system of belief whose sheer illogicality and latent sadism the poem then cynically endorses. On neither account can Milton be seen as coming off with much credit. Empson suggests that both views are wrong, and that the power of Milton's poetry comes from his attempting to defend a creed against which his reason and his feelings alike were constantly crying out. 'If you regard the poem as inherently nerve-wracking in this peculiar way, you do not feel that any separate justification is needed for its extraordinary style. . . . its style is necessary for the effect.' Hardline neo-Christians underrate Milton's moral intelligence (or plain human decency) by taking the poem at its own official word, as a determined vindication of Christian belief. Well-meaning liberals hang on to their faith by detaching the poem from its context of hard-pressed theological argument and thus rendering it safe for the purposes of vaguely ecumenical uplift. On the contrary, says Empson: the poem is so good because Milton had both the intellectual nerve to take on Christianity at its most repellent, and the decency of feeling (at whatever 'unconscious' level) to resist its powers of irrational persuasion.

This helps to explain why Empson's interests veered away so sharply from the style of analytical close reading for which he is probably still best known. He came to feel that such techniques were positively harmful when divorced from the attitude of broad-based tolerant understanding which went along with an enlightened rationalist outlook. Otherwise the emphasis on conflict and paradox was liable to lead – as it had at various points in *Seven Types* – towards regions of depth-psychological motive which could always be mined and exploited by the neo-Christian zealots. Hence perhaps the shift of period-emphasis, in *Complex Words*, from those poets of the early seventeenth century (notably Donne and Herbert) whose work offered such a rich field for this style of quasi-theological exegesis, to the later Restoration and Augustan writers in whom Empson found a more congenial emphasis on the 'rational prose virtues' as manifest in key-words like 'sense' and their structures of implied normative judgement. Perhaps the best example is his chapter on Pope ('Wit in the "Essay on Criticism" ') where Empson follows out the intricate logic of a style finely poised between the rival claims of 'wit' and 'sense'. The rather self-supporting dialects of 'wit' are shrewdly played off against a note of moderating judgement which insists on the merits of plain 'good sense' or the *sensus communis* of civilized reason. 'To play this trick on such a scale', Empson writes,

> comes at last to suggest more dignified notions; that all a critic can do is suggest a hierarchy with inadequate language; that to do it so well with so very inadequate language is to offer a kind of diagram of how it must always be done.
>
> (*CW*, p. 85)

Of course this refers as much to Empson's own 'inadequate' language – his machinery of paraphrase, semantic equations, logical operators, etc. – as to Pope's more polished and elegant turns of style. To offer a 'kind of diagram' may be the furthest that a theory like Empson's can go towards explaining the extraordinary subtlety and strength of that style. Yet the 'trick', after all, is much the same in Empson as in Pope: to keep the high gyrations of 'wit' in play while constantly suggesting a larger background of tacit values and assumptions. 'Putting the complex into the simple' – Empson's root definition of Pastoral – here becomes a kind of working faith for the theorist-interpreter of complex words.

This is what I mean by suggesting that the book's two dimensions of argument – the theoretical and the ethical-normative – fit together in a way that must appear deeply problematic to those who insist on the difference (the unbridgeable gulf, as some philosophers would have it) between these orders of truth-claim. The following passage will give some idea of how this process works with the key-word 'sense', a crucial example from Empson's point of view since it carries such a range of meanings – or compacted arguments – bound up with the shift from a theocentric to a rational-humanist outlook. 'Our present structure of the word', he writes,

> was invented around the time of the Restoration; speakers then took to regarding the 'good judgement' use as a simple metaphor, in the course of a general drive toward simplification. And the two types of equation, 'A is like B' and 'A is typical of B', come into play together; the rise of *sense* for 'good judgement' goes hand in hand with the rise of

73

sensationist or plain-man philosophies.... The suasive power of the word seems to come from treating all reactions or good judgements as of one sort, though, in fact, they presumably range from the highest peaks of imaginative insight, or the greatest heart-searchings of 'enthusiasm', to fundamental but humble processes like recognising a patch of colour as a table. *Sense* tells you to concentrate on the middle of the range, the man-size parts where we feel most at home; and it can do this because the simple use of the trope (which is now taken as a pattern) is an appeal to you to show a normal amount of good judgement, 'like every-body else'.

(*CW*, p. 262)

Now clearly there is a sense in which any such usage will manifest a certain 'period' character, the result of its having developed – as Empson notes – in response to new forms of collective aware-ness or modes of 'commonsense' perception. To this extent the above passage must be read as a commentary on one particular phase of post-Renaissance European thought. Roughly speaking, this would be the phase that started out with the questioning of divinely sanctioned or absolutist principles of social order, and which arrived at its highest, most developed stage with the advent of a rational-humanist paradigm grounded in the notion of a 'public sphere' identified with the supposedly self-evident, uni-versal values of 'good sense', reason, and enlightened self-knowl-edge. This is why, as Empson says, 'the historical approach can profitably be used'; because key-words like 'sense', despite their implicit universalizing claims, in fact bear witness to changing structures of consciousness – whether 'residual', 'dominant', or 'emergent', to adopt Raymond Williams's useful terms of analysis – which cannot be understood apart from their historical context. But Empson then goes on – in the very next sentence – to assert what appears a contradictory claim: that 'it is not true that *sense* could only get from "sensations" to "good judgement" by a meta-phor under specific conditions' (p. 262). That is to say, there is a 'grammar' of complex words – a range of structural-semantic possibilities or modes of communicative grasp – which may indeed emerge to most striking effect in certain kinds of usage and at certain historical junctures, but which none the less consti-tutes a permanent feature of the human capacity for using and interpreting such language. And it is Empson's argument that words like 'sense' are best suited to demonstrate this underlying grammar since they involve the kind of reflex, self-implicating logic – the 'humour of mutality' allied to a sense of broad-based public appeal – which allows language the freedom to develop these complex semantic resources.

In short, the main point about 'sense' and its various cognates is that they open up a space of 'communicative action' (in Jürgen Habermas's phrase) where it is assumed *first* that speakers have an interest – a rational interest – in achieving the best possible degree of enlightened mutual understanding, and *second* that any real advance in this direction will involve criticism of existing ('commonsense') ideas and values where these serve only to promote some partisan, self-authorized, or class-based set of interests.[66] That the word can move across such a range of meanings – and convey such a variety of meaningful relations between them – is what gives it the scope for playing this role in the articulation of a 'public sphere' progressively detached from religious or other sources of imposed doctrinal usage. More specifically, it enables language to break with those types of irrationalist 'equation' – from the paradoxes of Christian doctrine to the slogans of Orwellian Newspeak – which exploit the ever-present tendency of thought to get into muddles by accepting some form of illicit analogical transfer or 'primitive' identity relation. Thus

> in reasonable language the notion of identity can shift to that of a relation between the elements, as in the English sentence, and the covert assertion becomes for instance 'A is included in the larger class B', 'A entails B', or 'A is like B in possessing a character prominent in B'.
>
> (*CW*, p. 255)

Such logical nuances in the semantic 'grammar' of complex words mark a real stage of intellectual and social advance since they offer at least some measure of defence against those various dogmatic creeds and ideologies which can otherwise so easily capture our minds.

This is why Empson insists very firmly (perhaps with a backward glance to the problems encountered in *Seven Types*) that 'I am trying to write linguistics; something *quite* unconscious and unintentional, even if the hearer catches it like an infection, is not part of an act of communication' (p. 31). Here as in Habermas, the word 'communication' carries a strong normative weighting, a commitment to certain basic working principles – among them the good of improved communicative grasp and the potential for a genuine 'public sphere' of enlightened consensus values wherein such a promise might at last be redeemed – which mesh with Empson's 'theoretical' concerns at every point in the book. This is not to say that he blithely ignores all the problems that philosophers have put in the way of any straightforward passage from judgements of fact (or theoretical truth-claims) to judgements of value. Nor – as we have seen – does Empson want to suggest that a key-word like 'sense' could take on its role as a bearer of secularizing impulses and attitudes quite apart from the relevant background context of historically specific values and beliefs. In fact these are two aspects of the same basic problem: namely, how to reconcile the general and the particular in matters of interpretive judgement, or how to make allowance for the sheer variety of cultural codes, conventions, belief-systems, 'commonsense' ideologies and so forth, while none the less offering some explanatory *theory* by which to render their differences intelligible. For any such theory will always come up against the question of its own value-laden character, its commitment to principles – like Empson's rational-humanist outlook – which to some extent determine what shall *count* as evidence in favour of the theory concerned.

Thus:

> till you have decided what a piece of language conveys, like any literary critic, you cannot look round to see what 'formal features' convey it; you will then find that some features are of great subtlety, and perhaps fail to trace some at all.
>
> (*CW*, p. 437)

Empson's target here is the behaviourist school of structural linguistics exemplified by Leonard Bloomfield, an approach which – according to Empson – erects a false idea of 'scientific' objectivity and so ignores a basic truth about language, that we could not attain the least idea of its workings 'if we had not a rich obscure practical knowledge from which to extract the theoretical' (p. 438). But this point clearly applies to *any* theory – including Empson's own – which lays claim to an order of validity (in his case, a 'grammar' of logico-semantic entailment)

76

beyond mere *ad hoc* observation or interpretive flair. For there is plainly a sense in which the particular kinds of 'subtlety' that most interest Empson are those which on the one hand answer to his strongly held rational-humanist beliefs, and on the other display exactly the kinds of 'formal feature' that his method is predisposed to seek out. What is more, *Complex Words* might appear to present an extreme – almost vicious – variant of the 'hermeneutic circle' in so far as it discovers its historical home-ground in precisely that period of semantic development when words like 'sense' were undergoing a shift towards their modern (distinctively secular) range of meaning. And yet, as we have seen, it is Empson's claim that these changes do have a larger, representative significance; that the kinds of semantic 'machinery' involved are not just the products of a certain ideological or period-specific world-view but indicate capacities of the human mind which amount to a 'grammar' of interpretive competence, a generalized theory of what goes on in the production of and reception of language. Such is at any rate the argument implied if one puts together the analysis of 'sense' and its various cognates ('sensation', 'sensibility', 'good sense', etc.) with the treatment of 'grammar' as a word that conveys – 'self-reflexively', so to speak – certain features of its own semantic performance which can then be extended to other such complex words.

This point may be clarified by taking account of some remarks from his Appendix on 'Theories of value', written when the book was almost ready for press – that is to say, when most of the 'practical' chapters had been completed – and based on Empson's reading around in the relevant philosophical literature. His main concern here is to offer some rejoinder to the emotivist theory of ethical value propounded by Charles Morris, C. L. Stevenson and other influential thinkers of the period. Empson thinks the doctrine misleading – as one might expect – in so far as it cuts value-judgements off from any process of rational appraisal, any means by which to analyse their various entailments with regard to both the logic of evaluative language and the wider domain of human activities, interests, and practical involvements. 'Value,' he says,

> seems to come into the sphere of fact of its own accord, rather like imaginary numbers into the solution of real equations; but for rigorous logic you then have to go back

77

and alter the definitions of the numbers in the equations – they were always complex numbers but with null imaginary parts.

(*CW*, p. 421)

In other words, there is a genuine puzzle here – a puzzle duly noted by philosophers at least since Hume – but it is still a basic truth of human experience that we *do* make the passage from 'is' to 'ought' (or reach evaluative judgements on a cognitive basis) every day of our lives. And moreover, as Empson's mathematical analogy suggests, this process must involve much more in the way of complex ratiocinative thought – at whatever 'subconscious' or 'preconscious' level – than could ever be allowed for by theorists who adopt the straightforward emotivist doctrine.

So there is a close relation between Empson's treatment of the fact/value antinomy and his thinking on the question of 'theory' as applied to matters of historical-interpretive judgement. In both cases – so the argument runs – it is a fallacy to suppose that theoretical truth-claims are somehow undermined by their involvement with various kindred evaluative attitudes, or by the fact that they first took rise (like the complex of ideas around the key-word 'sense') at a certain stage of cultural-linguistic development. Such findings are no doubt of genuine interest from the standpoint of critics – Empson included – who seek to explain how language plays a role in the social evolution of values and beliefs specific to this or that period. Thus 'a word may become a sort of solid entity, able to direct opinion, thought of as like a person ... [and] to get some general theory about how this happens would clearly be important' (*CW*, p. 39). But one could only claim to possess such a 'general theory' on condition that the underlying principles involved – like the 'grammar' of complex words – held good across a decently extended range of historical examples, and thus offered something more than an insight into the local (period-specific) workings of select lexical items. And it is here that Empson's book stands squarely opposed to the relativist drift that has overtaken various disciplines – chief among them philosophy, sociology, and literary theory – during the past two decades.

The point can best be made through a series of indicative (though no doubt overly schematic) comparisons. As against the poststructuralists and followers of Saussure Empson *denies*

78

(1) that language is a network of purely 'arbitrary' codes and conventions; (2) that these conventions are best understood in terms of the likewise 'arbitrary' link between signifier and signified; (3) that any aspirant 'science' of structural linguistics will respect this condition and hence not concern itself with issues of truth, reference, propositional meaning or other such 'extraneous' factors; and (4) that such a 'science' must in any case acknowledge its own inevitably culture-bound character, its textual constitution or transient status as a product of this or that localized 'discourse' lacking any claim to ultimate validity or truth. On the contrary, he argues: there is a 'grammar' of complex words which corresponds to certain basic logico-semantic operations, and in the absence of which we would be unable to interpret even the simplest forms of verbal behaviour. Thus 'much of what appears to us as a "feeling" (as is obvious in the case of a complex metaphor) will in fact be quite an elaborate structure of related meanings' (*CW*, pp. 56–7). In which case the Saussurean paradigm is plainly inadequate since it takes no account of those signifying structures – or relations of logical entailment – that operate both at the level of discourse (i.e. of extended propositions) and at the level of individual words in so far as they carry 'compacted arguments', or implied semantic 'equations'. Here, as we have seen, Empson is much closer to philosophers in the Anglo-American 'analytical' tradition – thinkers like Frege, Russell and Quine – than to anything in the French poststructuralist line of descent.

He also provides strong arguments against the kind of ultra-relativist outlook (associated nowadays with Foucault and the avatars of so-called 'New Historicism') which reduces all questions of truth, method and validity to so many stratagems of 'power/knowledge', or products of the epistemic will-to-power that drives the various forms of knowledge-constitutive interest.[67] What *Complex Words* enables us to grasp – and this is perhaps its most important contribution in the present climate of debate – is the fallacy or patent *non sequitur* involved in all such relativist doctrines: namely, the idea that, *just because* truth-claims take rise from some given (historically contingent) set of socio-cultural values and beliefs, *therefore* they can possess no validity beyond or outside that original context. To Empson's way of thinking – call it 'rational-humanist' – this simply ignores all the evidence of real intellectual advances (and improvements at the level of communicative grasp) achieved, very often, against sizeable odds of entrenched dogma and prejudice. As he put it most concisely in a book review of 1930: 'it is unsafe to explain discovery in terms of a man's intellectual preconceptions, because the act of discovery is precisely that of stepping outside preconceptions.'[68] Any theory that fails to take account of this fact – like currently fashionable forms of poststructuralist and neo-pragmatist thinking[69] – will thereby be forced into an ultra-relativist position where it becomes simply *unthinkable* that communication could ever take place between different language-games, paradigms, discourses, or cultural 'life-forms'. Such arguments may have a certain heady appeal but they can hardly begin to explain how we interpret even the simplest – let alone the most complex and challenging – forms of verbal utterance.

This may help to make sense of Empson's claim that his 'equations' have a normative as well as a historically specific or period-based character. It is a claim that he asserts most explicitly in a passage from the chapter 'Sense and Sensibility', in many ways the philosophic heart of the book since the key-words in question – along with their structures of semantic entailment – raise quite a number of relevant issues in the realms of epistemology, ethics, psychology, interpretation theory and so forth. In the case of such words, Empson writes:

> it is because the historical background is so rich and still so much alive . . . that one can fairly do what seems absurdly unhistorical, make a set of equations from first principles. When you have so unmanageable a history behind a stock opposition the words get worked down till they are a kind of bare stage for any future performance. It is no longer the first question about the words to ask when and how, in history, the various elements were introduced, which the full form makes possible. What the user needs, and feels that he has, is an agreed foundation on which to build his own version; a simple basic difference between the words from which the whole opposition can be extracted. One is forced to ask what it can be; I suggest that it is a difference in the order in which the similar elements in the words are equated, and that any subsequent difference is put in by developing the type of equation as required.

> (*CW*, p. 269)

This is not to deny that a word like 'sense' could only have developed as it did at this time – i.e., acquired a range of distinctively secular and rational-humanist overtones – as a result of changes in the social and ideological sphere which allowed such a shift to occur. In fact, it is one of Empson's main arguments throughout *Complex Words* – and another clear sign of his distance from the current poststructuralist orthodoxy – that critical theory is a useless endeavour if it doesn't take advantage of a splendid resource like the *Oxford English Dictionary* by way of reconstructing those semantic changes through a detailed study of particular case histories. That is to say, there is no point in having a theory of language that operates on strictly 'synchronic' principles, thus excluding any reference to the way that words have actually developed in response to such pressures (or new-found opportunities) in the realm of social exchange. It is in this sense that language – as Empson understands it – both registers and actively works to promote the most far-reaching shifts of 'public opinion' on issues of religion, politics, or ethical concern. There is, he concedes, 'a puzzle for the linguist about how much is "in" a word and how much in the general purpose of those who use it'. But on the other hand it is this 'shrubbery' of half-acknowledged values and beliefs, 'a social and not a very conscious matter, sometimes in conflict with organized opinion, that one would expect to find only able to survive because somehow inherent in their words' (*CW*, p. 158). In which case clearly the critic's main task is that of reconstructing the development of such words 'on historical principles', like the *OED*, and not coming up with some abstract theory in the structural-synchronic mode.

EMPSON AMONG THE THEORISTS

The obvious comparison here – and one that deserves more extended treatment – is with Mikhail Bakhtin and his lifelong project for a 'sociological poetics' alive to the diversity of meanings and values that jostle for priority in each and every act of communicative utterance.[70] Like Empson, Bakhtin mounts a trenchant critique of those 'idealist' theories of language – Saussure's pre-eminent among them – which think to achieve the condition of a genuine 'science' by defining their object in rigorously abstract terms (*la langue*), and hence disregarding the variety of contexts, of rival ideologies or competing value-systems which are everywhere at work in real-life socialized discourse.[71] There is also common ground between the two critics in their marked preference for words, genres or modalities of usage that challenge the values of official ('monological') discourse by opening it up to all the counter-currents of subversive popular sentiment. For Bakhtin this tradition starts out with the rise of Menippean satire (as opposed to more decorous, 'classical' forms); achieves perhaps its fullest expression with Rabelais and the style of unbuttoned 'carnivalesque' humour directed against every form of authority, religious and secular; and then comes to characterize 'novelistic' discourse in so far as the novel – at least when not subjected to didactic or moralizing purposes – displays a high degree of 'dialogical' exchange between various (overt or implied) narrative voices.[72] For Empson likewise, language attains to its best, most rewardingly complex uses when it manages to break with those (mainly theological) systems of instituted value and belief which had hitherto placed firm limits on the range of permissible thought and sentiment.

This may be an important matter for any society, he thinks, 'because its accepted official beliefs may be things that would be fatal unless in some degree kept at bay' (*CW*, p. 158). And again, in a passage that will surely strike a familiar note with readers of Bakhtin:

> The web of European civilization seems to have been slung between the ideas of Christianity and those of a half-secret rival, centring perhaps (if you made it a system) round honour; one that stresses pride rather than humility, self-realisation rather than self-denial, caste rather than either the communion of the saints or the individual soul.
>
> (p. 159)

Moreover, both critics show a similar tendency to conflate theoretical and normative claims, since they both – as I have noted already of Empson – find their central ideas about language most strikingly embodied in certain speech-forms, idioms or genres that invariably carry a strongly marked ethical or evaluative toning. A good example is Empson's unpacking of the key-word 'honest', giving numeral values to the various head senses, letters to the predicates imposed by context, and plus or minus signs by way of denoting what he calls 'appreciative' and 'depreciative'

82

pregnancy. The development of this word during the seventeenth and eighteenth centuries

> was supported by the philosophical ideas of the Enlightenment, which have not yet been given up, nor should I want to give them up myself; the man who satisfies his own nature ('3+') and is honest to himself ('4+') is expected to have generous feelings ('1b+') from his own unobstructed nature, not from the rules of '1–' or the effort of principle in '2'.
>
> (*CW,* p. 216)

What is interesting about this passage – aside from the complex apparatus of notation – is the way that it moves across so readily from a generalized defence of 'Enlightenment' values to a paraphrase of 'honest' (or its grammar of semantic implication) which clearly offers backing for that same set of values by claiming both descriptive adequacy and ethical-normative force. From this point of view there is simply no separating questions of value from issues in the realm of theoretical and cognitive enquiry.

All the same it would be wrong to press too far with the comparison between Empson and Bakhtin. For one thing, Empson has some pointed reservations about raising 'rogue-sentiment' into a kind of systematically inverted morality, an ethics of purely anarchic, antinomian or subversive character which – as Bakhtin would have it – somehow works to promote the communal good by casting down all the idols of custom and conventional restraint. 'Chat about rogues and other Rabelaisian figures tends to be cosy from a safe distance', Empson writes; 'they may have been of great value to our society but very nasty' (*CW,* pp. 158–9). And indeed his book provides some striking examples of the way that such words ('rogue', 'dog', 'fool', 'honest', even 'sense') can take on a range of pathological meanings – or twisted cynical implications – sharply at odds with their usual sentiment of tolerant mutual regard. Where he differs from Bakhtin is in offering the means – the normative and logico-semantic resources – by which to explain such markedly deviant structures of meaning and understand how they managed to get a hold under certain specific social and historical conditions. His chapters on ' "Sense" in *Measure for Measure*' and ' "Honest" in *Othello*' are predictably the two essays where this approach finds its most challenging material. Thus it is hard not to feel that the way everybody [in *Othello*] calls Iago honest amounts to a criticism of the word itself; that is Shakespeare means 'a bluff forthright manner, and amusing talk, which get a man called honest, may go with extreme dishonesty'. Or indeed that this is treated as normal, and the satire is on our nature not on language.

(*CW*, p. 219)

But the main point about Shakespeare's cynical variations on the word is that they only work at all – or can only achieve their singular dramatic effect – by making such a contrast with the structure of meanings more normal at this time, that is to say, the implicit 'humour of mutuality' that allowed 'honest' to develop as a token of secular-humanist values. In short,

it is the two notions of being ready to blow the gaff on other people and frank to yourself about your own desires that seem to me crucial about Iago; they grow on their own, independent of the hearty feeling that would normally humanize them.

(p. 221)

And of course this claim takes for granted the idea that there exists a normative 'grammar' of complex words, a capacity for grasping such superinduced ironies – parasitic on the usual structure of meaning – which requires both a highly developed sensitivity to nuances of historical usage and a grasp of those other, more basic forms of semantic entailment whose logic Empson sets out to explain.

One could summarize the divergence of approach between Empson and Bakhtin in terms of the differing emphasis they place on theory (or the claims of analytical reason) *vis-à-vis* the multiplicity of languages, speech-genres, value-systems, socialized codes and conventions, etc. Bakhtin's attitude – roughly stated – is one that holds 'the more the merrier', an outlook of undifferentiating pluralist 'free play' that celebrates diversity for its own sake and equates such values as reason, truth and method with the workings of a grim paternal law of oppressive 'monological' discourse. For Empson, conversely, this amounts to a species of what might be called 'infantile leftism', a failure to grasp that such anarchic tendencies can just as well lean over into forms of vicious irrationalist sentiment – like those he analyses in Iago's

84

'honest' – which scarcely justify Bakhtin's claims for the radical or liberating power of language when released from all normative values and constraints. 'To get some general theory about how this happens would clearly be important; if our language is continually thrusting doctrines on us, perhaps very ill-considered ones, the sooner we understand the process the better' (*CW*, p. 39). And this also has clear implications for the issue of priority (if such it is – and Empson would I am sure reject such a claim) between 'historical' and 'theoretical' approaches to literary criticism. For on his view it is evident that both come in at an early stage in the process of interpretation; that you can't get any sense of how an author is using some particular 'complex word' – or range of such words in context – without *first* learning as much as possible about the relevant historico-semantic background, and *second* attempting to fit the various period senses into a working structure, a 'grammar' of implicit semantic equations by which to understand their argumentative force. But this would involve a good deal more in the way of 'theoretical' exposition than Bakhtin and his followers seem willing to provide.[73]

One area where these questions have an obvious bearing is that of lexicography, or the long-running debate – taken up by Empson in his chapter 'Dictionaries' – on how best to cover the historical ground while also giving users a practical grasp of the semantic resources (as well as the pitfalls) encountered by language-learners and specialists alike. Empson begins by stating plainly 'what I hope is already obvious, that such work on individual words as I have been able to do has been almost entirely dependent on using the majestic object (the *OED*) as it stands' (*CW*, p. 391). But he then goes on to offer a series of proposals for a different, less cumbersome and hence more effective practice of dictionary-making, one that would not simply list the various senses of a word in roughly chronological (or topic-based) order, but apply something more like Empson's own system of extracting the relevant semantic 'equations' and thus conveying a sense of the operative 'grammar' that needs to be grasped by any competent user. 'This amount of symbolism, however indecorous it might appear, really does seem to be needed, because it is important to make the reader notice that the senses can combine and interact' (*CW*, p. 396). And again, more explicitly:

what they [native speakers as well as foreign learners] need

is an English-to-English dictionary which is guaranteed
against circularity, does on the other hand give working
rules to distinguish near-synonyms, and also gives warnings
of the unexpected tricks that a word might play, especially
by an unlooked-for sense poking up.

(*CW*, p. 397)

Empson's chief point with these proposals – worked out in
some detail across a range of more or less problematical cases –
is that even the most dedicated efforts of archival research or
philological scholarship won't much help the dictionary user if
they don't give some account of the semantic grammar – or the
logic of (often unnoticed) propositional attitudes – that defines
what passes for a 'competent' use of the word or idiom in question. And this links up in turn with his approach to questions of
interpretive method in the literary-critical chapters. That is to say,
it combines a lively sense of the historical relativities of language
usage with a firm persuasion – on argued theoretical grounds –
that one can only explain these semantic and socio-cultural shifts
from a rationalist standpoint which leaves one sufficiently prepared to analyse the logic of their various (more or less covert)
structures of implication. Hence his quarrel with Raymond
Williams over the latter's book *Keywords*: a fine piece of dictionary-
hunting, Empson thought, offering lots of handy source-material,
but apt to give the wrong impression by treating language-users
as passive creatures of habit, entirely at the mercy of their pet
words and slogans. Thus Williams

> decides that many of our common words regularly tempt
> us to accept wrong beliefs, usually political ones.... He
> does not say that resistance to them is beyond human power,
> which would make his book entirely useless, but his intro-
> duction offers very little hope from the technique he
> provides.[74]

Not that Empson was inclined to underestimate the suasive power
of such words, or the extent to which people's thinking could be
influenced, on a wide range of moral and political questions, by
exactly these kinds of subliminal prompting. His own experience
of wartime propaganda work was enough to make Empson keenly
aware of this fact. But he saw no reason to treat it as a basic truth
about language – a grimly Orwellian truth – that such rhetorical

effects (so to speak) went all the way down, so that no kind of analysis along logico-semantic lines could hope to explain or indeed counteract their influence. Oddly enough, Empson cites a whole series of examples from Williams's book – like the entries on 'interest', 'materialist', 'common', and 'educated' – where Williams *does* in fact offer something very like his own type of argument on rational-reconstructive lines. It is hard not to feel that his response in these cases has more to do with politics – or with Empson's suspicion that Williams has smuggled in a Marxist ideological agenda under cover of his seemingly 'disinterested' method – than with any deep-seated theoretical difference. (Thus 'many of the entries are not political, and they show great breadth of mind, especially in showing that a controversial word contains both sides of the controversy in itself'.)[75] But his argument here, as always, is that you can't really separate questions of method (or 'theory') from questions of substantive ethico-political 'interest'; that theory does best when it acknowledges the sheer variety of such interests at work in language; and that any method which narrows down the range of intelligible motives and meanings is sure to miss the point in some potentially harmful way.

It is in this sense, as I have argued, that Empson's complex words (or the 'machinery' he offers by way of understanding them) can be seen to controvert any doctrinaire version of the fact/value antinomy. They involve on the one hand a *theory* of interpretation – an account of how we, as competent language-users, habitually 'do things with words' – and on the other an *ethics* of mutual understanding with its own distinct set of human-ist and rationalist values squarely opposed to all forms of religious or proto-theological dogma. Of course these are principles hardly likely to commend Empson's book to literary theorists who uncritically endorse the current strain of anti-humanist, non-cognitivist, counter-enlightenment or 'postmodern' thought. If one had to cast around for a present-day figure who agrees on all the main points at issue then undoubtedly Habermas would be the prime candidate. Like Empson, he sets out a strong defence of 'enlightenment' values and truth-claims, basing that defence on a theory of language (or 'communicative action') which involves both descriptive and normative elements.[76] What Empson has to say about the reciprocal character – the self-implicating logic or 'humour of mutuality' – manifest in key-words like 'sense' finds a parallel in Habermas's regulative notion of an 'ideal speech-situation', a public sphere or optimal context of free and open debate where the various parties would no longer be subject to the distortions, injustices and failures of communicative grasp brought about by currently prevailing social conditions. Moreover, one could point out a similar shift of emphasis in the course of their respective enquiries into language, meaning and interpretive method. Thus where Habermas moves from the 'subject-centred' or epistemological concerns of a work like *Knowledge and Human Interests*[77] to the language-based approach of his later writings (notably *Communication and the Evolution of Society*), Empson follows a similar path – as I argued in more detail above – from the analysis of complex mind-states (*Seven Types*) or modalities of reflective self-knowledge (*Some Versions*) to the study of language in its logico-semantic and more broadly social dimension. Above all, they are both committed to the basic principle – as against the current drift of postmodernist fashion – that thinking cannot simply abandon those 'enlightenment' values of truth, reason and critique that have come to define what Habermas calls the 'unfinished project of modernity'.

All the same there is one major point of disagreement between Habermas and Empson, a point that is so significant as to constitute the most original and striking aspect of *Complex Words*. For it is Habermas's contention that poetry – or literary language in general – belongs to an order of 'world-disclosive', aesthetic or imaginative discourse quite distinct from those other kinds of language (science, philosophy, law, ethics, literary criticism, etc.) which have separated out during the past two centuries in the course of evolving their own specific standards of cognitive and evaluative truth. Such is indeed the precondition of maintaining that enlightened 'public sphere' of differential truth-claims which Habermas sets out to defend against its current detractors. Thus he sees nothing but error and confusion in any attempt to erase the 'genre-distinction' between literature and philosophy, a charge which Habermas – wrongly, I think – tries to lay at Derrida's door, but which certainly applies to many others in the postmodern-neopragmatist camp. This argument is worked out in great detail by Habermas in his book *The Philosophical Discourse of Modernity*.[78] My only point here is that it sets him decidedly at odds with Empson, since the latter's central claim – refined and developed throughout *Complex Words* – is that one cannot (or should not) treat poetic language as somehow existing in a realm quite apart from the logic of truth-conditional discourse, the standards of cognitive accountability, or the interests of rational understanding. Such, after all, is Empson's chief objection to Richards's theory of 'emotive' meaning, as well as to the American New Critics and their talk of 'irony', 'paradox', and other privileged tropes, as a result of which poetry is conceived to exist in a self-enclosed realm of aesthetic values devoid of truth-telling warrant. Thus from Empson's point of view there could be no justification – aside from immediate polemical concerns – for Habermas's exclusion of literary language from the 'public sphere' of enlightened discourse where truth-claims are properly tried and tested through the process of uncoerced critical debate.

So the comparison with Habermas, though useful and suggestive, breaks down at the point where Empson asserts his most distinctive literary-critical claim: that poetic understanding is *in no way discontinuous* with the kinds of sense-making judgement and analysis brought to bear upon other (whether 'everyday' or specialized) genres of language usage. And this applies even to metaphor, traditionally thought of – at least since Aristotle – as a hallmark and touchstone of language in its creative or 'literary' aspect. Thus, as Empson puts it, 'a metaphor goes outside the ordinary range of a word, [while] an equation "argues from" the ordinary range, treating it as a source of traditional wisdom' (*CW*, p. 332). But even so one can offer a more elaborate scheme of equations, analogical transfers, 'appreciative pregnancies', contextual cues, structures of compacted argument, etc., by which to explain how metaphors work without resort to woolly notions of 'emotive' meaning or mysterious modes of 'primitive', 'prelogical' or irrationalist thought. Thus:

> The mind does not in general use words without attaching to them both a class and its defining property, however vaguely, but owing to the creative looseness of the mind it can sometimes use defining properties which, apart from the aggregate of experience which can be tapped by one word, remain obscure. Cases where a word seems to leave its usual range successfully often occur when the conscious mind has its eye on a few important elements in the situation and the classifying subconscious is called on for a suggestive word. . . . The process may be like a 'construction' in Euclidean geometry; you draw a couple of lines joining

points which are already in the diagram, and then the proof
seems obvious, though till then the right 'aspect' of the
thing was nowhere in sight.

(*CW,* p. 335)

Empson's chapter on metaphor can thus be seen as a firm repudiation of theories that assert some basic, irreducible difference
between literal and figural modes of language, or those which
maintain – like Habermas – that it is simply wrong, a species of
category mistake, to apply the standards of cognitive (truth-
seeking) discourse to language in its 'world-disclosive', metaphor-
ical, or literary aspect. If Empson is right – and his ideas about
metaphor have been strongly endorsed by (among others) the
philosopher Donald Davidson[79] – then there is no good reason
to adopt this line. Such arguments would be seen as amounting to
just another form of that widespread irrationalist or aestheticizing
tendency in present-day thought which Habermas, ironically, sets
out to challenge in *The Philosophical Discourse of Modernity.*

But what of the poets – Wordsworth especially – whose language resists such treatment to the point where Empson's rationalist semantics seem very nearly played off the field? In *Seven
Types,* as we have seen, he devoted some strenuous but finally
rather baffled commentary to the climactic lines from Wordsworth's 'Tintern Abbey', professing to admire the poem whole-
heartedly, yet finding its logical grammar 'shuffling and evasive'
when it came to the high points of pantheistic doctrine. The
major advance in *Complex Words* is the fact that it can address
these problems without arriving at an ultimate deadlock – or a
kind of uneasy stand-off – between the claims of reason and
those of Wordsworth's inspirational rhetoric. Thus the chapter in
question (' "Sense" in *The Prelude*') explores the more benign or
less actively misleading kinds of paradox involved in the language
of Romantic nature-mysticism. And it is able to do so by virtue
of the shift from a somewhat mistrustful depth-psychological
approach to one that operates with a better understanding of the
logical grammar – the order of unconscious but none the less
describable truth-claims or 'equations' – that characterize Wordsworth's high prophetic strain. Thus 'the whole poetical and philosophical effect', Empson writes, 'comes from a violent junction
of sense-data to the divine imagination given by love, and the
middle term is cut out' (*CW,* p. 296). That 'middle term' is

the commonsense ground of moderating rational judgement, as contrasted (say) with the high dialectics of 'wit' in Empson's reading of Pope's 'Essay on Criticism'. By using language in such a way as to jump clean over this stage in the argument Wordsworth moved into regions of paradox pregnant with irrationalist hints and possibilities. In effect, he persuades the reader to accept his pantheist creed through the 'firmness and assurance' of these Type IV equations, structures of implied argument 'whose claim was false, because they did not really erect a third concept as they pretended to' (p. 305). Yet Empson still very readily admits that 'the result makes good poetry, and probably suggests important truths' (ibid.).

His reading thus steers a difficult path between two opposed philosophies of language, truth and meaning. It refuses the straightforward emotivist option of ignoring the truth-claims and taking what Wordsworth has to offer in the way of inspirational uplift or luxuriant sentimental appeal. At the same time it sees that there are powers of suggestion vested in poetic language which might always elude any normative grammar based on too rigid or prescriptive a use of the logico-semantic categories. '[This] ecstasy both destroys normal *sense* and fulfils it, and the world thus shown is both the same as and different from the common one' (*CW*, p. 295). Of course such perplexities could be simply set aside by assuming that poetry just *is* paradoxical, that it exists *sui generis* in a realm quite apart from the entailments of rational prose meaning or commonsense logic. Thus 'what Wordsworth wanted to say', according to Cleanth Brooks, 'demanded his use of paradox . . . , could only be said powerfully through paradox.'[80] But this does no more than translate the emotivist view into a language of high formalist principle that can offer no convincing account of the difference between Wordsworth's exalted 'language of the sense' and the semantic perversions of Orwellian Newspeak. Empson's point is that the reader (or the competent reader) is indeed capable of making such distinctions, most often by going through a series of tentative efforts to sort the meaning into some kind of logical structure, and then – if the passage still puts up resistance – allowing for the presence of rhetorical effects that finally elude such treatment.

Thus valuable (as opposed to meretricious or merely propagandist) examples of the kind will tend to call out a much greater range of possible meanings and structures, even if none of them turns out to satisfy the strictest requirements of logical sense.

> 'Sensation is Imagination' is a possible slogan, but both this and its inverse seem very open to misunderstanding without making the real point. 'Sensation and Imagination are included in a larger class' is merely dull; besides, the important thing may well be that they overlap to form a narrower class. 'Sensation and Imagination interlock' seems the best way to put it. But I think it is fair to say that Wordsworth had not got any translation ready; he was much better at adumbrating his doctrine through rhetorical devices than at writing it out in full.
>
> (*CW,* pp. 299–300)

Empson's involvement with Basic English – a cause he took up at Richards's behest during the years of preparatory work on *Complex Words* – is very evident in this passage.[81] Along with the experience of teaching in China and Japan, it led him to conclude that complexity in language need not (indeed should not) become an excuse for adopting the kind of high-toned obscurantist attitude that placed poetry beyond reach of plain-prose rational explanation. 'Writing it out in full' is not all the same thing as pedantically murdering to dissect, or refusing the wisdom and enjoyment that poetry has to offer for the sake of some hard-bitten intellectualist creed. On the contrary: it is the best way to understand a poet like Wordsworth, one who expressly believed that 'poetry had better be made out of the "simple language of men", though he made good poetry out of hard words as well'.[82]

This sentence comes from a 1940 broadcast talk on 'Wordsworth and Basic English', one of several pieces that Empson wrote by way of trying out the Basic programme as a technique of practical criticism. Such an exercise is useful, he thinks, not because it gets the full meaning across through an adequate prose paraphrase, but because it sets one off in the right direction – or the right frame of mind – for finding out where the problems lie and then going on to make another, better attempt. 'In looking for the reason why your first answer was wrong, you are sent on to the important questions about poetry. So this process makes the structure of the poetry much clearer.'[83] And again:

> We do not commonly get the ideas opened up, and see

the reasons for the feelings. So all this argument about the effect of the lines has come straight out of our attempt at putting the sense into Basic. Without that start we would probably not see what was important, in the structure of the thought.[84]

In retrospect it is clear that this was already the attitude behind Empson's passages of multiple paraphrase in *Seven Types* – such an affront to orthodox New Critical doctrine – as well as bearing a distinct kinship to the root notion of Empsonian pastoral, that of 'putting the complex into the simple'. But it was only with the writing of *Complex Words* that he managed to bring these interests together in a generalized theory of language and interpretation that could encompass both the normative logic of everyday discourse and the kinds of paradoxical truth-claim implied by a poet like Wordsworth.

When he reviewed A. J. Ayer's *The Foundations of Empirical Knowledge* in 1941 Empson was already convinced that 'the whole development of rationalism since the sixteenth century has been playing round "sense" '.[85] As might be expected, it is a broadly sympathetic review, approving Ayer's attitude of sturdy commonsense reason and also – up to a point – his attack on 'metaphysics' in the name of a logical-positivist programme grounded in the methods, procedures or evidential protocols of modern science. All the same Empson points to certain difficulties with Ayer's phenomenalist talk of 'sense-data' and his suggestion that 'we can only build up our knowledge out of what the senses give us'. Such is of course the doctrine (or the structure of implied equations) that Empson discovers in one major use of the keyword 'sense', that is to say, an outlook of secular and rationalist confidence in the basic reliability of the senses and the power of human reason ('sense' = 'good judgement') to arrive at a knowledge of the world on this basis. But if one pushes the normative claims too hard – as by equating 'rationality' with a refusal to go beyond the evidence of the senses, or by treating metaphysics *tout court* as a species of mystified word-magic – then one ends up by endorsing a phenomenalist creed where 'sense-data' (or unmediated sensory perceptions) are the only valid items of experience, and where nothing could count as evidence against some 'commonsense' delusion presently imposed by the limits of our physical powers of observation. Thus:

the plain man may remark that the universe has been sturd-
ily indifferent for eons to the observers to whom reality is
reduced; Mr Ayer will reply that we only *can* be referring to
logically possible observations. But he seems very anthropomorphic about observers. Bees see ultra-violet light; perhaps
birds feel the points of the compass; some people say atoms
have dim sensations – is it logically possible for me to be
an atom? The objection to assertions about matter is that
we can't conceivably observe it. How are we better off by
reducing it to sense-data which we can't conceive ourselves
as having? Here again, we know less about the sense-data
than we do about the things.[86]

This amounts to a defence of commonsense reason against the
kinds of philosophical perplexity that arise when the same set of
values – as carried by a key-word like 'sense' – is allowed to
harden into abstract dogma. But Empson also makes the point
that even scientists couldn't get along with anything like so rigid
a conception of what counts as genuine (veridical) knowledge.
Thus 'one impulse "active in the phenomenalist" is a desire to
push out of sight the immense queerness necessary in the universe before we can get any knowledge of it at all'.[87] This argument is partly a Kantian response to Ayer's strain of Humean
radical empiricism: a response which holds that we had better
start out from 'the fact that the universe is one which can be
observed by the creatures it contains', creatures – that is to say –
whose knowledge-constitutive interests and capacities are highly
evolved and likely to reflect a fair measure of truth about that
universe and its physical laws. There may indeed be 'innumerable
other universes', but ours is after all 'the only one that could
produce a book describing itself'.

However, Empson's main objection to the hardline logical-
positivist programme – or to Ayer's narrowly phenomenalist con-
strual of the sense of 'sense' – is that it cuts out so many of those
meanings and beliefs that have developed alongside the discourse
of scientific rationalism, thus providing a context, a 'public
sphere' of differential truth-claims, values, etc., by which to
adjudicate in matters of wider (non-scientific) concern. This is
why, as Empson says, 'to a literary man his [Ayer's] idea of the
purposes that govern a choice of words seems naive; there are
generally several purposes at once, and even the chooser may

not be clear about them till later'.[88] So a rationalist semantics –
even a strong version of the thesis like Empson's – must also find
room for varieties of language that don't make sense on the
narrow (positivistic) account, but which may none the less both
suggest important truths and supply some 'machinery', some
grammar of equations, by which to interpret them. It was this
line of argument that he later took up in the chapter on Wordsworth in *Complex Words*, a chapter which tests his theory to the
limit by focusing mainly in those passages where 'sense' carries
the whole weight of high Romantic argument. Thus

> the word, I maintain, means both the process of sensing
> and the supreme act of imagination, and unites them by a
> jump; the same kind of jump as that in the sentence about
> crossing the Alps, which identifies the horror caused by the
> immediate sensations with the exaltation that developed
> from them.

> (*CW*, p. 304)

What Empson is describing here is of course that revelatory
moment of transition from the order of sensuous (phenomenal)
experience to the order of 'suprasensible' ideas which critics and
philosophers since Kant have treated as the mark of sublime
imagining. Clearly he approaches such claims with a measure of
scepticism, or at any rate an attitude of principled doubt with
regard to their epistemological and ethical correlates. To this
extent (and despite all the differences I have noted) Empson
anticipates the thinking of a critic like Paul de Man, especially
those essays – among them 'The rhetoric of temporality' – where
de Man challenges the privileged terms of mainstream Romantic
scholarship, terms such as metaphor and symbol which purport
to establish a relation of direct, unmediated union between mind
and nature, subject and object, language and the realm of organic
processes and forms.[89] Here also the critique proceeds by way of
a meticulous attention to details of language – most often discrep-
ant or anomalous details – which in turn signal the presence of
elements irreducible to any such mystified organicist doctrine.
Thus the valorization of symbol and metaphor (the master tropes
of Romantic discourse in the German and English traditions)
gives way, on this account, to the more prosaic figures of
metonymy and allegory, figures that are linked – as de Man
argues – 'in their common demystification of an organic world

postulated in a symbolic mode of analogical correspondences or in a mimetic mode of representation in which fiction and reality could coincide' (*BI*, p. 222). Hence his objection to the orthodox reading of Romantic poetry proposed by theorists such as M. H. Abrams and Earl Wasserman: that they adopt what amounts to a fideist position, accepting the truth-claims of metaphor and symbol at face value, and failing to notice those complicating factors – those moments of aporia or non-coincidence between meaning and intent – which effectively undermine such a reading.[90] Thus Abrams typically 'makes it seem . . . as if the romantic theory of imagination did away with analogy altogether and that Coleridge in particular replaced it by a genuine and working monism' (p. 195).

In the essays of his last period de Man traced this tendency back to its origins in the widespread misreading of Kant – especially of Kant's passages on the sublime in his third *Critique* – which first gave rise to the 'aesthetic ideology' by ignoring the various problematical tensions that characterized the discourse of Romanticism.[91] And he did so primarily in order to resist that powerful strain of post-Kantian idealist thought – starting out with Schiller's *Letters on Aesthetic Education* – which raised the idea of the 'organic' artwork, or its subjective correlative, the balanced and harmonious consort of human faculties, into a model for the conduct of human affairs under their ethical, social and political aspects. 'The "state" that is here being advocated', he writes, 'is not just a state of mind or of soul, but a principle of political value and authority that has its own claims on the shape and the limits of our freedom.'[92] For it is partly by way of this aestheticizing drift – this extension of organicist themes and motifs from nature, through art, to the realm of morality and politics – that subsequent ideologues were able to envisage the nation-state as an ideal expression of the unified collective will, an expression manifest at every level of language, culture and history. At very least there is a strong elective affinity between doctrines of a late Romantic transcendentalist cast – especially the idea of symbolic language as achieving a consummate synthesis of particular and general, the local and the universal, contingency and necessity, etc. – and those potent forms of nationalist mystique that exploited a similar rhetoric in pursuit of more sinister political ends.

It is worth noting in this connection that Empson's talk on

'Wordsworth and Basic English' was broadcast at the outset of the Second World War, and that it makes some of its points through a comparison of the late (1850), more conservative and doctrinaire version of *The Prelude* with the original 1805 text. What Empson brings out by means of his parallel reading is a general falling-off in the poet's powers of detailed local observation, along with a marked increase in the number of first-person pronouns (putting Wordsworth, rather than nature, at the centre of his own imaginative world), and also – most importantly – a coarsening of the verbal textures whereby words like 'sense' came to lose a great deal of their previous suggestiveness and semantic range. The effect, Empson says, is like 'turning the guns around from firing at the Germans and pointing them against the French',[93] a simile whose application at that time must have carried somewhat more than a casual force. The implication, I think, is that a lot more hangs on the usage of such words – whether in poetry, politics, or everyday parlance – than could ever be explained on any version of the emotivist or non-cognitivist approach. And this idea is reinforced by the implicit analogy that Empson draws between the older Wordsworth's revisionist stance – his disenchantment with French political events and desire to cover the traces of his own revolutionary past – and the troubled situation of 1940 when Europe was once again entering a period of extreme ideological turmoil. It hardly needs saying after recent revelations about de Man's wartime journalism that in his case also the experience must have left a keen sense of the wider political issues bound up with these seemingly specialized concerns in the realm of linguistic and interpretive theory.[94]

This is not the place for a detailed exposition of de Man's writings on aesthetic ideology. Suffice it to say that he, like Empson, holds out against any too willing acquiescence in paradox or other such (supposedly) characteristic marks of 'literary' language; that they both find this attitude potentially complicit with forms of deep-laid ideological mystification; that de Man's deconstructive strategies of reading are aimed, like Empson's, at uncovering the sources of precisely this suasive or rhetorical power vested in the discourse of Romantic poetry and criticism; and finally, that Empson and de Man both insist on maintaining some version of the working distinction between logic, grammar and rhetoric, in de Man's case more explicitly by suggesting a return to the forensic model of the classical *trivium*,[95] and with

Empson – by the time of *Complex Words* – through a detailed attention to the structures of logico-semantic 'grammar' that can always be short-circuited (as by poets like Wordsworth) to produce a whole range of paradoxical truth-claims or 'Type IV' equations inherently resistant to the powers of rational understanding. De Man makes this point most often by locating the moments of 'aporia' (or interpretive undecidability) which result from the conflict between literal and figural, logical and rhetorical, or constative and performative dimensions of language. What he won't accept – unlike the 'old' New Critics – is any notion that logical criteria (or standards of truth and falsehood) have to be suspended in the reading of literary texts, since these embody an order of 'paradoxical' wisdom above and beyond the require-ments of plain-prose reason. And for Empson likewise it is a suspect move – a strategy of evasion or line of least resistance – for the critic to adopt such a blandly accommodating view of the relation between logic, grammar and rhetoric. One must, he says,

> distinguish a 'fallacy', which depends on your not noticing
> the logical contradiction, from a 'paradox', in which it is
> recognised and viewed as 'profound'. It is only the paradox
> which is apprehended as a contradiction, and could become
> a candidate for listing as 'X = –X'.

> (*CW*, p. 53n)

But it is clear from what Empson has to say elsewhere in *Complex Words* – especially the chapters on Wordsworth and Milton – that very often these cases cannot easily be distinguished, so that the fittest state of mind in which to appreciate poetry is one that casts around for some rational machinery by which to reformulate the paradox, and only then (when the available options run out) falls back on the 'profound' interpretation. Otherwise, as he felt, the way was wide open to the kinds of really harmful irrationalist mystique that could always crop up when rhetoric got the upper hand over logic, or when Type IV equations were taken on faith as 'deep' paradoxical truths, beyond reach of rational or com-monsense judgement.

So some kind of 'theory' was evidently needed in order to resist this recurrent strain of literary-critical fashion. On the other hand, Empson disliked the way that 'Eng. Lit.' was becoming a geared-up affair of competing systems and theories. Often they struck him as rationalizations of a new technique for drilling the students into an attitude of religious or political orthodoxy. Most offensive were those 'Symbolist' readings (of Shakespeare especially) which equated profundity with a total lack of interest in commonplace worldly motives and values.[96] During the 1960s Empson reviewed quite a number of books – mostly by American academics – in which he detected this perverse 'neo-Christian' ideology at work. Of Maynard Mack's *'King Lear' in our Time* he remarked that the professors only seemed to feel safe with a Lear who had renounced all claim to sanity and entered a state of near-lunatic transcendental 'wisdom'. 'It is a very Eng. Lit. theory; developed I think because an impressive obscurantism, teaching the kids to revere things that are very odd or plainly evil, is imagined to be the only way to prevent them going red.'[97] In the face of such readings Empson insisted over and again on the importance of 'attending to the story' and not giving in to the prevalent cant of other-worldly meanings and values.

This was probably the chief reason why Empson turned aside from the relatively specialized interests of *Complex Words* and devoted most of his time over the next three decades to the task of resisting this pervasive drift towards pious orthodox creeds. It led him flatly to reject any 'theory' which distracted attention from the urgent business of rescuing Shakespeare, Donne, Milton, Coleridge or Joyce from the hands of their perverse modern exegetes.[98] What these critics were attempting, Empson thought, was a wholesale annexation of literary studies to the High Church monarchist values handed down by Eliot and his numerous acolytes. The canonical 'tradition' of Eliot's devising had already been effective in closing many students' minds to the virtues of any poetry (like Shelley's) that might set them thinking about politics or doubting the truth of Christian revelation. The radical side of Milton had likewise been pushed out of sight by a technique of focusing on (largely irrelevant) 'problems' of style and thus excluding any serious discussion of the poet's life-history, political involvements, and – above all – his embattled theological stance. It remained for the critics to take a poet like Donne – central to Eliot's 'tradition', but uncomfortably prone to heterodox ideas – and make him safe for modern readers by reinterpreting the poems so as to keep those ideas out of view. Empson noticed this technique at work in some of Eliot's own later writing on Donne.[99] The trick was to concede that the ideas were there, but only as a springboard for the poet's neat turns of 'irony', 'paradox', or metaphysical 'wit'. The 1920s view of Donne as radical *thinker* – in matters of sexual politics, science and religion alike – could thus be ignored and the poems reclaimed for a latter-day ethos of pious conformist zeal.

Empson became increasingly gloomy about the prospects of turning back this tide of militant unreason. In 1967 he was still relatively sanguine, holding out the hope that literary studies might yet be saved from these effects of doctrinal and ideological distortion. Such gross abuses 'are bound to crop up', Empson writes, 'and might destroy it; but with periodic sanitary efforts it can probably be got to continue in a sturdy, placid way, as is needed'.[100] But as time went on the situation worsened, so that Empson felt obliged to devote himself almost full-time to countering the trend in its various forms. In the case of Donne this meant taking on not only the critics (including, most recently, John Carey's hard-boiled debunking approach)[101] but also the editors whose attentions – in Empson's view – were increasingly apt to disfigure the poetry. Brought up on Grierson's pioneering edition of 1921, Empson now found numerous instances where the latest texts either muffled an argument or reduced the poem to a cynical caricature of 'decent' human feelings. The editors (whether wittingly or not) were in league with the critics in using these techniques to distort the plain sense of what they read.[102] Empson's own poems of the Cambridge years had been written partly in excited response to the current 'rediscovery' of Donne, encouraged both by Eliot's early essays and Grierson's classic edition. All the greater was his sense of betrayal when Eliot's influence turned out to promote a very different and (to Empson) very damaging line of literary-critical fashion. This took the form of ignoring Donne's arguments and imputing various kinds of subtle irony (or 'deep' symbolic meaning) to ensure that any ideas left over were deprived of all real argumentative force. The blame for this approach he placed squarely at the door of Eliot and those who had developed and refined his technique. 'Mallarmé and Verlaine, it seems fair to remember, did not employ their treasured Symbols to insinuate scandal, as at a cats' tea-party; this bold application of the method was invented by our pious Establishment critics.'[103] As with Donne, so with Milton, Coleridge, Joyce and others: the plain task now (Empson thought) was to clear away the fog of creeping orthodox revisionism which threatened to obscure these authors from view.

It is hardly cause for surprise that Empson's later writings have often been ignored by those who would assign him a handy slot in the history of modern criticism. *Seven Types* is still seen as his greatest single achievement, with *Some Versions* a somewhat puzzling sequel (not least on account of its ambivalent politics), and *Complex Words* a curious mixture of homely commonsense wisdom and clanking theoretical machinery. Beyond that, *Milton's God* is sometimes picked upon for polemical reasons, but otherwise treated (by 'serious' Milton scholars) to a virtual conspiracy of silence. Empson, after all, reached the point of rejecting just about every movement of ideas in contemporary critical debate. Theory itself became suspect in so far as it propped up perverse and damaging creeds (like the anti-intentionalist doctrine) which then gave rise to objectionable readings. 'A critical theory is powerful indeed', as he once remarked of Bentley and Pearce on Milton, 'if it can blind its holders to so much beauty' (*SVP*, p. 129). Yet Empson has a certain admiration for those eighteenth-century rationalist scholars whose methods, he feels, at least had the merit of not giving in to the forces of unreason or letting the issues go by default. In *Some Versions* he thinks it a cause for regret that they 'lost so many points' in the wrangling over Milton, since their defeat in the long run 'had a bad effect on criticism' (p. 130). And in *Seven Types* he puts this more strongly with reference to the earliest editors of Shakespeare and their attempts to make rational sense of disputed or obscure textual details. As Empson remarks: 'we no longer have enough faith to attempt such a method, but its achievement must be regarded with respect, because it has practically invented some of Shakespeare's most famous passages' (*ST*, p. 82). There is much the same ambivalence about Empson's theorizing in *Complex Words*. On the one hand it is needed in order to rebut the more harmful forms of emotivist doctrine and provide at least the basis – the enabling groundwork – for an alternative approach to such questions. On the other it threatens to get in the way of a critic's intuitive responses, an objection that Empson cannot afford to disregard since his main point about words like 'sense', 'fool' and 'honest' is that their structures developed out of a rich background of tacit values and assumptions, a background which the reader has to grasp intuitively before he or she can make a start in understanding the logico-semantic 'machinery' involved. Thus

101

we must not develop tender feelings towards our little bits of machinery; they need to be kept sharply separate from the delicacy and warmth of the actual cases they are to be used on. . . . there might really be a harmful effect from using this kind of analysis if the two things were liable to get mixed up.

(*CW*, p. 19)

Hence the often startling fluctuations of tone, between passages of hard-pressed verbal explication and others where he seems content to adopt a more intuitive line of approach.

This is what makes it impossible to claim Empson for either side in the current, drastically polarized debate about 'theory' and its uses in literary criticism. In *Seven Types* he aligned squarely with those who put their faith in 'analysis', rather than mere 'appreciation', as the fittest state of mind in which to understand a poem. Forty years on he reaffirmed that position in response to an American critic who seemed to regard it (symptomatically, Empson thought) as just a species of youthful eccentricity.

In the year when I. A. Richards was tutoring me some of my friends at Cambridge . . . thought that his 'scientism' was philosophically very absurd, and I could usually, after my weekly hour with Richards, go and tell them some particularly absurd thing he had just said. They, of course, were following T. S. Eliot, early members of the Neo-Christian movement.[104]

'Scientism' here stands in for the attitude of open-minded rational debate which Empson so admired about intellectual life at Cambridge in the 1920s. He never lost faith in this idea, and showed little patience with those (like Leavis) who made a wholesale crusade out of rejecting science, 'technocratic' reason and all their works. Having theories and testing them against the evidence was part of the normal way in which the mind got to grips with experience. And besides, as Empson's poems had shown, there was no firm line to be drawn between the speculative interests of modern science – especially astronomy and nuclear physics – and the needs of a rich emotional life. Yet along with this belief went a feeling that theory could easily harden into dogma and produce all kinds of vicious result. 'The trouble with modern criticism, a wonderfully powerful instrument, is that it is always liable to be applied upside down.'[105] This remark occurred in the course of a letter on the topic (once again) of Orwell's *Nineteen Eighty-Four*. The 'Eng. Lit.' equivalents of Doublethink and Newspeak were, he thought, fairly harmless by comparison, but still required a sturdy effort of mind to resist their corrupting effects.

Empson was disappointed but not altogether surprised that *Complex Words* had met with such a negative response among its early readers and reviewers. He hoped one day to get down to a full-scale revision of the book which would bring the theoretical portions more closely in line with the chapters of 'practical' criticism. In the end this comes back to the old problem of 'analytical' versus 'appreciative' criticism, an issue he had addressed in that early response to John Sparrow, and which crops up again at various points in *Complex Words*.

> The thing becomes disagreeable to read, and also likely to excite suspicion, quite rightly I think, because the only way to decide about the examples is by 'taste' (granting that taste needs a good supply of examples and an adequate assurance that contrary ones have not been suppressed), and if you are being badgered by theory at the same time it is hard to keep taste in focus.
>
> (p. 202)

Even so, the book as it stands is by far the most original and sustained effort of literary theory to have appeared in this country during the past fifty years. Nor should its importance be lost upon the linguists, analytical philosophers and (above all) the adepts of poststructuralist or deconstructive criticism, since Empson's argument engages at so many points with the issues thrown up by these otherwise disparate schools of contemporary thought. But it is likely that Empson will always resist any attempt to annex his writings to this or that corporate academic enterprise, no matter how avowedly 'interdisciplinary' its interests. In a note to one of his poems Empson remarked (with a sidelong glance at Leavis) that 'this being over-simple . . . is itself a way of escaping the complexity of the critic's problems'.[106] It was Empson, more than anyone, who held out against such simplified solutions and worked to keep the problems steadily in view.

NOTES

1 William Empson, *Seven Types of Ambiguity*, 3rd edn, revised, Harmondsworth: Penguin, 1961. All further references given by *ST* and page number in the text.
2 These issues are addressed from a range of philosophical standpoints in Martin Hollis and Steven Lukes (eds), *Rationality and Relativism*, Oxford: Basil Blackwell, 1982.
3 For his own views on this matter, see Empson, *Argufying: Essays on literature and culture*, ed. John Haffenden, London: Chatto & Windus, 1987, especially the various articles and reviews gathered in the final section, 'Cultural perspectives: ethics and aesthetics, East and West'. This volume is a splendid work of dedicated scholarship and I have been grateful to Haffenden for his efforts in bringing such a mass of often fugitive material to light.
4 See especially Donald Davidson, 'On the very idea of a conceptual scheme', in *Inquiries into Truth and Interpretation*, London: Oxford University Press, 1984, pp. 183–98.
5 Benjamin Lee Whorf, *Language, Thought and Reality*, ed. John B. Carroll, New York: Wiley, 1956.
6 See W. V. O. Quine, *From a Logical Point of View*, Cambridge, Mass.: Harvard University Press, 1953.
7 See for instance Paul K. Feyerabend, *Against Method: Outline of an anarchist theory of knowledge*, London: New Left Books, 1975.
8 The most often-cited defence of this Wittgensteinian argument may be found in Peter Winch, *The Idea of a Social Science and its Relation to Philosophy*, London: Routledge & Kegan Paul, 1958.
9 See Christopher Norris, *Deconstruction and the Interests of Theory*, London: Pinter Publishers and Baltimore: Johns Hopkins University Press, 1988, for an exposition and critique of these movements in contemporary cultural theory.
10 Empson, *Collected Poems*, London: Chatto & Windus, 1969.
11 See Feyerabend, *Against Method*.
12 Empson, *The Structure of Complex Words*, London: Chatto & Windus, 1951. All further references given by *CW* and page number in the text.
13 Roland Barthes, *Critique et vérité*, Paris: Seuil, 1956.
14 I. A. Richards, *Principles of Literary Criticism*, London: Routledge & Kegan Paul, 1927.
15 See for instance W. K. Wimsatt, *The Verbal Icon: Studies in the meaning of poetry*, Lexington, Ky.: University of Kentucky Press, 1954; and Cleanth Brooks, *The Well Wrought Urn*, New York: Harcourt Brace, 1947.
16 Empson, 'O miselle passer' (response to John Sparrow), in *Argufying*, pp. 193–202.
17 Ibid., p. 197.
18 Ibid., p. 198.
19 Ibid., p. 197.
20 See especially Sigmund Freud, *Totem and Taboo and other works* in

The Standard Edition of the Complete Psychological Works of Sigmund Freud, vol. XIII, trans. James Strachey, London: Hogarth Press, 1961 reprint.

21 Empson, *Some Versions of Pastoral*, Harmondsworth: Penguin, 1966. All further references given by *SVP* and page number in the text.

22 See for instance René Girard, *Violence and the Sacred*, trans. Patrick Gregory, Baltimore: Johns Hopkins University Press, 1977.

23 See Neil Hertz, 'More lurid figures', *Diacritics* 20:3 (1991), pp. 2–27.

24 See for instance Hertz, *The End of the Line*, New York: Columbia University Press, 1985; Peter de Bolla, *The Discourse of the Sublime: History, aesthetics and the subject*, Oxford: Basil Blackwell, 1989; Paul Crowther, *The Kantian Sublime: From morality to art*, Oxford: Clarendon Press, 1989; Hugh J. Silverman and Gary Aylesworth (eds), *The Textual Sublime: Deconstruction and its differences*, Albany, N.Y.: State University of New York Press, 1990; and Jean-François Lyotard, *The Differend: Phrases in dispute*, trans. George van den Abeele, Minneapolis: University of Minnesota Press, 1988.

25 See Paul de Man, 'The dead-end of Formalist criticism', in *Blindness and Insight: Essays in the rhetoric of contemporary criticism*, London: Methuen, 1983, pp. 229–45.

26 See especially Empson, 'Still the strange necessity', and 'Thy darling in an urn', in *Argufying*, pp. 120–8 and 282–8.

27 Empson, 'Still the strange necessity', p. 124.

28 Empson, 'Herbert's quaintness', in *Argufying*, pp. 256–9; p. 257.

29 Empson, 'The verbal analysis', in *Argufying*, pp. 104–9; p. 108.

30 Paul Ricœur, *Freud and Philosophy*, New Haven: Yale University Press, 1970, p. 496.

31 See Stanley Fish, *Is There a Text in this Class? The authority of interpretive communities*, Cambridge, Mass.: Harvard University Press, 1980.

32 See Raymond Williams, 'Pastoral and counter-pastoral', *Critical Quarterly* 10 (1968), pp. 277–90.

33 G. W. F. Hegel, *The Phenomenology of Spirit*, trans. A. V. Miller, London: Oxford University Press, 1977.

34 For a useful selection of relevant texts see David Simpson (ed.), *The Origins of Modern Critical Thought: German aesthetics and literary criticism from Lessing to Hegel*, Cambridge: Cambridge University Press, 1988.

35 Paul de Man, 'The dead-end of Formalist criticism'. All further references given by *BI* and page number in the text.

36 Martin Heidegger, *Poetry, Language, Thought*, trans. Albert Hofstadter, New York: Harper & Row, 1971.

37 See de Man, 'The rhetoric of temporality', in *Blindness and Insight*, pp. 187–228; also de Man, *The Rhetoric of Romanticism*, New York: Columbia University Press, 1984.

38 See especially de Man, *The Resistance to Theory*, Minneapolis: University of Minnesota Press, 1986.

39 Empson, 'Thy darling in an urn', in *Argufying*, p. 285.

40 Empson, 'The calling trumpets', in *Argufying*, pp. 137–41; p. 141.

41 Empson, 'Advanced thought', in *Argufying*, pp. 516–21; p. 516.

42 For a critique of these and related notions, see Christopher Norris,

What's Wrong with Postmodernism? Critical theory and the ends of philosophy, London: Harvester-Wheatsheaf and Baltimore: Johns Hopkins University Press, 1990.

43 Haffenden records some of Empson's (to say the least) negative remarks about Derrida, Barthes and the new French theorists in his Introduction to *Argufying*, pp. 51–3.

44 Raymond Williams, *Keywords: A vocabulary of culture and society*, London: Fontana, 1976.

45 Empson, 'Compacted doctrines', in *Argufying*, pp. 184–9; p. 188.

46 Ferdinand de Saussure, *Course in General Linguistics*, trans. Wade Baskin, London: Fontana, 1974.

47 See Christopher Norris, *What's Wrong with Postmodernism?*; also Norris, 'Deconstruction, naming and necessity: some logical options', in *The Deconstructive Turn*, London: Methuen, 1983, pp. 144–62; and Norris, 'Sense, reference and logic: a critique of post-structuralist reason', in *The Contest of Faculties*, London: Methuen, 1985, pp. 47–69.

48 See especially Roland Barthes, *S/Z*, trans. Richard Miller, London: Jonathan Cape, 1975.

49 Leonard Bloomfield, *Language*, London: Allen & Unwin, 1935.

50 W. V. Quine, *Quiddities: An intermittently philosophical dictionary*, Harmondsworth: Penguin, 1987, p. 156.

51 Ibid., p. 157.

52 See especially Paul de Man, 'The resistance to theory' and 'The return of philology', in *The Resistance to Theory*, pp. 3–20 and 21–6.

53 Bertrand Russell, 'On denoting', *Mind* 14 (1905), pp. 479–93.

54 Gottlob Frege, 'On sense and reference', in Max Black and P. T. Geach (eds), *Translations from the Philosophical Writings of Gottlob Frege*, Oxford: Basil Blackwell, 1952, pp. 56–78.

55 Empson, *Milton's God*, 2nd edition, London: Chatto & Windus, 1965, p. 30.

56 See Donald Davidson, *Inquiries into Truth and Interpretation*.

57 See Quine, *From a Logical Point of View*.

58 I. A. Richards, *Interpretation in Teaching*, New York: Harcourt Brace, 1938.

59 Plato, *Theaetetus*, trans. and ed. Robin A. R. Waterfield, Harmondsworth: Penguin, 1987; Gilbert Ryle, 'Letters and syllables in Plato', in Ryle, *Collected Papers*, vol. I, London: Hutchinson, 1971, pp. 54–73.

60 See, for instance, Noam Chomsky, *Aspects of the Theory of Syntax*, Cambridge, Mass.: MIT Press, 1965; also Chomsky, *Current Issues in Linguistic Theory*, The Hague: Mouton, 1966.

61 See Frege, 'On Sense and reference'.

62 See especially Noam Chomsky, *Language and Politics*, ed. C. P. Otero, Montreal: Black Rose Books, 1988.

63 Empson, *Milton's God*, p. 58.

64 See Empson, 'Orwell at the BBC', in *Argufying*, pp. 495–501.

65 C. S. Lewis, *A Preface to 'Paradise Lost'*, London and New York: Oxford University Press, 1942.

66 See especially Jürgen Habermas, *Communication and the Evolution of Society*, trans. Thomas McCarthy, London: Heinemann, 1979.

67 See for instance Michel Foucault, *Language, Counter-Memory, Practice*, ed. D. F. Bouchard and S. Simon, Oxford: Basil Blackwell, 1977; also *Power/Knowledge*, ed. Colin Gordon, Brighton: Harvester, 1980; and H. Aram Veeser (ed.), *The New Historicism*, London: Routledge, 1989.

68 Empson, review of E. A. Burtt, *The Metaphysical Foundations of Modern Science*, reprinted in *Argufying*, pp. 530–3; p. 531.

69 See for instance Stanley Fish, *Is There a Text in This Class?*; Richard Rorty, *Consequences of Pragmatism*, Minneapolis: University of Minnesota Press, 1982; and the essays collected in W. J. T. Mitchell (ed.), *Against Theory: Literary theory and the new pragmatism*, Chicago: University of Chicago Press, 1985.

70 See especially Mikhail Bakhtin, *The Dialogic Imagination*, ed. Michael Holquist, trans. Caryl Emerson and Michael Holquist, Austin: University of Texas Press, 1981.

71 See V. N. Volosinov, *Marxism and the Philosophy of Language*, trans. L. Matejka and I. R. Titunik, New York: Seminar Press, 1973.

72 See for instance Bakhtin, *Rabelais and his World*, trans. Helene Iswolsky, Cambridge, Mass.: Harvard University Press, 1968; *Problems of Dostoevsky's Poetics*, ed. and trans. Caryl Emerson, Minneapolis: University of Minnesota Press, 1984; *Speech Genres and Other Late Essays*, ed. Caryl Emerson and Michael Holquist, trans. Vern W. McGee, Austin: University of Texas Press, 1986.

73 For some well-informed and often sharply critical commentary, see Ken Hirschkop and David Shepherd (eds), *Bakhtin and Cultural Theory*, Manchester: Manchester University Press, 1989. Other recent studies include Katerina Clark and Michael Holquist, *Mikhail Bakhtin*, Cambridge, Mass.: MIT Press, 1984; Tzvetan Todorov, *Mikhail Bakhtin: The dialogical principle*, Manchester: Manchester University Press, 1984; David Lodge, *After Bakhtin: Essays on fiction and criticism*, London: Routledge, 1990.

74 Empson, 'Compacted doctrines', in *Argufying*, p. 184.

75 Ibid., p. 187.

76 See Habermas, *Communication and the Evolution of Society* and *The Theory of Communicative Action*, vol. I, trans. Thomas McCarthy, London: Heinemann, 1984.

77 Habermas, *Knowledge and Human Interests*, trans. Jeremy Shapiro, London: Heinemann, 1984.

78 Habermas, *The Philosophical Discourse of Modernity: Twelve lectures*, trans. Frederick Lawrence, Cambridge: Polity Press, 1987.

79 See Donald Davidson, 'What metaphors mean', in *Inquiries into Truth and Interpretation*, pp. 245–64.

80 Cleanth Brooks, *The Well Wrought Urn*, p. 138.

81 See Empson, 'The hammer's ring', 'Remembering I. A. Richards' and 'Basic English', in *Argufying*, pp. 216–31.

82 Empson, 'Basic English and Wordsworth', in *Argufying*, pp. 232–8; p. 232.

83 Ibid., p. 234.
84 Ibid., p. 238.
85 Empson, 'The foundations of empirical knowledge', in *Argufying*, pp. 583–4; p. 583.
86 Ibid., p. 584.
87 Ibid.
88 Ibid., p. 583.
89 Paul de Man, 'The rhetoric of temporality'.
90 See especially M. H. Abrams, *The Mirror and the Lamp: Romantic theory and the critical tradition*, New York: Oxford University Press, 1953.
91 See for instance de Man, 'Phenomenality and materiality in Kant', in Gary Shapiro and Alan Sica (eds), *Hermeneutics: Questions and prospects*, Amherst: University of Massachusetts Press, 1984.
92 De Man, 'Aesthetic formalization: Kleist's *Uber das Marionettentheater*', in *The Rhetoric of Romanticism*, pp. 263–90.
93 Empson, 'Basic English and Wordsworth', p. 238.
94 See de Man, *Wartime Journalism, 1939–43*, ed. Werner Hamacher, Neil Hertz and Thomas Keenan, Lincoln, Nebr.: University of Nebraska Press, 1988; also *Responses: On Paul de Man's wartime journalism*, ed. Hamacher, Hertz and Keenan, Lincoln, Nebr.: University of Nebraska Press, 1989; and Christopher Norris, *Paul de Man: Deconstruction and the critique of aesthetic ideology*, New York and London: Routledge, 1988.
95 See de Man, *The Resistance to Theory*.
96 See for instance Empson, 'The cult of unnaturalism' and 'Literary criticism and the Christian revival', in *Argufying*, pp. 627–31 and 632–7; also 'Hunt the symbol', *Times Literary Supplement*, 23 April 1964, pp. 339–41.
97 Empson, review of Maynard Mack, *'King Lear' in Our Time*, *Essays in Criticism* 17 (1967), p. 95.
98 See especially the articles and reviews collected in Empson, *Using Biography*, London: Chatto & Windus, 1984; and *Essays on Shakespeare*, Cambridge: Cambridge University Press, 1986; also 'Donne the space man', *Kenyon Review* 19 (1957), pp. 337–99; 'The Ancient Mariner', in *Argufying*, pp. 297–319; and the various shorter pieces on these and other authors brought together by Haffenden in *Argufying*.
99 Empson 'Donne in the new edition', *Critical Quarterly* 8 (1966), pp. 255–80.
100 Empson, letter in response to Roger Sale, *Hudson Review* 20 (1967), pp. 534–8 (p. 538).
101 John Carey, *John Donne: Life, mind, art*, London: Faber, 1981; see also Empson's review, 'There is no penance due to ignorance', *New York Review of Books* 28 (3 December 1981), pp. 42–50.
102 Empson, 'Donne in the new edition'.
103 'Volpone', *Hudson Review* 21 (1969), p. 659.
104 Empson, reply to James Jensen's article 'The construction of *Seven Types of Ambiguity*', *Modern Language Quarterly* 27 (1966), p. 257.

105 Empson, 'Orwell's *Nineteen Eight-Four*' (letter), *Critical Quarterly* 1 (1959), pp. 157–9 (p. 159).
106 Empson, *Collected Poems*, p. 110.

2

OEDIPUS WRECKS? OR, WHATEVER HAPPENED TO DELEUZE AND GUATTARI?

Rereading *Capitalism and Schizophrenia*

Nick Heffernan

Of all the intellectual events that can be said to have arisen in France in the wake of those other, more socially disruptive, 'events' of May 1968, the reception accorded Gilles Deleuze and Felix Guattari's *Anti-Oedipus* (1972) remains among the most noteworthy. It is perhaps also true to say that the book itself, unlike the productions of other French theorists whose 'stardom' was either secured or heightened during the post-1968 intellectual fallout, has remained notably untouched by widespread academic appropriation and application, particularly by an Anglo-American readership. Whether this is because Deleuze and Guattari's ideas are especially resistant to such a process of recuperation and adaptation, or whether it is more a matter of the English-speaking academic world increasingly being overfaced with attractive French theoretical options is an open question. For now, though, it is interesting to note that British commentators in particular have found it difficult to account for the enormous 'popular' success and influence of *Anti-Oedipus* among the French intelligentsia of the early 1970s as anything other than a time-bound intellectual phenomenon. Keith Reader, in his study *Intellectuals and the Left in France since 1968*, judges that 'the interest of *L'anti-Oedipe* . . . resides in its reception and impact as much as in the ideas it elaborates', and goes on to account for 'the rapid obsolescence of much of it' as an effect of its being, in retrospect, 'little more than a rhetorical excursus'.[1]

Such an evaluation would see *Anti-Oedipus* – and the instant celebrity of its authors – as 'symptomatic' of a certain cultural moment in which some of the euphoric spirit of the May events was consciously rekindled and mobilized in a theoretical assault against what were perceived as the two great betrayers or oppressors of that spirit – on the one hand institutionalized psychiatry and psychoanalysis, understood as a theory and practice of 'normalization', and on the other, the ossified Marxism of the French Communist Party (PCF). With the passing of this moment, then, the ideas of Deleuze and Guattari would lose what relevance and force they might have had and *Anti-Oedipus* itself would remain of importance only as a historical document. The twin questions of power and desire which the book did so much to foreground could more profitably be pursued through the more purely historical, philosophical or psychoanalytic work of Michel Foucault, Jean-François Lyotard and Jacques Lacan respectively.

This, at least in British intellectual circles, seems to be the fate of Deleuze and Guattari's ideas. In the United States their work *has* been translated and more actively promoted, most energetically by the journals *Semiotext(e)* and *Substance*, both of which have had special issues on Deleuze and Guattari.[2] However, their work has received minimal attention in comparison with the penetration into the American academy achieved by the ideas and texts of Derrida, Lacan, Foucault and more recently Lyotard. The only 'major' theoretician to have consistently taken Deleuze and Guattari into account has been Fredric Jameson,[3] and he too has tended to regard them from a metacritical position, purely as an instance of a certain historically specific style of postmodern critical discourse.[4]

Outside their native cultural milieu then, the names of Deleuze and Guattari have entered into critical and theoretical discourse only at the expense of being thoroughly historicized – locked into a post-1968 pre-Mitterand time-warp, or dissolved into some wider historical phenomenon called poststructuralism. While I would want to acknowledge the necessity and importance of taking such a contextual and historical view of cultural and intellectual production, it also seems that, in the case of Deleuze and Guattari, the dominance of this approach has had the effect of deferring any prolonged engagement with the ideas and texts themselves. Furthermore, it remains to be said that *Anti-Oedipus* was only the first instalment of a larger theoretical project which Deleuze and Guattari called 'Capitalism and Schizophrenia', and to write off the whole enterprise at a stroke as obsolete without awaiting its completion might be judged premature.

The appearance (1980) and translation (1988) of the second volume of *Capitalism and Schizophrenia, A Thousand Plateaus,* would therefore indicate that it is now possible to take another look at Deleuze and Guattari, to read the new book in the light of *Anti-Oedipus* and to formulate an evaluation of the project as a whole.

This study is such an attempt. It therefore follows a path that runs between the exposition of Deleuze and Guattari's ideas on the one hand and the critical analysis of them on the other. In the first instance, I treat the respective volumes of *Capitalism and Schizophrenia* as books in their own right, seeking to highlight the major concepts and arguments and relate them to wider questions and other theorists. I then focus on particular aspects of Deleuze and Guattari's project – the literary and the political, though the separation can never be absolute, and I have tried throughout to be attentive to the political implications of their work whatever its ostensible focus. Finally, a short conclusion brings the intellectual and cultural context up to date and ventures a brusque judgement of the validity of the kind of 'reading' of Deleuze and Guattari arrived at by Keith Reader above.

First, though, a consideration of the period prior to the emergence of *Anti-Oedipus* is necessary in order to establish the cultural and intellectual context of Deleuze and Guattari's project for, as Vincent Descombes has convincingly argued in his survey of contemporary French philosophy, 'The recent orientation of the debate in France is a delayed effect of the experience of May 1968.'[5]

1968

It would appear that there are as many versions of the 'events' of May 1968 as there are commentators to account for them or participants to memorialize them.[6] Treatment has ranged from lofty patrician dismissal of the events as a short-lived outburst of juvenile dissent, rapidly quelled by an encounter with authority, to their consecration as a crucial turning-point in post-war French history, which left traditional notions of radical political and cultural action in ruins.[7] The constant factor in all this, however, is the sheer persistence with which the events have demanded attention from those seeking to address almost any aspect of French

cultural life of the last twenty years, not least the
intellectual production. Indeed, the events, as Keith F
pointed out, 'while in many ways anti-intellectual, wei
able from the universities, where they started and w
most lasting effects were felt'.[8] And though it is outside the scope
of this essay to treat the May events in detail, it is none the less
necessary to begin with them as the historical precondition for an
intellectual and political situation in which Deleuze and Guattari's
theoretical intervention was conceived and whose limitations it
sought both to expose and to transcend.

The significance of the May events for French intellectual history might be schematically illustrated by means of a 'before'
and 'after', the two terms standing respectively for the pre-May
dominance of structuralism as a mode of intellectual enquiry,
and its subsequent problematization in, and displacement by,
what came to be loosely defined as poststructuralism. It has even
been suggested that the events themselves were in part motivated
by Parisian student resentment and hostility towards the oppress-
ively deterministic view of social relations that structuralism, in
its more rigorous forms, implied. While this notion in itself is
fantastic (it is questionable, for instance, whether structuralism
was quite the academic orthodoxy it was perceived to be in
retrospect), the fact that it could be offered as an explanation of
the events highlights the extent to which intellectual movements
and trends are bound up with politics (usually of the Left) in
French culture. Thus the failure of the prevailing modes of structuralist thought to provide an adequate intellectual framework
for both participants and analysts to think through the events and
their implications seriously compromised its credibility among a
student body and an intellectual elite which tended to align
themselves 'naturally' with the political Left.

This was most damagingly the case for the brand of structuralist
Marxism personified by the philosopher Louis Althusser. Indeed,
Althusser's brusque dismissal of the events at the time as insignificant in revolutionary terms confirmed, for many who experienced them as the most significant personal and political moment
of their lives, the final eclipse of politics by theory in his work.
Moreover, the PCF, of which Althusser was a prominent member,
also distanced itself from the events, and this failure of the largest
Marxist organization in the country, along with its leading theoretician, to grant the events any large political importance seemed

to call for a drastic revision of the way politics and revolutionary action had been hitherto conceived by the organized Left.

In effect then, structuralism in both its 'straight' academic or overtly Marxist incarnations could offer no productive intellectual tools with which to tackle the two major questions posed by the success and failure of the May events, namely: How and why does such a vigorous and apparently spontaneous challenge to state power materialize? Why and how is power so swiftly able to reassert its dominance? The fundamental structuralist reliance on a synchronic and systemic conception of societal relationships, derived from the Saussurean notion of *langue*, seemed to allow no place for the unpredictable oppositional 'event' that May so evidently was; nor did its stress on the thoroughly determining nature of the structures which articulated such relationships admit of the possibility for human agency aimed precisely at transforming those very structures. In short, orthodox structuralism was weak on the problem of *power*, how it operated and how it might be conquered; there was no room in the structuralist schema to ask *why* certain structures were related to particular forms of social and political organization, or to allow for contradiction and struggle between them. This limitation found its equivalent in Althusserian Marxism's evacuation of the problem of power into an all-encompassing notion of ideology which, projected into the deepest crevices of human subjectivity, foreclosed certain key political options such as class struggle and individual or collective revolutionary agency. Vincent Descombes is therefore able to judge that 1968's prevalent theory of history – historical materialism of a distinctly Althusserian complexion – was itself 'the obstacle that separated [French intellectuals] from history at the very moment when history was knocking at the door'.[9]

Yet despite Althusser's humiliation in the face of the events and their aftermath, it was another variant of structuralism – one to which, paradoxically, Althusser was deeply indebted – that most successfully weathered them to emerge strengthened (but not entirely unproblematized) by May's intellectual upheaval. This was the structural psychoanalysis of Jacques Lacan; and for Sherry Turkle, who charts the rise of Lacanian theory in her study of 'French Freud', 1968 is the crucial moment in the growth of a widespread 'psychoanalytic culture' in France.[10] The reasons for this are both theoretical and experiential. For while the process of argument, discussion and radical self-questioning that accompanied and followed the May events rapidly exposed the theoretical shortcomings of structuralism touched on above, this process in itself was a qualitatively new and difficult experience for many who participated in the strikes, demonstrations and occupations, and for those whose political hopes rested with them. This difficulty was intensified by the 'failure' of the events: their brevity, the ease with which the Gaullist regime restored 'order' and reassumed 'normality', and the acquiescence of hitherto rebellious sections of the population in this restoration seemed to require explanation in terms that went deeper into the participants' own personal, even psychic, investments in 'revolution' than the more orthodox categories of ideological or economic analysis could go. Furthermore, there was the style or 'spirit' of the events with which to come to terms, encapsulated, according to Keith Reader, by the word 'imagination',[11] and bearing all the features of a festival or ritual of liberation.[12] In this respect May represented a dramatic conjunction of personal desire and revolutionary action that seemed light-years removed from the dour notions of a politics centred on the industrial working class. Thus it is not surprising that the process of reappraisal and self-scrutiny that the events set in train should focus on the relation of the self to political action and societal structures, nor that this discourse should find in Lacanian psychoanalysis its most accommodating theoretical vehicle.

Like much of the structuralism that was found wanting in 1968, Lacan's work was greatly concerned with the ways in which individual human subjects come to be constituted by powerful and impersonal structures of communication and interrelation of which they remain largely oblivious. *Unlike* most other structuralisms, however, Lacan's did not view this process with equanimity, or as unproblematic for subjectivity itself. For him, subjectivity was conferred with the infant human organism's entry into the collective social domain of language and of human signification generally. In essence, the Oedipus process consisted in the passage from the Imaginary realm of unstructured infantile experience to the Symbolic realm of social languages and laws, and this necessarily involved a degree of internalization, transformation and loss that was exceedingly traumatic and painful for the developing psyche. Thus, while Lacan's account of subjectivity as the internalization of social and cultural structures – primarily language and the family – seemed to promise some kind of theoretical access to the point at which the personal and the political met and intertwined, his insistence that the subject and its desire were born out of crisis, pain and loss spoke powerfully to many veterans of May for whom the events had marked the abrupt flowering and demise of revolutionary desire itself.

Indeed, there were those for whom Lacan's reformulation of Oedipus achieved in theory precisely what the May events had attempted to accomplish in practice – the destruction of the boundary between self and society.[13] It became possible to interpret the utopian impulse of the events in Lacanian terms as an attempt to shatter society's Symbolic constraints and return to the presocial and Edenic experience of the Imaginary. In certain respects this was the development of a theme previously stated by such Freudo-Marxians as Herbert Marcuse and Norman O. Brown, whose Reichian equation of political and sexual repression led them to propose infantile polymorphousness as a model of fundamental human liberation.[14] After the events this theme was modified further by writers such as Julia Kristeva, whose proposal of the 'semiotic' as a site of prelinguistic flux and freedom was clearly related to Lacan's theorization of the Imaginary. But what marked these political idealizations of a hypothesized realm of presymbolic experience was their divergence from the Althusserian interpretation of Lacan developed in an influential essay of 1964.[15]

For Althusser, Freud and Lacan's 'decentring' of the human subject was crucial to a Marxism which came to view subjectivity as an effect of ideology. Lacan's Symbolic order was the truly 'Human Order' – and hence the truly political – into which every human being is 'inserted' through a process of 'ideological misrecognition' to become subject (in all senses of the word) to the 'Law of Culture'. As has been suggested earlier, such an equivalence of the Symbolic and the Ideological had disabling implications for any notion of political struggle or change, and the post–1968 focus on the Imaginary can be seen as an attempt to circumvent this theoretical impasse by reversing the political hierarchy of Symbolic over Imaginary insisted upon by Althusser.

Such a reversal, though, was certainly not suggested by Lacan himself, who was much closer to Althusser in stressing the inevitability and constitutive power of the Oedipal moment of entry into the Symbolic order. Rather, what seemed to be required was a critique[16] of Lacanian theories of subjectivity which would necessarily return to the politics of the Oedipal moment only to refuse the inevitability of its outcome. Feminists especially were to perceive the limitations of Lacan's work, particularly his account of the strict modulations of desire under the sign of the phallus,[17] but it was Gilles Deleuze and Felix Guattari (himself a psychoanalyst trained in Lacan's methods) who, in *Anti-Oedipus*, seemed at the time to have most successfully assimilated Lacanian theory (and, not insignificantly, Lacanian *style*) in order to turn it against itself in defence of the spirit of 1968.

ANTI-OEDIPUS: CAPITALISM AND SCHIZOPHRENIA I

Perhaps the most striking aspect of *Anti-Oedipus* is its style, which one American reviewer characterized as 'skittish' and 'appropriately nutty'.[18] This refusal to 'make sense', however, is crucial to the book's political ambitions, for Deleuze and Guattari subscribe absolutely to the avant-garde modernist investment in the politics of style – particularly in its subversive, defamiliarizing possibilities. This was also a credo of Lacan's, whose elusive textual strategies were not only necessitated by a discourse that sought to trace the subjective disruptions of language and challenge traditional notions of authorship, but also reflected a close personal association with Surrealism, a relationship which exemplifies a tendency for 'radical' theory in France to identify with and borrow from the more 'radical' schools of artistic and literary production. More importantly, it was through style that Deleuze and Guattari sought to reconnect theory with social and psychic reality and recapture some of the May events' disruptive force. For, as Vincent Descombes points out,

> the great wealth of the ferment of May 1968 is not to be found in the ideas propounded at the time. . . . [its] interest lies rather in the *impertinence* of its dissent, in the *unseemly* character of its criticisms. It was form above all that was seriously shaken.[19]

At one level, then, the book's frenetic pitch, its irreverence and its lack of respect for disciplinary boundaries or expertise stem directly from the critique of received forms of intellectual and political life that seized 'the traditional meeting place of the two, the university',[20] during 1968. At another level, this refusal of formal orthodoxy embodied one of *Anti-Oedipus*'s major themes – its critique of the genital organization and symbolic orientation of the so-called 'normal' subject which, for both Freud and Lacan, it was the function of the Oedipus complex to secure.[21] The question of style also points to another of the book's pervasive concerns – power. Not surprisingly, Michel Foucault – the arch-theorist of power – touches on this in his admiring preface to the book, whose style he sees as an attempt to 'neutralize the effects of power'.[22] Deleuze and Guattari's textual devices are not derived from rhetoric, which is a coercive linguistic practice; rather they are what Foucault calls 'traps' or escape routes from the oppressive structures of discourse – 'so many invitations to let oneself be put out, take one's leave of the text and slam the door shut'.[23]

Such a sensitivity to the way language might freeze into oppressive discourses and formations was part of a wider poststructuralist reaction against the 'high' structuralist tendency to submit every area of cultural life to the explanatory operations of the Saussurean linguistic paradigm. Along with it went an attentiveness to those microscopic slippages and elisions of sense which inhabit the very texture of language and which work to undermine its larger, totalizing movement towards meaning and closure. Derrida's direct assault on Saussurean linguistics in his 1967 essay, 'Différance', anticipated 1968's attempts to 'reinvent' language the better to resist authoritarian forms and reconnect more authentically with immediate subjective experience, an impulse which is embodied in the style of *Anti-Oedipus*.[24] Yet, after Lacan, the critique of language and the critique of subjectivity could hardly be separated, and the deployment of radically disruptive compositional strategies was also a principal device by which poststructuralist writers could both describe and *enact* the 'crisis of the subject' that was so central to their view of modernity. In this respect, at least, they were loyal inheritors of the structuralist tradition, though they approached the problem in radically different terms, scorning the exhaustive rationality of their predecessors in favour of a Nietzschean irrationalism and anarchistic playfulness. This constituted what both Keith Reader and Vincent Descombes, in their discussions of the period, see as a 'refusal of theory' – an antagonism towards large interpretive theoretical superstructures and a concern, rather, to develop mobile, constantly changing and essentially *provisional* analytic frameworks, a concern which can be felt in *Anti-Oedipus* in both its style and its grounding opposition between the disruptive, even revolutionary, profusion of elements on the 'molecular' level and their recuperation into repressive structures and forms on the 'molar' level.

For Deleuze and Guattari the primary theoretical device of such recuperation in our particular period of late capitalism is the Oedipus process, understood as 'the moment of transition from presocial to social man, the moment of "Oedipization", the passage from the imaginary to the symbolic'.[25] This is the moment at which the organs of the body receive their final, fixed meaning and organization, at which language enters and constitutes the subject through the agency of the familial triangle, and at which desire is reined in and tied to this triadic representation of 'Daddy, Mommy, me'. This, at least, is Oedipus according to Freud. Lacan, however, had pushed the notion further in illustrating the extent to which Oedipus was an ideologically and culturally determined, and determining, process. Deleuze and Guattari seize on the Lacanian definition of Oedipus as containing the means of its own deconstruction, in that it highlights the central role played by 'Oedipization' in the reproduction of capitalism, and thus any challenge to capitalism must first seek to unseat Oedipus.

The critique of Oedipus was contained within a larger attack on theories and philosophies of representation generally, and on hermeneutics in particular, which Fredric Jameson identifies as the major characteristic of poststructuralism as an intellectual movement.[26] Such philosophies, according to Deleuze and Guattari, seek to subject the complex, heterogeneous and contradictory materials of actual social and subjective experience to a drastic process of revision and totalization by which, through the application of an all-powerful interpretive 'key', they can be rendered representable – and thus meaningful – in terms other than their own. What is denied or suppressed by this rewriting is nothing less than the *real* itself, 'the whole rich and random multiple realities of concrete everyday experience';[27] and for Deleuze and Guattari the real is inseparable from *desire*, which invests and produces the real at every turn. Psychoanalysis, as the ruling interpretive discourse on desire, is therefore guilty of colonizing desire and restricting it to a reductive and limited set of representations – a dismal 'theatre' of dream, fantasy, Greek myth and family romance.[28] The Oedipus complex is, to use a Derridean formulation, the 'transcendental signifier' in this apparatus, the final, fixed term beyond which meaning, interpretation and desire itself are forbidden to stray. In possession of the Oedipal 'key', then, the psychoanalyst is installed as the modern despot/priest of desire. Oedipus therefore becomes the regulated and diminished representation of desire in our times – the point at which desire 'lets itself be caught'.[29]

Against the psychoanalytic version, Deleuze and Guattari posit a conception of desire that is prior to representation and everywhere escapes and undermines it. This is desire as a primordial 'flow' of libido, a fundamental condition of human beings in nature, or of matter itself, whose modulations constitute the real. Deleuze and Guattari invoke the Greek term, *hyle*,[30] meaning 'basic world stuff'[31] which, for all their hostility to Freud, is an intensification of his notion of the 'primary process'. The organs of the human body – 'machines' as Deleuze and Guattari call them – cut into and are themselves shaped by this flow to form the partial objects that constitute reality. Desire thus 'produces the real' at the most basic level; it is in effect 'desiring production',[32] while human bodies, parts of bodies or groups of bodies in conjunction work as 'desiring machines', interrupting and modulating the flow of desire and its material investment.

Just as Lacan had insisted that the third major term in his theoretical schema, the Real, could not be represented but could only be approached (and at the same time *obscured*) in the subject's movement between the Imaginary and the Symbolic, so Deleuze and Guattari maintain that desire, as that which *produces* the real, cannot be represented. Indeed, they exceed Lacan in detaching desire from any pre-existing level of physiological need, not only regarding it as a prelinguistic phenomenon but making it always already there, in operation from the beginning. This can be seen as a manœuvre intended to purge desire of the negativity Lacan had given it in predicating it on lack or absence, thus condemning desire to the interminable pursuit of representations of the missing object, thereby linking its operations to those of language, in whose symbolic structures it was thus deeply inscribed. Liberated from its Lacanian sentence of nostalgically tracing the irretrievable object across an endless relay of 'empty' linguistic signifiers, desire was free to become an active, productive, and hence revolutionary force. For although desire was prelinguistic, it was by no means presocial. Deleuze and Guattari equate 'desiring production' with 'social production', and every-where wish to see desire as a more thoroughly collective and political agent than psychoanalysis, with its cloistered familial terms of reference, will allow. Deleuze and Guattari's 'machinic unconscious' is not the Oedipal realm of internalized capitalist power relations that it is for Freud and Lacan, but is rather a pre- or an-Oedipal site in which the pressure of a much wider range of social, political and libidinal forces is felt. Yet, and crucially, desire is at the same time a profoundly anti-social force in the sense that its productions are always 'molecular multiplicit-ies', while society, or capitalism in particular, proceeds by violently subordinating the productions of desire to 'molar aggregates' and 'formations of sovereignty'.[33]

The molar/molecular opposition in *Anti-Oedipus* is clearly a derivation and an inversion in terms of political importance of Lacan's Imaginary and Symbolic realms. Deleuze and Guattari privilege the molecular as that which is immediate, fragmentary and proceeds by flows, breaks and intensities. The molar, on the other hand, is the level

> of all those large, abstract, mediate and perhaps even empty and imaginary forms by which we seek to recontain the molecular: the mirage of the continuity of personal identity, the organizing unity of the psyche or the personality, the concept of society itself;[34]

it is in effect the level at which the profusion of libidinal energies assumes ideological forms – the subject, the family, the nation, the state.[35] This valorization of the molecular is not only directed at psychoanalysis, whose function is to organize desire into a series of molar representations; it is a further critique of Marxism, which Deleuze and Guattari see as another totalizing discourse anxious to pin desire down to representations such as class, society and ideology. Indeed, their characterization of Oedipus as an impoverished 'theatre of representations'[36] is at once a rebuke to Freud and to Marxism in the person of Louis Althusser who, in his essay on Freud and Lacan, had referred to the Oedi-pus complex as a ' "theatrical machine" imposed by the Law of Culture on every involuntary, conscripted candidate to humanity'.[37] This was central to Althusser's notion of ideology, which he based on Lacan's theorization of the Symbolic; but for Deleuze and Guattari, who refuse absolutely to recognize the category of ideology, it was another betrayal of desire (reflected in Althusser and the PCF's 'reactionary' role in the May events) which confirmed the need to transcend the prevailing Marxist and Freudian parameters if the revolutionary potential of desire was to be released.[38]

Paradoxically, though, the means of this transcendence were furnished by Marxism itself – desire, as we have seen, was made productive; it became, in Marxian terms, infrastructural, in fact the fundamental force of production. Thus, while Keith Reader notes that 'The dethroning of economism from its place at the centre of left wing thought is the most pervasive and abiding legacy of May',[39] he might also have mentioned that this marks less the disappearance of a concern with political economy than its absorption into an expanded notion of 'libidinal economy', central also to the post-1968 work of that other major 'philosopher of desire', Jean-François Lyotard. Freud and Marx might, for Deleuze and Guattari, be classically oppressive 'bad fathers', but it is out of their dismembered parts that *Anti-Oedipus* is constructed. The influence of Marx is increasingly evident when Deleuze and Guattari attach the revolutionary capacity of desire to the nature of present-day capitalist organization; indeed, their whole understanding of capitalism is couched in terms of a 'universal history' that recalls the Marxist conception of the historical process as a succession of increasingly complex modes of production.[40]

Deleuze and Guattari posit three main phases of human history, each characterized by a distinct kind of 'social machine' and a related mode of representation that together constitute a regime under which desiring production operates. These are the Primitive-Territorial machine, the Barbarian-Despotic machine, and the Civilized-Capitalist machine, and they can roughly be said to correspond to Marx's historical schema of primitive accumulation, Asiatic, and finally capitalist modes of production.[41] Furthermore, in *Anti-Oedipus* history is a process by which desiring forces are progressively 'deterritorialized', or released from fixed points of investment in the earth, the body or the socius to become increasingly abstract and volatile 'flows' – a notion which suggests an almost classical Marxist view of history in which the forces of production outstrip the relations of production to revolutionary effect.

For Deleuze and Guattari the historical process commences in the primitive territorial stage, which is in many ways the least repressive of the three social machines, having little requirement for complex systems of subordination. It is characterized by the relatively free distribution of human beings across the earth's surface according to tribal 'codes' which might be sedentary or nomadic. The primary mode of representation in these societies is inscription – collective inscription of the patterns of tribal settlement on the earth itself, and inscription in the form of tattoos, scars and marks on the individual human body. Social organization in this stage is based on debt and physical cruelty, encapsulated in the biblical philosophy of 'an eye for an eye' which, Deleuze and Guattari insist, is not to be understood as an early form of exchange – itself a particularly capitalist notion.

The territorial stage is succeeded by the barbarian stage when primitive patterns of distribution and investment come to be 'overcoded' on the isolated body of the despot or king. Social relations are thus 'deterritorialized', or abstracted from their previous sites of investment, and refocused on a single figure who becomes the personification of those relations which now function in terms of the state. Indeed, the Barbarian machine is characterized by the emergence of a state apparatus, with its reliance on more complex structures of subjection and control, and with this stage, Deleuze and Guattari proclaim, an *Urstaat* 'springs fully armed into being':[42] terror replaces cruelty, and the structures of subjection are internalized and spiritualized (this stage marks the arrival of Christianity), whereas in the Primitive machine relationships had been inscribed on the body's, or the earth's, exterior. Writing is the primary barbaric mode of representation, in which the voice and the graph are joined under the despotic rule of the signifier; and while this represents a further deterritorialization of relationships into an abstracted realm of communication, writing also imposes new forms of regulation, and particularly of subjectification, in terms of grammar and the structuring of enunciation. In short, then, the Despotic machine initiates on a large scale the double and contradictory process of deterritorialization and overcoding that is brought to a potentially revolutionary climax within the Capitalist machine.

Deleuze and Guattari use the term 'Civilized-Capitalist' ironically, as for them it is the most violent and cynical of the three types of social machine. In it a destabilizing profusion of abstracted 'flows' is released under the aegis of the principle of exchange; money, property, labour and so on circulate as relatively deterritorialized flows of surplus value, detached from any particular locus of investment in the social formation. These are part of capitalism's 'language' of decoded flows, empty signifiers and lines of deterritorialization which is in a constant state of flux. For Deleuze and Guattari, like Marx, capitalism is the very figure of modernity in which 'all that is solid melts into air', and in which the rate of social, political, economic and even subjective change far outstrips any attempts to arrest it long enough for definitive or total analysis. Even writing is an archaism in the modern socius, for capitalism effects a McLuhanite shattering of the Gutenberg galaxy which releases a proliferation of 'empty' forms of signification without referent.[43]

In the midst of this welter of flux and intensity, however, capitalism, for the sake of its continued reproduction, everywhere reabsorbs, recuperates and recodes, or 'axiomatizes', the very flows it releases into ever more repressive formations – the police, the army, psychoanalysis. Consequently the 'revolutionary path' is not to *resist* the fundamental dynamic of capitalism, or to *protest* its disastrous social effects, but rather to *intensify* these:

> To go still further. . . . For perhaps the flows are not yet deterritorialized enough. . . . Not to withdraw from the process but to go further, to 'accelerate' the process as Nietzsche put it: in this matter, the truth is that we haven't seen anything yet.[44]

And for Deleuze and Guattari, desire is the crucial agent of this acceleration: 'if we put forward desire as a revolutionary agency, it is because we believe capitalist society can endure many manifestations of interest, but not one manifestation of desire, which would be enough to make its fundamental structures explode.'[45]

The overwhelming question that remains for such a conception of history, and of capitalism in particular, must therefore be: What is the fate of desire in the modern social formation? Given historical conditions ideal for the liberation of desiring production, how is capitalism – 'the limit of all societies' – able somehow to turn itself back into 'a gigantic machine for social repression–psychic repression, aimed at what nevertheless constitutes its own reality – the decoded flows'?[46] This 'failure of history',[47] as one commentator puts it, necessarily returns us to Oedipus, the point at which desire 'lets itself be caught' by the 'capitalist order of representation'.[48] Deleuze and Guattari are compelled to ask 'How is this possible?' And, given that an explanation in terms of ideology is ruled out, as desire is that which can never be deceived, their answer must be that *desire is divided against itself*, that it conspires in its own capture. Just as capitalism consists in a dual and contradictory movement of deterritorialization and axiomatization, so desire is doubled, oscillating between the molecular, 'schizophrenic', and the molar, 'paranoiac' poles of investment.[49] Furthermore, and with baleful political consequences, 'It appears that the oscillation *is not equal*, and that as a rule the schizoid pole is *potential* in relation to the *actual* paranoiac pole.'[50] Thus *Anti-Oedipus* proceeds towards the somewhat despairing conclusion that, as Foucault puts it in his preface to the book, 'there is a fascism in us all' which causes us 'to desire the very thing that dominates and exploits us'.[51]

The fate of desire in capitalism, then, is that it is pathologized, and this fate is demonstrated in the quintessentially modern, or 'capitalist', condition of clinical schizophrenia. For Deleuze and Guattari, the schizophrenic comes closest to *experiencing* capitalism in precisely the way they *theorize* it – as a teeming profusion of forces, signs and meanings which refuse to be organized or coded into a manageable hierarchy of forms. Like their notion of desire, the schizophrenic is at once thoroughly social – living the world in all its molecular immediacy – and deeply anti-social – refusing, or being unable, to enter into its conventional molar structures and representations. Schizophrenia is, in effect, a refusal of Oedipus – especially in the sense that it is the symbolic function of language that the schizophrenic has most difficulty in accepting. However, the incompatibility of schizophrenic desire with social existence means that it must be excluded, pathologized. Therefore, if Oedipus is the 'displaced *interior* limit of capitalism', then schizophrenia is its 'exorcized *exterior* limit',[52] and the schizophrenic embodies the modern fate of desire as it 'congeals' into 'sickness'.[53]

Deleuze and Guattari are anxious to distinguish between schizophrenia as a 'process' and as an 'entity'. 'Our' capitalist schizophrenics represent the *failure* of revolutionary desire, its capture and organization into the form of an illness. What is required is rather the activation of schizophrenia as a process, its liberation from the paranoid molar forms of societal representation. Yet there is still a strong sense in which the schizophrenic is for

Deleuze and Guattari a revolutionary 'innocent', a 'natural' being more closely in touch with presocial and presubjective energies than the rest of us. This reflects a persistent vitalist strand in Deleuze's work which had previously been evident in his writing on Bergson and Nietzsche, and which thoroughly informs the conception of desire in *Anti-Oedipus*. It is also related to Guattari's involvement in the movement against institutionalized definitions of deviancy and madness – a prevailing concern at the Clinique de la Borde where he works – and to his connection with the British anti-psychiatry of Laing and Cooper, for whom the schizophrenic was also privileged, though largely for moral-existential, rather than overtly political, reasons. Such concerns – the nature of the 'life force', the political meaning of madness – belonged to a strong 'current of political naturalism' which Sherry Turkle sees emerging from the May events' valorization of, and attempted return to, 'a model of a presymbolic age of direct, fusional relationships, of spontaneity, of primitive, unmediated desire'.[54] And in retrospect, this aspect of *Anti-Oedipus* appears not only its most dated, but also its most politically disabling, theme; for it reflects, as Peter Dews observes, an essentially 'naive' naturalism which, by assuming access to an a priori, prereflexive realm – 'the primary process in itself' – dismisses as 'metaphysical' those compromised secondary structures in which the political, for most of us, consists.[55]

This limitation particularly flaws Deleuze and Guattari's notion of 'schizoanalysis' – the radical practice by which schizoid investments, so far doomed either to 'congeal' pathologically or remain forever 'potential', can be reconnected and 'actualized'. For schizoanalysis, a term for revolutionary theoretical action, 'has strictly no political program to propose'.[56] Rather, its task is 'negative' – it 'must be violent, brutal: defamiliarizing, de-Oedipalizing, decastrating' in its attempts to trace the 'molecular lines of escape that already define the mechanic's task of the schizoanalyst'.[57] While this not only begs the question of formulating in advance any notion of what the politics of desire *wants* to, or envisages *will*, happen to capitalism under 'accelerated' conditions (other than its 'explosion'); it also neatly installs the schizoanalyst, or 'mechanic' of desire (or Parisian intellectual leftist?), in a position of political and epistemological supremacy over even the failed revolutionary schizophrenic him/herself. Moreover, the schizoanalyst's task seems to be unduly focused upon aesthetic and intellectual investments of desire, rather than upon its more properly political manifestations. (Admittedly, Deleuze and Guattari would not recognize such a distinction.) 'Our' arts and 'our' sciences receive considerable attention as possessing a 'revolutionary potential' capable of causing 'increasingly deterritorialized and decoded flows to circulate in the socius ... to the point where the artist and the scientist may be determined to rejoin an objectively revolutionary situation.'[58] Such an emphasis betrays a strongly avant-gardist conception of artistic and scientific production, to which schizoanalysis, with its defamiliarizing function, is explicitly linked;[59] and not surprisingly, Deleuze and Guattari's first venture into schizoanalysis proper took as its object the literary modernism of Franz Kafka, in which the politics of desire, finding its strategies anticipated in literature, substituted the notion of the revolutionary schizophrenic *text* for that of the failed revolutionary schizophrenic *person*.

That schizoanalysis can propose no positive political formulations beyond a kind of avant-garde guerrilla warfare is the result of a weakness in Deleuze and Guattari's conception of desire. For if desire can ultimately desire its own repression then there is in fact no political opponent other than itself, and the revolution is therefore always betrayed: '*betrayals ... are there from the very start.*'[60] Thus desire is caught in a political impasse in which struggle is pre-empted and to which the only available response is to intensify the contradictions of the immediate situation in the hope of some indeterminate 'explosion'.

As Fredric Jameson has commented, the political force of desire is thus essentially transgressive, 'as though [it] ... must always have a repressive norm or law against which to burst and against which to define itself'; and therefore by 'presupposing' that against which it works, desire actually 'reconfirms' its oppressor.[61] Indeed much poststructuralist theory is beset by a kind of 'doubling' which has seriously hampered its developing a convincingly constructive political critique of modernity: Derrida's theorization of the double and contradictory dynamic of language and reason, Foucault's 'power' which always contains its opposite – these notions derive their force from, and in many ways depend for their existence on, the particularly oppressive structures of which they are supposedly a critique. And for Deleuze and Guattari this is doubly disabling when the oppressor is nothing less than desire itself. Consequently, they are unable to specify what might guide a revolutionary investment of desire, or precisely what effects such an investment would have, largely because desire, like *différance* and 'power', is *without history* – only the forms of its repression are historical. Desire is thus a historical constant – always working, always the same, always fatally divided against itself in a way that recalls Freud's theorization of libido as a timeless opposition of Eros and Thanatos. Bereft of such 'orthodox' political notions as historical struggle, ideological conflict and human agency, or such compromised representational categories as class and society, Deleuze and Guattari are forced to pin their conception of revolutionary social transformation on 'the efficacy of a libidinal break at a precise moment, a schiz whose sole cause is desire'.[62] This is historical change conceived absolutely in terms of the 'moment' of May 1968 – as a 'rupture with causality that forces a rewriting of history on the level of the real, and produces a strangely polyvocal moment when everything seems possible'.[63]

It is therefore ironic that a project which set out to purge desire of Lacanian nostalgia and negativity, and to displace both Marxist and Freudian problematics with a Nietzschean enterprise of critical affirmation,[64] should be undercut by a nostalgia for the very historical moment – May 1968 – whose 'failure' made it a political necessity in the first place. Ultimately, *Anti-Oedipus* remains locked into a theoretical impasse similar to Althusser's, with potentially revolutionary desiring machines (or 'subjects' for Althusser) everywhere betrayed by paranoia (or 'conscripted' by Althusserian ideology) and made to participate in their own oppression. Indeed, the status of the various molar forms of recuperation is not resolved in the book, for there is a strong sense in which they are but fictional representations with no claims to actual historical existence whatever, yet their *effects* are none the less historical and real, disastrously so for the prospects of desire.

These shortcomings were to become increasingly evident as the moment of May 1968 receded; yet in 1972 *Anti-Oedipus* spoke forcefully to an audience which thought and debated in psychoanalytic terms and carried May's legacy of dissatisfaction with political and intellectual norms. The book's major distinction – an index especially of its fundamentally modernist dynamic and political orientation – was its scandalizing effect on Parisian psychoanalytic and theoretical discourse. But the completion of

Capitalism and Schizophrenia would take place in conditions increasingly removed from, and hostile to, the spirit of May, and in which many of the limitations of the philosophy of desire, sketched out above, could not be disguised.

A THOUSAND PLATEAUS: CAPITALISM AND SCHIZOPHRENIA II

Anti-Oedipus had stated the 'negative' task of schizoanalysis, yet any positive dimension to this task remained obscured by the fierce anti-psychoanalytic polemics of the book. Thus the more laborious duty of discovering 'the entire interplay of the desiring machines and the repression of desire'[65] was to be the focus of the second volume of *Capitalism and Schizophrenia*, approached through the framework of the 'universal history' and the particularly powerful characterization of contemporary capitalism that *Anti-Oedipus* had established. Indeed, the persistence and elaboration of the universal historical perspective is one of the strong continuities linking the two volumes against which the discontinuities can be measured; for while *A Thousand Plateaus* continues to assault the repressive representational structures of disciplines such as psychoanalysis, linguistics, philosophy and literary criticism, it also introduces a number of significant new terms and changes of emphasis into the schizoanalytic project overall.

Most notable among the latter is the greatly reduced importance of the schizophrenic who, as revolutionary hero, had been the central character of *Anti-Oedipus*. By the end of the 1970s the wave of interest in anti-psychiatry and the politics of deviancy and madness, that had swept that book to notoriety, had crested,[66] and the schizophrenic merits only few and desultory appearances in *A Thousand Plateaus* as an 'empty' and 'catatonic' figure of the pathos of 'perverted' desire. This is just one manifestation of an aura of caution and strategic restraint that informs the later book in contrast to the self-consciously iconoclastic tone of its predecessor which, it could be argued, reflects the impact of a general rightward shift in French culture since 1968. Indeed, the fate of the schizophrenic is, for the Deleuze and Guattari of *A Thousand Plateaus*, a singularly cautionary tale of the dangers of too hasty or ill-considered an investment of desire: 'Were you cautious enough? Not wisdom, caution. In doses. As a rule immanent to experimentation: injections of caution. Many have

129

been defeated in this battle.'[67] And it would seem that such an emphasis on the vulnerability, as opposed to the unbounded revolutionary power, of desire forms part of the changed strategic priorities necessitated by a 'positive' rather than a 'negative' political project. For along with the admonitory tone, Deleuze and Guattari mobilize in *A Thousand Plateaus* a constellation of new terms and concepts through which to further their project in which there is a gradual displacement of the notion of schizoanalysis by those of 'pragmatics', 'rhizomatics' and 'nomadology'.

On one level, this variation and permutation of terms is a typical poststructuralist device – a concern to release a profusion of interchangeable, but not identical, linguistic units lest any sequence of ideas or texts should coagulate into a new and oppressive theoretical orthodoxy and lose its subversive power. However, in *A Thousand Plateaus* it also signals both the downgrading of schizophrenia as a positive political quantity and the development of a new organizing principle for the mobilization of desire – rhizomatics.[68]

For Deleuze and Guattari, the rhizome – a kind of horizontal subterranean stem by which certain plants proliferate – is important because it is a structure *without* structure, with no transcendent law of development, which can assume 'very diverse forms, from ramified surface extension in all directions to concretion into bulbs and tubers'.[69] A rhizome is thus that *decentred* structure least likely to reduce multiplicity or difference by subordinating it to some higher developmental unity, and most likely to produce it – for one of the major emphases of *A Thousand Plateaus* is that multiplicity 'must be made' not simply 'released' as *Anti-Oedipus* had implied.[70] As such, the rhizome is the model for a new kind of thought, of writing, ultimately of a whole new spatio-temporality, which Deleuze and Guattari counterpose favourably to the prevailing 'arborescent' model of thought derived from the more orthodox (botanically speaking) root–radicle structure. It is this latter form that has served as the model for the growth of 'arborescent culture' – including psychoanalysis and linguistics[71] – which operates according to the 'principle' and 'outcome' of 'the structure of Power'.[72] Thus Deleuze and Guattari posit an opposition between a 'dendritic' or 'arborescent' model that imposes identity (its linguistic form is the verb 'to be'), and an acentred model that proceeds by conjunction, difference and multiplicity (described linguistically by the sequence 'and . . . and . . . and . . .') and works towards the 'uprooting' of identity.[73] In spatial terms, Deleuze and Guattari state that a root–radicle system is composed of static 'points' and 'positions', whereas in a rhizome 'there are only lines' which constantly move and intersect;[74] thus 'it is always by rhizomes that desire moves and produces'.[75]

This opposition is clearly a version of the grounding molar/molecular polarity of *Anti-Oedipus*, and its translation into organic terms deepens the emphasis on desire as a primordial natural force and illustrates Deleuze and Guattari's conviction that 'thought lags behind nature'. Furthermore, the rhizome is a more thoroughly spatial concept than any that had appeared in the earlier book, and as such is central both to the activity of mapping, which Deleuze and Guattari see as a crucial political task, and to the general spatialization of history which *A Thousand Plateaus* seeks to effect.

Indeed, for Deleuze and Guattari the rhizome *is a* map, but a map understood as an 'open' and 'connectable' productive agent 'oriented toward an experimentation in contact with the real', rather than as a 'tree-like' representation or 'tracing' of a static topographical arrangement.[76] Thus conceived, cartography is not valued for any cognitive function but for its active transformational capacities: a map does not reproduce any pre-existing reality or serve to reorient the misdirected consciousness, but is in a state of perpetual flux, open to entry and modification at all points by 'individual, group, or social formation', and thus functions to produce 'connections between fields'.

In the sense that it is a response to the massively complex and volatile configurations of modernity, and stands to some extent for the attempt to redefine and make this space inhabitable, Deleuze and Guattari's 'cartography' anticipates another influential notion of political map-making proposed by Fredric Jameson, and the two will be contrasted later in this discussion. But what is immediately evident is the connection between the notions of 'map' and 'rhizome' as spatialized concepts of transformation, and the particular form and construction of *A Thousand Plateaus* itself. For this is the book-as-rhizome, opposed to the 'dendritic', centralized and structured model of the book into which even the fragmented modernist or postmodern 'text' can be recuperated according to some higher 'cyclic' unity that would construe it in terms of the 'Total Work or Magnum Opus'.[77] Just as *Anti-Oedipus* was structured in a deliberately non-Oedipal manner, so its successor is designed to embody that radically different 'anti-structure' with which its authors seek to displace the conventional notion of the book; and the principal element of the book-as-rhizome is the plateau.

The plateau replaces the chapter of the orthodox book, substituting 'lines of communication' for the chapter's more restrictive points of 'culmination and termination'. Again, there is a metonymic relation between the plateau and the rhizome, for both are defined as 'any multiplicity connected to other multiplicities by superficial underground stems'.[78] But 'plateau' carries a peculiar sexual connotation, referring to an extended state of arousal or intensity which contrasts with the abrupt rise and fall of orgasmic climax. While this recapitulates the stance taken against normative genital organization in *Anti-Oedipus*, it is more important as the basis for what might be called a 'plateau theory of history'; for the 'intensities' that constitute a plateau have particular historical locations and determinations, and it is these historical zones of intensity that *A Thousand Plateaus* seeks to 'map' and make available to the present.

Each plateau is assigned a 'date' which marks a point of particular volatility in the historical opposition of molar and molecular forces. This is a return to the problematics of desire in history that *Anti-Oedipus* had established but failed to resolve. Yet rather than produce a history of desire (which is impossible since desire *has* no history, being always already there) Deleuze and Guattari conceive of *A Thousand Plateaus* in terms of a 'nomadology', which is 'the opposite of a history'.[79] For them, history is always written from a 'sedentary' point of view which takes as its model the state apparatus with its subordinating dynamic of incorporation and totalization. Nomadology, on the other hand, produces history and the book in terms of a 'war machine', the antithesis of the state formation which is less a model than an 'assemblage' whose function is to disrupt thought, undermine the 'cultural book', and connect the world with an 'outside' instead of simply reproducing it.[80] *A Thousand Plateaus* can thus be read as an *anti-history* of desire, with desire, like Derrida's *différance*, as the extra-textual 'other', everywhere 'producing' history as the traces of its blockages and escapes, yet everywhere refusing to come on stage itself or be represented. The plateaus are thus key historical sites of the operation and repression of desire and as such yield important strategic information about the production and recuperation of multiplicity. Deleuze and Guattari pursue this concern through a series of polarities – root/rhizome, state apparatus/war machine, sedentary/nomadic, striated/smooth – which serve to delineate the operations of desire in history and constitute the theoretical framework for the practice of schizo-analysis and its various offshoots – rhizomatics, pragmatics, strato-analysis, micropolitics and nomadology – interchangeable terms which for Deleuze and Guattari also 'function as plateaus'.[81]

While *A Thousand Plateaus* is 'rhizomorphous' in that it has multiple points of entry and exit and no overall formal organiz-ation, it is none the less concerned with four fundamental ques-tions which, separately, emerge as the focus of particular plateaus and, taken together, constitute the 'problematic' to which the book is addressed. These are: the question of the subject, or of desire in the body; the question of 'nature', or of terrestrial, even cosmic, desire; the cultural question of desire in language and art; and the 'political' question of collective desire in history. All these problems are of course political and none can be regarded as independent of the others, even if the plateaus themselves are to be taken independently in a discontinuous reading practice.[82] There is, moreover, a consistent concern with the relations between knowledge and power, with the tendency for various disciplines and institutionalized practices to impose restrictive forms on desire in the name of some higher unity such as the subject or the state. This Foucauldean thematics was behind the critique of psychoanalysis in *Anti-Oedipus*, but is expanded across a whole range of disciplines and practices in *A Thousand Plateaus* so that Deleuze and Guattari can describe the latter book as an 'anti-genealogy' or an 'anti-memory,'[83] twisting Foucault's notions of 'genealogy' and 'counter-memory' to suggest less the painstaking historical retracing of particular cultural and intellec-tual practices to reveal both their constitutive and oppressive aspects, than the wilful appropriation and manhandling of such histories in the spirit of Nietzsche's 'active forgetting', a strategy frequently endorsed by Foucault but rarely practised by him in his own books.[84]

The first plateau of Deleuze and Guattari's anti-history reopens the question of the unconscious and bodily desire by returning to the familiar territory of psychoanalysis. It is dated 1914 for the composition of Freud's famous 'Wolf Man' case history which, for Deleuze and Guattari, is a crucial moment in the (mis)representation of desire and the repression of multiplicity. Their point is that the Wolf Man's central dream was populated by six or seven wolves which Freud, in a characteristic interpretive gesture, reduced to single wolf in order to 'discover' the presence of the fundamental Oedipal figure, the Father. Similarly Freud imposed an interpretive reduction on the myriad pores of the Wolf Man's skin, with which the patient was morbidly obsessed, converting a proliferation of holes into a singularity which could then be made to signify castration and confirm the Oedipal scenario.[85] But for Deleuze and Guattari dreams and fantasies do not represent or 'signify' anything; they are, rather, actualizations of desire, multiplicities by nature to which the processes of the dream-work – overdetermination, displacement and secondary revision – simply do not apply. The Wolf Man's dreams and fantasies are thus not to be *interpreted* but taken literally, as instances of desire working to destabilize the identity of an individual subject and initiating what Deleuze and Guattari call a 'becoming' – a disintegration of unitary subjectivity into a shifting multiplicity. Freud, then, resists the Wolf Man's 'becoming-multiple' and 'becoming-wolf' (wolves, like rats and ants, are privileged beings for Deleuze and Guattari in that they live in a mobile and relatively dehierarchized multiplicity – the pack or swarm) by imposing a reductive interpretive frame on his patient's desire and yanking him back into the molar enclosure of 'normal' subjectivity.

This is tragic and politically regressive for, according to Deleuze and Guattari, any becoming consists in a movement towards the 'Body without Organs' (BwO), an ideal of thoroughly desubjectified desire that is the antithesis of both the monadic bourgeois subject and the relatively decentred Althusserian–Lacanian subject, locked as the latter is into ideology and language. In this sense the liberation of desire and of the body are one and the same, and the primary form inhibiting such liberation is the *organism*, understood as the particularly static 'organization' of organs and parts which Deleuze and Guattari contrast to the BwO's 'molecular multiplicities' and 'bands of intensity'.[86] They thus join Foucault in relocating the question of the subject firmly in the body, where Marcuse and Brown had put it in the 1950s and 1960s, but from where structuralism and the more text-centred versions of poststructuralism had subsequently displaced it into the area of cognitive activity.

The notion of the BwO is itself derived from a text of Artaud which declares war on the organs as part of a larger strategy of sloughing off metaphysical forms. Yet in the plateau dated by the composition of this text Deleuze and Guattari are at pains to point out how the BwO can be 'botched' by a too hasty desubjectification which can result in the 'empty', 'sucked-dry' bodies of the schizo, the masochist, the hypochondriac and the drug addict.[87] These are becomings which have been hijacked by the 'death-drive' and converted into 'self-destructions'; and it seems that subjectivity must be *worked through* rather than exploded, for 'You have to keep enough of the organism for it to reform each dawn . . . and you have to keep small rations of subjectivity to enable you to respond to the dominant reality.'[88] Such counsel is intended to inject a dimension of strategy and negotiation into what, in *Anti-Oedipus*, seemed to be a politics of total deracination; yet it also represents the difficulty of constructing a positive *modus operandi* within the parameters of a system which is deemed absolutely metaphysical or oppressive – a difficulty which besets poststructuralist politics in general.

A successful 'becoming' is one that constructs a BwO by connecting with the 'plane of consistency', Deleuze and Guattari's term for a primordial level of pure, unmediated matter in flux: 'a plane of immanence, univocality, composition upon which everything is given, upon which unformed elements and materials dance . . . a fixed plane of life upon which everything stirs, slows down or accelerates.'[89] This is the 'plane of Nature', the level of the 'Real' itself,[90] in relation to which the self and other such molar formations are but thresholds to be exceeded by the force of a becoming or a deterritorialization.[91] It is conceived on an infinite or 'cosmic' scale and represents not so much absolute and primordial origin as it does the perpetual condition of possibility of the limitless forms and states into which matter–energy can be combined – a 'mechanosphere' or 'rhizosphere'.[92] Indeed the earth itself is drawn from the plane of consistency in that it too is a BwO which has undergone 'stratification' – a kind of elementary territorialization of matters and energies into distinct and limited elements and spheres, or 'contents' and 'expressions'.[93] The plane of consistency is thus a pure or ideal potentiality from which the various 'strata' that constitute reality are drawn as limited instances of substance, form or practice which intersect and combine in 'machinic assemblages'. Any 'destratification', or release of energies from one point of organization into, or away from, another, necessarily involves a movement towards the plane of consistency, a movement 'effectuated' for Deleuze and Guattari by what they call an 'abstract machine' – a principle of 'pure Matter Function', or kind of ideal 'diagram', which distributes and to some extent determines the relations between plane and strata.[94] For example, the 'hand–tool assemblage' consists in a particular relation between a human-organic stratum (the hand) and a stratum of 'formed matters' (the tool) of which the 'hand–weapon assemblage' is a relative deterritorialization. The difference between these assemblages does not so much involve the literal replacement of the tool by the weapon, as the 'becoming-weapon' of the tool in a process of 'accleration' or use-transformation (an axe can be either tool or weapon), the 'diagram' of which is an abstract machine, likened by Deleuze and Guattari to a 'map' (in the rhizomatic sense) which 'one can lay out on the plane of consistency.'[95]

There is, however, another plane – the 'plane of organization' – which, rather than 'pure immanence', is a 'hidden principle ... which at every instant causes the given to be given, in this or that state' and which 'can only be inferred, induced, concluded from that to which it gives rise'.[96] This plane produces forms and subjects and inhibits becoming; and as it appears to be the principle of social and symbolic forms there is an implied nature/culture duality at work here, in which Deleuze and Guattari see the body-as-subject trapped. In accordance with this opposition, several of the plateaus focus on moments at which certain cultural discourses and practices – writing, linguistics, Christianity, cartography – have effected a particular organization of the body, the unconscious or the earth itself.

Among these, Deleuze and Guattari regard Christianity as crucial to the formation of modern subjectivity, in that it installs a regime of 'faciality' in which social relations are deterritorialized from material inscription, recoded into spiritualized form and made amenable to the process of internalization by which the obedient subject, or 'soul', is constituted.[97] The face, of which the all-seeing and ubiquitous visage of Christ is the emblem, is thus 'a politics', an 'economy of power' which, inasmuch as its definitive property is an expressiveness which demands interpretation from a willing subject, functions in terms of signification. Faciality thus marks the emergence of a regime or 'semiotic' based on a combination of signifying and subjectifying power, and as the face is the machinic representation of the 'White Man' then these powers define our own 'semiotic of modern White Men, the semiotic of capitalism'.[98]

The notion of the White Man refers less to any specific ethnic, sexual or social grouping than to a more general conception of 'majority'. For Deleuze and Guattari the White Man is the figure of majority, understood not in a numerical sense but in terms of the prevalence and subordinating power of the 'norm', from which position history is traditionally made and written. In opposition to the White Man, any becoming must proceed by way of 'minority', and in this context animal becomings (such as the Wolf Man's) and 'becomings-woman' – with which 'all becomings begin . . . and pass through' – are especially significant.[99]

An important site of 'becomings-minor', particularly within capitalism, is language; for if capitalism can be said to have a single operating principle it is, for Deleuze and Guattari, a version of the primarily linguistic process of signification. The deterritorialized flows unleashed within capitalism are themselves a kind of language which is 'axiomatized' by the capitalist semiotic into molar formations of state power, a process similar to that by which the discipline of modern linguistics seeks to assign a structure to the flows and transformations of language itself.[100] By imposing an interpretive grid on what, for Deleuze and Guattari, is a transformative collective flow, linguistics, like psychoanalysis in the realm of unconscious desire, is performing the work of capitalism and its implications must therefore be resisted at every level. For example, Deleuze and Guattari assert that the basic unit of language, the statement, is always politically rather than semantically motivated: it is – after Lenin and Bakhtin – an 'order word'. In this respect 'language is not made to be believed but to be obeyed, and to compel obedience'.[101] Grammar is a principal agent of such linguistic compulsion or 'axiomatics', a structure of power rather than syntax whose function is to produce the individualized, Oedipized and compliant 'subject of enunciation'.[102] Deleuze and Guattari, on the other hand, recognize only 'collective enunciations' which produce 'collective assemblages'; language consists primarily in ' "free" indirect discourse' in which there is individuation of neither subjects nor utterances, only the actuation of 'all the voices present within a single voice'.[103]

Language, like the desire which inhabits it, thus slides between two poles, the one represented by capitalist axiomatization at the molar extreme, the other by the polyvocality of collective enunciation at the molecular extreme. Here Deleuze and Guattari describe a 'doubling' of language similar to Derrida's, and align with him in targeting linguistics as a deeply problematic discipline in its tying together of subjectivity and the systemic view of language. In its stead they propose 'pragmatics' – a practice which refuses to separate language as a system from its instances of use and from the bodies which use, and are used by, it.[104] Pragmatics adheres to a more general poststructuralist agenda in placing language firmly in the productive sphere as opposed to the representational; thus statements 'do not belong to ideology, but are already at work in what is supposedly the domain of the economic base'.[105] Yet there remains in Deleuze and Guattari's formulation traces of a nostalgic Rousseauean naturalism, a legacy perhaps of 1968's dream of shattering and reinventing language, in that for them 'Language is not life, it gives life orders. Life does not speak; it listens and waits'[106] – a view which in many ways conflicts with the deconstructionist notion of an all-encompassing textuality.

While language tends always to be the domain of the White Man, of the majority or power structure, it nevertheless harbours 'intralinguistic, endogenous, internal minorities' in the form of dialects, ghetto languages and composite tongues.[107] The task of pragmatics is thus to locate and activate these subordinate languages to effect a 'becoming minoritarian' of the dominant tongue.[108]

Such 'minor' languages are, for Deleuze and Guattari, the figure of autonomy and difference and are particularly forceful within the cultural domains of art and science. Kafka, for instance, a minority Czech Jew in the Austrian-dominated Habsburg empire, was able to turn the imperial language of German against itself in creating a literature that at once anatomized, and drew various lines of escape from, the oppressive state-bureaucratic 'machine' in which he found himself caught.[109] Similarly, Schumann effected a liberation of music from the increasingly dominant territorializing gesture of the refrain,[110] and for Deleuze and Guattari Schumannian chromaticism is a 'minor' pocket of resistance within a general, or 'majoritarian' adherence to the principle of modal composition. This is particularly important as music is the least representational, most abstract and therefore least compromised art form, and all becomings are in a sense 'becomings-music' in that music embodies vital lines of connection with the cosmos and the plane of consistency along which all deterritorializations must proceed.[111] There is, too, a 'minor science', which Deleuze and Guattari oppose to the Platonic conception of 'State', or 'Royal', science,'[112] and whose primary importance is its effect of deconstructing the solidities and volumes of Euclidean space into the 'patchwork' of surfaces and lines that characterizes Riemannian, or 'smooth' space.[113]

The political valorization of such pockets of disruptive minority reflects a general poststructuralist distaste for any politics of mass movements, organization or global perspective – in other words, for Marxism – and a penchant for local, specific and short-term struggles or, to use Deleuze and Guattari's formulation, 'micropolitics'. This notion anticipates Lyotard's influential characterization of the political nature of postmodern space in terms of its fragmentation into a profusion of ever-changing 'language-games' or 'paralogisms' which have come to undermine the 'grand narratives' of earlier, largely nineteenth-century, theorizations of social and historical change.[114] These connections will be touched on in due course, but for now it is important to note that *A Thousand Plateaus* tends thus to repeat the movement of *Anti-Oedipus* towards an emphasis on the revolutionary potential (now the capacity for becoming 'minor') of art and science. This inevitably entails the privileging of certain forms of artistic and scientific production over others, with the concomitant danger that these forms will cease to be viewed historically, becoming instead ontologized – enshrined as somehow 'essentially' revolutionary regardless of any historical, cultural and social specificities.

In this sense the schizoanalytic-rhizomatic project is perhaps best grasped as an 'aesthetic', as Fredric Jameson has observed[115] and as Michel Foucault described *Anti-Oedipus* in his preface to it. Indeed Deleuze and Guattari's modernist allegiances foster such a close identification of aesthetics and politics that the one is confused with, or substituted for, the other. Thus one implication of *A Thousand Plateaus* is that the book itself can become the figure of collective revolutionary action as the 'abstract machine' which connects the collective assemblage with the plane of consistency and sets the scene for a massive deterritorialization.[116] Given that language, writing and the book are such important sites of desiring production for Deleuze and Guattari, I will now consider the status of literature in their work and its implications for literary study.

SCHIZOPHRENIC WRITING

Like other poststructuralists, Deleuze and Guattari favoured for both aesthetic and political reasons a certain kind of writing that most 'spontaneously' conformed to their own agenda – a literary modernism whose fragmented and elusive linguistic forms apparently dramatized the dissolution of the subject that poststructuralism so eagerly endorsed. Yet such a view was of course the effect of an operation of *criticism* which read or constructed the favoured texts along certain lines; and as, for Deleuze and Guattari, the revolutionary potential of art in general 'appears all the more as one is less and less concerned with what . . . [it] means', then the schizoanalytic approach to literary texts would necessarily be anti-interpretive, producing a reading strategy that stressed use over meaning and sought to rid itself of the slightest hermeneutic impulse.[117]

In their work on Kafka, Deleuze and Guattari formulated a kind of psycho-biographical criticism that refused any relative distinctions, even of the 'last instance', between life and art, and approached writing as a thoroughly political site of desiring production in which the molar forms of subject, family and state are continually fractured and dispersed by the molecular flows and breaks of desire in language. Schizoanalysis thus 'produces' the literary text just as it 'produces' a non-Oedipal unconscious – by appropriating it for its own political ends. Its initial manoeuvre is to construct the book or text as an 'assemblage', a 'multiplicity', which is to be made to 'work': 'a book itself is a little machine. . . . the only question is which other machine the literary machine can be plugged into, must be plugged into, in order to work.'[118]

This 'work', however, does not consist in representation, for writing does not represent: Deleuze and Guattari are as much 'against the book as image of the world'[119] as they are against the view of literature as ideology.[120] Writing, rather, is *prior* to any such images or forms – it takes place 'on the same level as the real of an unformed matter, at the same time as that matter traverses and extends all of non-formal language'.[121] Such an insistence on writing's primal nature is at once a rejection of a powerful current of Althusserian criticism which sees literature as a privileged site of social signification in which ideological contradictions are highlighted,[122] and an extension of the Derridean emphasis on the materiality of writing. Indeed, the notion of writing as desiring production places Deleuze and Guattari in a more general poststructuralist tradition, concerned with drawing out the political implications of writing's connection with the body, to which the Barthes of S/Z and Pleasure of the Text, and feminist writers such as Luce Irigaray and Hélène Cixous, for whom the body is a crucial factor in an autonomous écriture féminine, belong.

Writing is thus invested with all the force of the real, of desire itself; and in this respect it does not signify but produce – it is infrastructural. Literary production is like the schizoanalytic notion of speech, understood not in the Saussurean sense of a performativity principle, nor in the Lacanian–Althusserian sense as a principle of symbolic subjectification, but rather in the sense that statements are *actions* capable of producing 'incorporeal transformations' within both the speaker and the addressee.[123] Literature is a rich site of such transformations or 'becomings', and it is the properly political function of literature and criticism to 'experiment' with these subjective deterritorializations rather than to interpret them.[124]

Writing's importance lies in its capacity to produce and 'survey' or map (in the rhizomorphous rather than representational sense) the disintegration of the subject that is so central to Deleuze and Guattari's project. It also has a visionary or Utopian function in that it can connect with 'realms that are yet to come'[125] – states of deterritorialized subjectivity not yet allowed by the capitalist axiomatic. Such a view of literature's task clearly influences the kinds of writing Deleuze and Guattari enlist to their enterprise, and one index of the shift in priorities from *Anti-Oedipus* to *A Thousand Plateaus* is the movement from a focus on the politics of madness in the earlier book to the politics of literary madness in the latter. The privileged figures in *A Thousand Plateaus* are writers who were either concerned with, or themselves affected by, extreme states of consciousness occasioned by madness, mental illness or drugs; and there is an obvious danger

141

in the celebration, for precisely this reason, of writers such as Kleist, Holderlin, Nietzsche, Artaud, Woolf and Burroughs of reproducing a clichéd and exoticized view of literature-as-madness, and of romanticizing the figure of the insane visionary genius.

This is not a danger Deleuze and Guattari entirely escape, despite their eagerness to destroy the notion of the author as subject and their insistence that drugs, madness and suicide are destratifications of the organism that proceed too rapidly towards the BwO and thus fall victim to the death drive. As they repeatedly counsel, the plane of consistency is not reached by 'wildly destratifying', and thus in terms of literature and language 'crazy talk is not enough'.[126]

While particular writers, then, are crucial markers of the force of desire in language, their importance is an index of the larger revolutionary potential writing harbours in its various forms. For Deleuze and Guattari both the novel and the novella are regions of intensity in which all varieties of subjective deterritorialization are produced. In schizoanalytic terms, 'the novel' is neither a body of texts defined by certain common formal properties nor a historically specific kind of writing constituted by an evolving structure of conventions; rather, it consists – in a manner that recalls Bakhtin's classification – in a particular quality, a 'novelness' which always has something to do with the processes of forgetting and disorientation.

The novel is defined as 'the adventure of lost characters who no longer know their name, what they are looking for, or what they are doing, amnesiacs, ataxics, catatonics'.[127] As such it becomes a virtually ahistorical essence, fluid enough for Deleuze and Guattari to place Beckett at its origin: 'Molloy is the beginning of the genre of the novel' inasmuch as Beckett's character distils the qualities of subjective dissolution in which novel-ness consists.[128] This is an almost Adorian emphasis: Adorno similarly privileged the modernist novel, and Beckett in particular, for its dramatization of the plight of the modern subject. But whereas for Adorno the modernist novel's theme was tragically nostalgic – a cry of pain for a lost and irretrievable subjective wholeness – and its political value ultimately cognitive, for Deleuze and Guattari the opposite is the case. The schizoid novel *celebrates* subjective disintegration, effecting less a 'tremor' of recognition in the reader in which he or she grasps the political nature of subjective pain, as the modernist novel did for Adorno, than a positive disorientation of the reader in the liberatory 'forgetting' of such meanings.

In this respect the novel's function is to draw a 'line of flight' from the subjectifying tyranny of the 'faciality machine', of signifying relations in general, into a 'black hole' of constructive amnesia.[129] Indeed, *lines* are the very substance of writing – a punning formulation which Deleuze and Guattari take seriously enough to make the measure of the novel's political importance. For example, the French novel, even Proust, lacks revolutionary potential in that it is too concerned with 'plotting points instead of drawing lines, active lines of flight or of positive deterritorialization'.[130] It is too subtle, too social, too psychological, ultimately too attached to the idea of salvation through art to open itself to the full force of language's desiring flow and see its precious forms blown apart. By contrast, the Anglo-American novel concerns itself precisely with the transgression of restrictive forms, with breaking borders and with escape. Clearly Deleuze and Guattari do not refer here to the tradition of Jane Austen but to that of Lawrence and Hardy, or Melville and Miller, writers who, they claim, do not escape 'into' art but use it as a tool for 'blazing life lines' – for to escape the molar in 'real life' 'requires all the resources of art, and art of the highest kind'.[131]

Deleuze and Guattari's characterization of Anglo-American literature owes a great deal to Lawrence's critical work, particularly his *Studies in Classic American Literature* which, in its concerns, anticipated an influential critical current of the 1960s and 1970s represented by the likes of Leslie Fiedler, Richard Poirier and Tony Tanner, who viewed writing, and style especially, as a kind of existential bid for freedom. A similar concern clearly informs Deleuze and Guattari's own practice in composing *A Thousand Plateaus*, as well as the conception of literary production and effect proposed there. However, such a view fosters an elision of any level of difference between writing and living and thus refuses to grant literary production any kind of specific historical and political dynamic by which its social nature and effects can be analysed. Moreover, it issues in an exalted idea of the writer him/herself, who is cast alternately as 'guidance device', a visionary and even a 'sorcerer'.[132]

The image of the writer as antisocial outsider or occult dabbler is not particularly helpful in analysing the social and political

function of literature and the network of cultural institutions
through which it is produced, articulated and consumed. But this
is not the concern of schizoanalysis, for which 'literature' is an
acceptably unproblematic category, referring to those conju-
gations of libidinal energy and primal matter which constitute
various textual 'becomings' – Melville's 'becoming-whale', Kafka's
'becoming-beetle, mouse' and so on. These are the acts of 'sor-
cery' that place the writer at the limits of subjective experience
and of society itself, a position that Deleuze and Guattari can
seriously offer as the explanation of 'many suicides by writers'.[133]
This fascination with the wilder aspects of the literary sphere
suggests a strangely masculinist conception of the writer which
undercuts Deleuze and Guattari's insistence that all writing
involves a 'becoming woman', even for the most phallocratic
writers such as Lawrence or Miller.[134] Indeed, their equation of
'becoming-woman' with an entry into a 'zone of indiscernibility'
(as in the novels of Virginia Woolf) prompts a suspicion,
expressed by Alice Jardine, that 'becoming-woman' has less to do
with the specific material oppressions suffered by real women the
world over, than it does with men, once again, borrowing
the figure of 'woman' for their own literary-political purposes –
purposes which seem to involve the precipitous disappearance of
women altogether.[135]

If the novel's particular essence is the dramatization of an
amnesiac wandering, then the essence of the novella lies in its
treatment of a 'universal matter' – the line. Deleuze and Guattari
devote a whole plateau to the novella, dated after the composition
of Henry James's 'In the Cage', in which they seek to demonstrate
how writing 'enacts postures of the body and mind' by conjugat-
ing its own lines with the profusion of other molecular lines out
of which 'we are made'.[136] For Deleuze and Guattari the novella
always poses a question – 'What happened?' – which does not
proceed to a discovery or resolution but remains rather the effect
of a fundamental secret. In the James novella a young telegraphist
enters into a secret relation with a couple who conduct a clan-
destine romance through her; and the important thing for
Deleuze and Guattari is that this relationship is never resolved
by the narrative. It thus describes a line of 'molecular' or 'supple
segmentarity' which cuts across the lines of 'molar' or 'rigid segmentarity' that define the telegraphist's other relationships to
her job, her family and her fiancé. The molecular line thus effects

a 'relative deterritorialization' of the molar line, which becomes in turn an 'absolute deterritorialization', or 'line of flight', as the secret is carried into the sphere of the telegraphist's own libidinal apparatus, where it transforms the nature of her desire all the more powerfully for remaining unstated and producing no narrative disruptions.

Deleuze and Guattari trace a similar dynamic of the line in Fitzgerald's novella, 'The Crack-Up'. Probing towards the secret of his nervous breakdown, Fitzgerald describes three types of line that 'compose a life': a segmentary line of 'oversighted breaks' constituted by the kind of binary choices typically presented by an outside world of social and cultural formations; a line of 'micro-cracks', of 'molecular changes in desire' which occur imperceptibly at a subjective level, and which Fitzgerald associates with his crack-up; and a line of 'rupture' or 'clean breaks', which develops out of the microline but 'explodes' all other kinds of line 'in favour of something else'.[137] This something else is arrived at in the shift from, or forgetting of, molar and orthodox forms of living and a movement onto the molecular level which demands a completely different kind of experience or 'seeing'. Pierrette Fleutiaux's novella, 'The Story of the Abyss and the Spyglass', with its distinction between 'near-seers' who can only perceive 'great binary divisions'[138] and 'far-seers' who perceive 'details of details . . . with all their ambiguity,'[139] enacts this transition.

Deleuze and Guattari's point is that, in writing, these lines 'continually intermingle', and it is the duty of literature and schizoanalysis to 'invent' lines of flight, thus making themselves 'like the art of the new'.[140] They insist, however, that 'no line is transcendent', wishing no doubt to guard against the solidifying of their notion into a new hierarchy of forms.[141] For similar reasons they declare that these lines 'mean nothing', they are not for interpretation, nor should they constitute an alternative literary-critical thematics, for the lines 'have nothing to do with language; it is, on the contrary, language that must follow them, it is writing that must take sustenance from them, *between* its own lines'.[142] Lines, then, are not textual figures but modulations of the real which 'compose us as they compose our map'; and in this sense writing is 'an affair of cartography', a zone of intensity in which new kinds of space and perception are actualized.[143] 'Minor' literature is thus an instance of 'nomad art', the importance of which lies in its transformation of orthodox optical space, based on Euclidean geometry, into radically different 'haptic' space.[144]

Haptic space is essentially non-perspectival and refuses any kind of orientation. Deleuze and Guattari liken it to the spatial experience of an artist working close up to a painting or, as the notion is not limited to visual application only but implies its own kind of temporality, a writer in the midst of composition working with short-term memory and 'forgetting' the overall pattern of the work. The 'haptic' is thus the spatio-temporality of the molecular – 'local, changing and interconnecting' – which is opposed to the kind of molar perception assumed to be necessary for the extraction of meaning from all kinds of phenomena. Moreover, it is another version of that 'smooth' space in which desire freely flows, and which Deleuze and Guattari oppose to the 'striated' space of the state apparatus and the molar points of desire's entrapment.[145] Geographically, it is the space of the desert or the steppe, or of the ocean prior to its stratification into a longitudinal grid, spaces inhabited by nomadic peoples whose mobile and relatively dehierarchized principles of organization constitute a 'war machine' rather than a state apparatus. On another level it is the space of the BwO, counterposed to the striated and stratified form of the organism; and further still, it is the historical space of global capital which creates a smoothness of abstract monetary flows only to reimpose the strictest striations of all.

In a large sense, *A Thousand Plateaus* is an extended argument for the existence and political importance of haptic or smooth space in whose actualization, or 'mapping', literature has a vital role to play. For Deleuze and Guattari this necessitates the repudiation of any interpretive approach to literature and the development of a rigorously anti-totalizing and functionalist reading practice. Yet, as Fredric Jameson points out, this 'amounts less to a wholesale nullification of all interpretive activity than to a demand for the construction of some new and more adequate immanent or anti-transcendent hermeneutic model'.[146] Some commentators see the schizoanalytic project failing in its own terms at this point: an anti-representational philosophy finds itself caught in the problematics of representation. Vincent Leitch, for example, concludes that Deleuze and Guattari fail to advance beyond the problematics of language and representation by refusing to develop a theory of the text and of textuality in the kind of terms deployed by Derrida.[147] He thus finds it unacceptable that they can live with a violent hostility to representation without formulating a strict theory of writing and reading which would breach its limits. For Elizabeth Wright, on the other hand, this is not an index of failure: Deleuze and Guattari recognize that they must *work through* representation in order to undermine it, and in doing so they inject a new energy into psycho-criticism and reopen the question of literary use value – 'What can you *do* with it?'[148]

Certainly Deleuze and Guattari are not concerned with theoretically unpicking the whole notion of representation. Their practice is rather, through literary texts, to undermine and break up the specific kinds of representation produced by other schools of criticism, particularly of the psychoanalytic and Marxist varieties. This practice explicitly resists the construction of a metalanguage or 'theory' of the text: texts are not to be *exchanged* for a theory, they are to be *used* for a purpose – that of demonstrating the interaction of desiring and social production and of reasserting the productiveness of the 'literary machine'. Yet while schizoanalysis-rhizomatics proposes no easily assimilable literary critical 'method', it does propose an aesthetic. In placing certain spatio-temporal characteristics at the centre of a revolutionary politics of desire, and in redefining literature in accordance with them, Deleuze and Guattari come close to evacuating politics into aesthetics.

This is perhaps a danger in particular for what J. G. Merquior calls 'litero-philosophy'[149] – a practice which tends to subordinate theoretical rigour to the attractions of a highly stylized 'borrowing' of contents from a heterogeneous variety of intellectual and artistic disciplines. Thus Deleuze and Guattari annex a particular version of 'literature' to their project with an anarchistic disregard for its institutional nature or historical articulation, a manoeuvre which ultimately – and paradoxically – undervalues literature's social and political significance in casting it in terms of a transhistorical essence. Consequently there is no attempt to distinguish between a dynamics of literary production on the one hand, and of consumption on the other. This must be a major shortcoming in any analytics of difference, for in effect it runs the two practices together and fails to grant the reader any social, historical or cultural autonomy from the site of writing, or moment of composition, itself. Deleuze and Guattari thus imply, against all their injunctions, a view of the reader as passive and subordinated, as someone who is simply 'led' by the schizophrenic-rhizomorphous text into areas already mapped by the writer. Moreover, the persistent identification of 'literature' with one very particular kind of writing reflects an unwillingness both to acknowledge the profusion of different writings that circulate in the cultural domain, and to address the question of a 'revolutionary' literature's relation to an audience – that is, of popularity and of a progressive popular culture.

The literary machine, then, remains a disappointingly high-cultural construct with a rather orthodox avant-garde function, ill equipped to become part of an effective contemporary cultural politics in its disdain for institutional or pedagogical structures. None the less, the connections established in *A Thousand Plateaus* between certain kinds of writing and the new political space of desiring production – haptic or smooth space – are particularly suggestive when considered in relation to the debate presently simmering around the question of a 'postmodern' literature. Indeed, Deleuze and Guattari's own writing constructs and inhabits a 'zone' similar to that found in the novels of such archetypically postmodern writers as Pynchon and Burroughs, a zone in which history is 'suspended' and flattened out into a depthless constellation of intensities in which disparate languages mix, congeal momentarily into provisional forms, and then fragment, causing wild and violent dissolutions of subjectivity. One critic has even gone as far as to declare the formal construction of such a zone to be the defining characteristic of postmodern writing;[150] but it is perhaps more important to acknowledge that the question of postmodernism in literature is finally a historical and political question about the nature and meaning of our own very real zone of global capitalism, and about the possibilities for its transformation into a more humane and habitable space for millions of people. As Deleuze and Guattari's crucial political formulation of smooth, haptic, or what we might now call postmodern space, derives from their particular view of history, and of capitalism especially, it is this aspect of their project that I will now consider.

POSTMODERN POLITICS

In *A Thousand Plateaus* the problem of politics, of the collective investment of desire in history, continues to revolve around 'the global question: Why does desire desire its own repression, how can it desire its own repression?'[151] Schizoanalysis cannot accept an answer in terms of either masochism – 'the masses certainly do not "want" to be repressed'[152] – or ideological 'misrecognition', as desire 'cannot be deceived'. Moreover, for the political impasse of *Anti-Oedipus* to be broken, an explanation must exceed the fundamental 'doubling' of desire proposed in that book; and thus Deleuze and Guattari seek, through the notion of 'micropolitics', to describe the precise molecular dynamic of political investments, particularly as it relates to the modern phenomenon of fascism – for them undoubtedly the most powerful case of the historical perversion of collective desire.

Whereas *Anti-Oedipus* had placed desire in oscillation between two poles, *A Thousand Plateaus* introduces the idea of 'micropolitics' in order to escape the binarist implications of the earlier formulation. In micropolitical terms, fascism is not simply a case of the 'capture' of desire by paranoiac tendencies and its organization into dominative molar structures – an analysis more applicable to totalitarian social formations, which conform to a model of the organism understood as a fixed and hierarchized distribution of attributes. Fascism, rather, is a 'cancerous body', not an organism, a 'mass movement', not an oppressive arrangement of domination, and as such implies a properly *molecular* dynamic or regime. There is, then, a 'microfascism', and this in part answers the 'global question' in that it suggests that there is not a molecular politics on the one hand and a molar politics on the other, but that 'every politics is simultaneously a *macropolitics* and a *micropolitics*'.[153] For Deleuze and Guattari it is 'too easy to be anti-fascist on the molar level and not even see the fascist inside you', and the particular danger of fascism lies precisely in its molecular power.[154] Desire would thus seem to be not so much divided or riven by internal contradiction than, as an effect of the very 'microtexture' which defines it, to bear fascism within itself as some kind of constant historical potentiality.

The likelihood of an actual manifestation of fascism, however, is closely linked to the existence of a certain kind of social space, which is determined by the particular historical nature of the

149

'social machine' which delineates and occupies it. Historically distinct social formations give rise to very different interrelationships of those lines, traced by Deleuze and Guattari in art and especially literature, along which 'life is spatially and socially segmented'.[155] Different 'segmentarities' prevail in different social formations. In so-called 'primitive' societies 'which have no fixed, central state apparatus, and no global power mechanisms or specialized political institutions' there is a 'communicability' between heterogeneous elements, a certain 'leeway' which is the characteristic of a 'relatively supple segmentarity'.[156] This gives way, however, to a modern regime of 'rigid' segmentarity as power comes increasingly to operate in terms of binary opposition, producing the major dualisms of class, sex, colour, age and so on by which a state apparatus functions. This does not so much represent an increase in the amount of power in the social formation as a change in the manner of its articulation from a principle of 'coding' to one of 'overcoding'. Yet the transition from the supple to the rigid line of segmentarity brings with it an increased tendency for deterritorializations to occur along a third line (also found in writing and literature), a 'line of flight'.[157] Indeed, as micropolitics inhabits every macroformation, the more rigid a segmentarity becomes the greater will be its potential for producing lines of flight, for with every molar recuperation 'something always escapes', so that every social system can be said to 'leak from all directions'.[159]

However, it also appears that the opposite is true: that there is an inversely proportionate tendency for lines of flight to 'return' to the molar organizations they escape, thus achieving less an 'absolute' deterritorialization than a 'reshuffling' of segments, an adjustment in the 'distributions of sexes, classes and parties'.[159] Thus capitalism, which itself describes an extreme deterritorialization of earlier social formations, belies its utterly decoded nature in being also the most repressive and horrifying of 'machines'. Within capitalism, the various national or state economies are simultaneously decoded and reintegrated into the 'mesh' of the global market, just as the great binarisms of terror, of East/West for instance, are upset only to reform elsewhere in new relationships like that of North/South. Yet the important thing for Deleuze and Guattari is that in this process the political nature of these relationships is altered, in that there is always a micropolitical transformation at work which releases a positive 'runoff' of energies.

The understanding and critique of modern social formations as founded on a terrorism of binary oppositions recalls the deconstructionist assault on the 'Western ethos' (what, for Deleuze and Guattari, is the rule of the 'White Man') in an attempt to install difference at the heart of identity. And just as Derrida's provisional overturning of opposites was supposedly a strategic manœuvre on the road to a completely different, non-identical mode of thinking and living, so Deleuze and Guattari's micropolitics is a strategic 'passing between' dualisms in order to 'get outside' them.[160] For both deconstruction and schizoanalysis politics are a matter of such strategies, of mapping and occupying those 'undecidable positions' of the 'included middle'[161] – a term derived from Information Theory to designate an area of uncertainty between two quanta (one and zero, true and false, sense and nonsense) which the binary operations of information systems typically exclude.

Politics is thus a matter of 'experiment', strategy, of 'groping in the dark';[162] for in this undecidable space no one line or kind of segmentarity is paramount or more desirable than another, and each kind of line presents the same set of 'dangers'. There is the danger of *fear* inducing a flight away from a line of flight already marking itself out; the danger that *clarity* will proffer some kind of 'truth' or 'understanding' about the politics of a situation that can only be false; and there is the danger that *despair* will transform a line of flight into a line of 'abolition' or 'death', a 'suicidal' line of flight such as the one described by the fascist deterritorialization of the state apparatus. Finally, there is the dangerous attraction of *power*, which is especially seductive since power has the same molecular nature as desire.[163]

The status of 'power' in Deleuze and Guattari's work is particularly slippery: at one pole it is the absolute other of desire, that which represses and dominates it; at the other pole it is coterminous with desire, sharing its characteristics and operations yet always producing negative political effects. The emphasis in *A Thousand Plateaus* is on power in this latter sense, not as the opposite of desire but as desire itself making the wrong connections. Unfortunately, Deleuze and Guattari are unable to say precisely why this should occur; and the problem to which the book as a whole is addressed can be only partially tackled by concluding that power and desire are homologous. This shading together of power and desire, this view of power as 'diffuse', 'dispersed', 'perpetually displaced'[164] and ultimately sensual in nature is very close to Foucault's influential theorization. Indeed, it has been argued that 'desire' as deployed by Deleuze and Guattari and Lyotard is the direct equivalent of Foucault's 'power', and that its elaboration as a revolutionary force was necessary to counteract the pessimistically determinist implications of the Foucauldean concept. Correspondingly, it can be said that Foucault supplies the fully fledged theory and analysis of the social and historical articulation of power that the philosophy of desire lacks.[165]

Certainly Deleuze and Guattari's notion of power refers directly to the 'disciplines' and 'micropowers' of Foucault's work, and like him they envisage its operations in terms of a constitutive and productive, rather than repressive, model. Thus the molar forms of the organism, the nation, the state, are not so much the effects of a domination imposed from above, as they are the productions of forces working deep within – power 'miniaturized . . . working in the details of detail'.[166] These 'micro-textures' are precisely 'what explain how the oppressed can take an active role in oppression';[167] yet power is not totally pervasive, equally distributed, or undifferentiated in its effects.

Power may be decentred but it can nevertheless be attributed 'zones' which mark variations in the extent of its control over the flows that constitute reality. Every power has a 'zone of its power', an area of almost total command or rigid segmentarity; a zone of its 'indiscernibility' where it shades out into a microsegmentation of elements; and a zone of its 'impotence' where the flows of matter escape it and where its control is most limited.[168] In this last zone, powers simply act as 'converters' of flows into 'segments', a process which is highly volatile and politically unstable as the dominant segment of any formation is always related to the most deterritorialized flow. For example, the dollar is the dominant segmentation of the flow of currency, yet the dollar does not represent the absolute extent of banking power as that power consists mainly in its first and second zones, represented by (a) the public central banks, and (b) these institutions' transactional relationships with other banks and borrowers. The third zone of banking power, the 'desiring flow of money', can only be converted into the terms of the other two, never determined or controlled; yet this is the zone on which banking power ultimately depends – the zone least assimilable to the model of a state apparatus.[169]

This concern to theorize power as a differentiated productive process in whose interstices resistance and transformation can occur coincides with a movement in the later work of Foucault towards a more politically hopeful view of power relations in which resistance is always inscribed.[170] Similarly, the kind of political practice implied by Deleuze and Guattari's micropolitics is a distinctly Foucauldean politics of the conjuncture, the local issue and the minority group, demanded by the fact that 'ours is becoming the age of minorities'.[171] In this respect, Deleuze and Guattari subscribe to the radically altered post-1968 agenda of political struggle focused on 'marginalised' groups and 'alternative' institutions, which contrasted with a more orthodox leftist concern with the molar oppositions of class within the contradictory state 'organism'. However, as Foucault himself admits, the danger of such an agenda is that of remaining 'unable to develop these struggles for lack of a global strategy or outside support';[172] and Deleuze and Guattari find themselves having to concede the precedence of conducting a molar politics in certain instances of 'minorities' – women, for example – who have yet to 'win back their own organism, their own history, their own subjectivity'.[173]

Deleuze and Guattari would no doubt claim that this was a 'strategic' concession to the momentary validity of reconstructing molar forms, for 'pure strategy' is the very essence of that particular assemblage to which deterritorialized desire, lines of flight and zones of impotence are always related – the 'war machine'.[174] The war machine is opposed to the state apparatus and all forms of thought and practice that take the state as their model; thus the state is always charged with the need to appropriate the war machine, to 'capture' and incorporate it. Even so, the war machine is finally irreducible and always exterior to a state apparatus – it is 'of another species, another nature, another origin'.[175]

Its origin is in fact nomadic – the plateau detailing the war machine is dated 1227 to mark the death of Genghis Khan – and nomads are an especially privileged group for Deleuze and Guattari in that their kind of organization, like that of pack animals, precludes the formation of boundaries, hierarchies and the sophisticated divisions of labour which are necessary for the development of a state apparatus. Moreover, the nomads have a particular relation to war which, adapting the Hobbesian notion of war's incompatibility with the state, Deleuze and Guattari see as the negation of the state: 'war is the mode of a social state that wards off and prevents the State.'[176] Thus while they can accept the hypothesis of a primordial repression, or of an *Urstaat*, Deleuze and Guattari also hold that this necessarily implies the equal priority of the war machine, for the law of the state is that of sovereignty through incorporation, based on an opposition of interior and exterior, and the state must therefore have 'always been in relationship with an outside and is inconceivable independent of that relationship'.[177] The war machine is precisely this 'pure form of exteriority' which resists the development of forms and 'exists only in its own metamorphoses'.[178]

The nomads are equally important in that they are the exemplary 'minority', so marginalized by molar social forms that for Deleuze and Guattari 'history is one with the triumph of States'.[179] Yet nomadic principles remain to inform the more generalized notion of a 'nomadology', a practice, or collection of practices, which aims to release thought from the state model and connect it to an 'outside' in the form of a war machine. This is close to Derrida's notion of *pensée dehors*, and in this respect there is an epistemology of the war machine which animates 'minor' or 'nomad' science which is Archimedean in conception – a science of variable forces, as opposed to the Platonic or 'State' model which seeks to construct a static order of reasons. Similarly, the war machine has a distinct affective regime which is passional rather than rational in nature, and in which feelings or sentiments (which imply interiority) give way to intensities and affects (implying the rapid cathexis of various surfaces, parts and flows). And just as importantly, there is the nomad aesthetic outlined on pages 132–3 above, by which writing, literature or the book can construct themselves as a war machine.

The various qualities of the war machine are an effect of its fundamental relation to an economy of violence – an economy of the weapon (speed, movement) rather than the tool (work, division of labour). Yet this is the essentially constructive violence of the hunted, who must learn to move with the flow of matter to survive, rather than of the hunter who seeks to capture and immobilize.[180] In this sense the war machine does not necessarily have war as its object. Deleuze and Guattari declare that war is 'supplementary' to the war machine, an accidental effect of its incompatibility with the state; indeed it is a mark of failure for a nomadic warrior or guerrilla fighter to be caught in a pitched battle. War only becomes the object of the war machine when it is captured by and subordinated to the state and its aims.

Like desire, then, the war machine has two poles – one at which it takes war as its object and turns a line of flight into a line of destruction (fascism is such a war machine), and another at which it draws a creative line of flight, effecting 'the composition of a smooth space, and the movement of people in that space'.[181] For Deleuze and Guattari this pole defines the 'essence' of the war machine, at which it is the 'constitutive element of smooth space'; and the final importance of the nomads is precisely their lived relation to space, for nomads 'have no history; they only have a geography'.[182] Nomadology thus seeks to *spatialize* history in order that thought might inhabit history just as the nomads traverse the smooth space of the desert or steppe.

Deleuze and Guattari thus concur with Foucault in his inversion of Clausewitz: 'politics is the continuation of war by other means';[183] and *A Thousand Plateaus* follows Foucault's injunction to conceive of history in the 'form of a war', and to place relations of power above relations of meaning in the construction of a 'strategic knowledge'.[184] Such a knowledge is principally to be aimed against the 'apparatus of capture' which annexes the war machine to the state apparatus. Particular historical forms of this capture include stockpiling, or primitive accumulation; the introduction of ground rent by which 'territory' is turned into 'land'; profit, which subjected bodily energy to the principle of labour; and taxation, which monetized the economy and marked the emergence of a regime of exchanges.[185] For Deleuze and Guattari all are forms of state violence, but taxation is crucial in that it completes the 'capitalization of power' or the 'articulation of capital' into a great 'megamachine' which constructs a space – the smooth space of exchange – dangerously similar to that of the war machine.[186]

In this respect capitalism is itself a war machine which has put the creation of smooth space at the service of the state. It extends this smooth space across the world in terms of a global market, and even beyond it through the deployment of ballistic missile systems, only to effect a 'striation' of this space by imposing structural, legal and juridical forms of violence upon it. These forms, which range from the great molar alliances of state military systems to the microformations of various cultural institutions and disciplines, always function to constitute precisely that which they take as their object. Nomadology thus demands the construction of a war machine 'capable of countering the world war machine',[187] but the striking coincidences between the operations of the two kinds of machine, capitalist and nomadic, go to prove that 'smooth spaces are not in themselves liberatory'; thus, Deleuze and Guattari counsel, 'Never believe that a smooth space will suffice to save us.'[188]

The political implications of such a conclusion are depressing. For it is clear that the war machine, despite the claims made for its exteriority, remains *within* capitalism as an unrealized potentiality or inflection – a revolutionary 'tendency' that requires the kind of 'acceleration' called for in *Anti-Oedipus* to become reality. Yet in some senses capitalism itself is precisely this kind of acceleration, in that its 'deepest law' is the continual setting and repelling of its own 'limits'.[189] This makes it at once *invincible*, a kind of transhistoric principle of self-regeneration, *and* the agent of its own destruction; and nomadology, lacking, like schizoanalysis, any positive political vision, ultimately rests on a somewhat suspect and 'teleological' faith in the capacity of history to work itself out favourably – a faith which would embarrass the most positivist of Marxists.

Capitalism is in effect the conceptual limit of nomadology–schizoanalysis, as nothing beyond it can be proposed. Thus the central political task for Deleuze and Guattari is not so much that of 'smashing capitalism' as of 'redefining socialism' in terms of the 'power of minority'.[190] Yet this is a task that socialists themselves, working in black, feminist, gay and green organizations, have been engaged on for at least two decades without feeling the pressing need to abandon wholesale either the totalizing historical perspective that Marxism provides, or the ultimate goal of seeing capitalism not merely 'smashed', but transformed into something radically different.

From this point of view, the most disabling strand of Deleuze and Guattari's work is its Nietzschean anarchism, its suspicion of any critical analysis that approaches its object seeking understanding, even truth, in terms other than those of the object itself. Thus Deleuze and Guattari are led to valorize politically those aspects of modernity which are at the same time the most characteristic signs of its brutality, violence and fragmentation. In this sense, according to Peter Dews, they repeat the typically poststructuralist gesture of refusing any integrated understanding of modernity, preferring instead to reproduce theoretically certain of its superficial characteristics in the drive to formulate a politics of affirmation. Poststructuralism in general thus abdicates its purportedly critical function and compares unfavourably with Adornian critical theory's attempts to tackle a similar problematic of nature in history from a broadly Marxist perspective,[191] one in which desire or nature was not seen as ultimately self-repressing, but as caught up in the increasing fragmentation of modern life into separate 'spheres', whose interrelationships could be traced in a historical dialectic.

Yet is it nevertheless possible to accept that the schizoanalytic project, along with other poststructuralisms, contains a potent descriptive 'truth' in its characterization of postmodern spatio-temporality and fragmented 'schizophrenic' subjectivity, while resisting its prescriptive formulation of just these qualities into a postmodern politics? Fredric Jameson believes it is.[192] The new 'world space of multinational capital' has been accurately described by poststructuralism, but it remains for a radically Marxist theory and practice to construct the 'new political culture' that will render this space amenable to effective political struggle and transformation.[193] Crucially, for Jameson, this involves making such a space *representable* in a reformulation of politics on symbolic terrain, bringing into play notions of ideology and the struggle over the *meaning* of postmodernity. Jameson's 'cartography' is thus a cognitive activity, involving the reinsertion of a vital critical difference between the subject and the space it must inhabit in order that a purchase on the volatile forms of postmodernity can be obtained. For Deleuze and Guattari, however, 'cartography' is precisely the *abolition* of critical distance in an active surrender to the rhizomorphous possibilities and intensities of late capitalist, or 'smooth', space. While a critical grasp of history is what for Jameson can furnish us with the means to construct a way out of our present social and spatial confusion, it is precisely history which is subjected in *A Thousand Plateaus* to a radical spatialization, a flattening which allows its surfaces to be freely traversed by the 'forgetful' nomadologist in search of a liberatory intensity.

As in the work of other poststructuralists, notably Derrida, Lyotard and Foucault, this synchronic view of history produces a conception of political struggle as necessarily fragmented, contingent and provisional, after the model of May 1968. Such a model cannot possibly be adequate to the degree of real political transformation demanded by the theorists themselves in their more rhetorical moments (of which there are many). Consequently there is a great temptation for certain writers to substitute theory for practice in an attempt to circumvent this problem. Deleuze himself, endorsing Foucault's notion of the 'specific intellectual' who engages in localized and specialist struggle, as opposed to the 'universal intellectual' who embodies or 'represents' certain global positions and attributes, concludes that 'representation no longer exists; there's only *action*'.[194] Thus, for the specific intellectual, theory 'is practice',[195] and we can see that the particularly aesthetic-modernist emphasis given to the gallery of political formulations that populates Deleuze and Guattari's work points consistently in this direction.

If this is so then it catches the schizoanalyst in a painful contradiction, for it implies that the book *is* the world, despite all protestations to the contrary: it is the ideal space in which the energies that the world inhibits and betrays can circulate and flow with maximum political efficacy. This is the Utopian gesture of the schizoanalytic project, and while it is in one sense a measure of political weakness at a molar, or conceptual, level, it is also the basis of a certain aesthetic pleasure at the molecular level of reading.

POSTSCRIPT

Deleuze and Guattari's enterprise is a bold attempt to come to terms with the social and subjective transformations of modernity and to arrive at a positive political evaluation of this condition. As such it occupies similar theoretical territory to the earlier work of Theodor Adorno, who also traced the historical subjugation of inner and outer nature by an increasingly degraded and instrumentalized rationality.[196] Like Deleuze and Guattari, Adorno saw fascism and the other organized barbarities of our century as the vengeful 'return' of repressed nature in the form of a collective and suicidal irrationalism. While for Adorno this was all the more reason not to succumb to a theoretical irrationalism, for Deleuze and Guattari, and indeed for poststructuralism in general, reason was itself fatally compromised by its constitutive role in the spread of rationalism and the coercive social, cultural and intellectual structures that were developed in its name. Thus poststructuralism rejected any kind of total or dialectical understanding of modernity in favour of harnessing its political project to those very aspects of modernity which were apparently subversive of, or beyond, reason's 'grand narrative' reach.

Consequently, the political thrust of poststructuralism – and of Deleuze and Guattari's work in particular – is towards deconstructing, or restructuring, certain 'metaphysical' notions such as history, the subject, thought, by making them commensurate with the decentred, fragmentary and depthless patterns of modern, or postmodern, reality. While it thus analyses many hitherto neglected dimensions of modern social and subjective experience, poststructuralism's rather too absolute identification of reason and power, and its paradoxically undifferentiated characterization of modern social space as 'totally' decentred, ungraspable or 'smooth', ultimately hinder its formulation of any effective political tools for the collective transformation of this space.

However, if we are to accept Peter Dews's argument, then the intellectual current of poststructuralism is presently nearing exhaustion; having been ousted from the position of supremacy it once held in its homeland, it 'can no longer be considered a living force in France itself'.[197] It has been dislodged, with considerable help from the French media and various publishing institutions, by the '*nouvelle philosophie*' – a renewed interest in metaphysical thought as a way into questions of religion, ethics and human rights. This rather backward-looking and conservative current views the revolutionary rhetoric and stylistic excesses of poststructuralism with distaste, characterizing it as part of that Marxist tradition whose death the *nouvelles philosophes* are so eager to announce.

A similar connection has been made by Jean Baudrillard, for whom the central poststructuralist problematic of power and desire represents the final nerve spasms of a thoroughly moribund Marxian and Freudian thematics. Baudrillard sees the work of Deleuze and Guattari and Foucault in particular as a last-gasp attempt to reinject a dash of life into what remains of the 'real' before it disappears completely in a welter of 'simulacra'. Theirs was thus an essentially nostalgic enterprise that sought, through an insistence on the primordial productiveness of power and desire, to preserve the categories of the real – society, the body, politics – against the irresistible encroachments of an empty and synthetic 'hyperreality' in which the truly postmodern consists.[198]

Thus the postmodern space central to the schizoanalytic project is already receiving new definitions and theorizations which propose drastically different estimations of its political significance, and which are marked by a willingness to pronounce the 'end' of ideology, of Marxism, of the political itself. In contrast to the belatedly pious anti-Stalinisms of the *nouveaux philosophes* or the modishly knowing ennui of a Baudrillard, the work of Deleuze and Guattari offers a far more productive and politically suggestive picture of the present historical situation. Yet its serious shortcomings can only have contributed to the rapid decline in its importance on the French and international intellectual scenes. *Capitalism and Schizophrenia* perhaps remained too true to the moment in whose spirit it was conceived – May 1968 – to have anything other than a relatively short shelf-life in the increasingly rapid turnover of theoretical consumer durables. But this 'truth' makes it an important document, a discursive 'symptom' of that historical space with which a more satisfactorily integrated, critical and broad-based politics must come to terms in order to transform.

NOTES

1 Keith A. Reader, *Intellectuals and the Left in France since 1968*, London: Macmillan, 1987, pp. 88–91.
2 *Semiotext(e)* II: 3 (1977), 'Anti-Oedipus'; *Substance 44/45* (1984), 'Deleuze'.
3 Jameson refers to Deleuze and Guattari throughout his *Political Unconscious* (Fredric Jameson, *The Political Unconscious: Narrative as a socially symbolic act*, London: Methuen, 1981), and makes use of their theorization of the molar and molecular levels of discourse in his *Fables of Aggression*, Berkeley: University of California Press, 1979, especially in the methodological 'Prologue', pp. 1–23. Moreover, his development of the notion of schizophrenia in the influential essay on postmodernism, 'The cultural logic of late capitalism', *New Left Review* 146 (July/August 1984), pp. 53–92, although not credited to Deleuze and Guattari, is clearly indebted to their description of 'Capitalism and Schizophrenia'.
4 Jameson, *The Political Unconscious*, p. 124.
5 Vincent Descombes, *Modern French Philosophy*, Cambridge: Cambridge University Press, 1980, p. 168.
6 Keith A. Reader, 'The anniversary industry', *Screen* 29: 3 (Summer 1988), pp. 122–6.

7 Reader, 'The May events, what were they?', *Intellectuals and the Left in France since 1968*, chapter 1.
8 Ibid., p. ix.
9 Descombes, *Modern French Philosophy*, p. 168.
10 Sherry Turkle, *Psychoanalytic Politics: Jacques Lacan and Freud's French Revolution*, London: Burnett Books, 1979 – introduction and chapter 3, 'May 1968 and psychoanalytic ideology'.
11 Reader, *Intellectuals and the Left in France since 1968*, p. 6.
12 Turkle, *Psychoanalytic Politics*, p. 72.
13 Ibid., p. 74.
14 Herbert Marcuse, *Eros and Civilization*, Boston: Beacon Press, 1955; Norman O. Brown, *Life Against Death*, Middletown: Wesleyan University Press, 1955.
15 Louis Althusser, 'Freud and Lacan', *Lenin and Philosophy*, London: Monthly Review Press, 1971, pp. 189–219.
16 Descombes, *Modern French Philosophy*, p. 173.
17 For example, Hélène Cixous, Luce Irigaray, Catherine Clément or, in a British context, Juliet Mitchell.
18 Jay Cantor, Review of *Anti-Oedipus* in *The New Republic*, 24 and 31 December 1977, pp. 36–7.
19 Descombes, *Modern French Philosophy*, p. 170.
20 Reader, *Intellectuals and the Left in France since 1968*, p. 2.
21 Cantor, Review, p. 37.
22 Michel Foucault, preface to Gilles Deleuze and Felix Guattari, *Anti-Oedipus*, London: Athlone Press, 1984, p. xiv.
23 Ibid., p. xiv.
24 Turkle, *Psychoanalytic Politics*, p. 145.
25 Ibid., p, 74.
26 Jameson, *The Political Unconscious*, p. 21.
27 Ibid., p. 22.
28 Deleuze and Guattari, *Anti-Oedipus*, pp. 30 and 266.
29 Ibid., p. 266.
30 Ibid., p. 36.
31 Elizabeth Wright, *Psychoanalytic Criticism: Theory in practice*, London: Methuen, 1984, p. 163.
32 Deleuze and Guattari, *Anti-Oedipus*, pp. 380–1.
33 Ibid., p 376.
34 Jameson, *Fables of Aggression*, p. 8.
35 Ibid., p. 9.
36 Deleuze and Guattari, *Anti-Oedipus*, p. 266.
37 Althusser, 'Freud and Lacan', p. 216.
38 Deleuze and Guattari, *Anti-Oedipus*, p. 63.
39 Reader, *Intellectuals and the Left in France since 1968*, p. 13.
40 Deleuze and Guattari, *Anti-Oedipus*, p. 139.
41 Ibid., pt III, 'Savages, barbarians and civilized men'.
42 Ibid., p. 261.
43 Ibid., p. 240.
44 Ibid., pp. 239–40.
45 Ibid., p, 379.

46 Ibid., pp. 245–6.
47 Descombes, *Modern French Philosophy*, p. 177.
48 Deleuze and Guattari, *Anti-Oedipus*, p. 262.
49 Ibid., p. 376.
50 Ibid., p. 376 (my emphasis).
51 Ibid., p. xiii.
52 Ibid., p. 251.
53 Ibid., p. 245.
54 Turkle, *Psychoanalytic Politics*, p. 83.
55 Peter Dews, *The Logics of Disintegration: Poststructuralist thought and the claims of critical theory*, London: Verso, 1987, p. 132.
56 Deleuze and Guattari, *Anti-Oedipus*, p. 380.
57 Ibid., pp. 381–2.
58 Ibid., p. 379.
59 Peter Burger, in *Theory of the Avant-Garde*, Manchester: Manchester University Press, 1984, sees the primary impulse of avant-garde art as an attempt to abolish the boundary between artistic production and social life, while the Russian formalist critics of the 1920s and 1930s defined literature, and modernist writing in particular, by its capacity to produce an effect of 'defamiliarization', or of 'estrangement' from 'normal' perceptions of reality in the reader.
60 Deleuze and Guattari, *Anti-Oedipus*, p. 379 (my emphasis).
61 Jameson, *The Political Unconscious*, p. 68.
62 Deleuze and Guattari, *Anti-Oedipus*, p. 378.
63 Ibid., p. 378.
64 Peter Dews traces this same 'drift' away from Freud and Marx towards the 'characteristic 1970's terminus of Nietzsche' in the work of the other major theorist of desire, Lyotard (*The Logics of Disintegration*, p. 31).
65 Deleuze and Guattari, *Anti-Oedipus*, p. 382.
66 Turkle, *Psychoanalytic Politics*, 'Conclusion'.
67 Gilles Deleuze and Felix Guattari, *A Thousand Plateaus: Capitalism and Schizophrenia II*, London: Athlone Press, 1988, p. 150.
68 Ibid., 'Introduction: rhizome'.
69 Ibid., p. 7.
70 Ibid., p. 6.
71 Ibid., p. 15.
72 Ibid., p. 17.
73 Ibid., p. 25.
74 Ibid., p. 8.
75 Ibid., p. 14.
76 Ibid., p. 12.
77 Ibid., p. 6.
78 Ibid., p. 22.
79 Ibid., p. 23.
80 Ibid., p. 24.
81 Ibid., p. 22.
82 Ibid., 'Authors' note'.
83 Ibid., p. 21.

84 Foucault's admiration for Deleuze's work is expressed in the preface to *Anti-Oedipus* and in 'Theatricum philosophicum', in D. Bouchard (ed.), *Language, Counter Memory, Practice*, Ithaca, NY: Cornell University Press, 1977, pp. 165–96.
85 Deleuze and Guattari, *A Thousand Plateaus*, p. 31.
86 Ibid., pp. 30–1.
87 Ibid., p. 150.
88 Ibid., p. 160.
89 Ibid., p. 255.
90 Ibid., pp. 266–7 and 69.
91 Ibid., p. 249.
92 Ibid., p. 74.
93 Ibid., p. 72.
94 Ibid., pp. 72 and 141.
95 Ibid., pp. 60–1 and 400–1.
96 Ibid., p. 265.
97 Ibid., p. 181.
98 Ibid., p. 182.
99 Ibid., p. 277.
100 Ibid., plateau 4, 'Nov. 20 1923: Postulates of linguistics'.
101 Ibid., p. 76.
102 Ibid., p. 76.
103 Ibid., p. 80.
104 Ibid., pp. 77–8.
105 Ibid., p. 81.
106 Ibid., p. 76.
107 Ibid., pp. 102 and 103.
108 Ibid., p. 106.
109 Gilles Deleuze and Felix Guattari, 'Kafka, toward a minor literature: the components of expression', *New Literary History* 16 (1985), pp. 591–608.
110 Deleuze and Guattari, *A Thousand Plateaus*, p. 323.
111 Ibid., pp. 308 and 316.
112 Ibid., p. 475.
113 Ibid., p. 485.
114 Jean-François Lyotard, *The Postmodern Condition: A report on knowledge*, Manchester: Manchester University Press, 1984.
115 Jameson, *Fables of Aggression*, p. 7.
116 Deleuze and Guattari, *A Thousand Plateaus*, pp. 72, 91 and 512.
117 Deleuze and Guattari, *Anti-Oedipus*, p. 379.
118 Deleuze and Guattari, *A Thousand Plateaus*, p. 4.
119 Ibid., p. 25.
120 Ibid., p. 4.
121 Ibid., p. 512.
122 For example, Pierre Macherey's *Toward a Theory of Literary Production*, London: Routledge & Kegan Paul, 1978.
123 Deleuze and Guattari, *A Thousand Plateaus*, p. 83.
124 Ibid., p. 139.
125 Ibid., p. 5.

126 Ibid., pp. 160 and 138.
127 Ibid., p. 174.
128 Ibid., p. 175.
129 Ibid.
130 Ibid., p. 186.
131 Ibid., p. 187.
132 Ibid., pp. 190 and 240.
133 Ibid., pp. 240 and 243.
134 Ibid., p. 276.
135 Alice Jardine, 'Woman in limbo: Deleuze and his br(others)', *Substance 44/45* 13: 3/4 (1984), pp. 46–60.
136 Deleuze and Guattari, *A Thousand Plateaus*, pp. 193–4.
137 Ibid., pp. 198–9.
138 Ibid., p. 200.
139 Ibid., p. 201.
140 Ibid., p. 203.
141 Ibid., p. 205.
142 Ibid., p. 203.
143 Ibid.
144 Ibid., p. 492.
145 Ibid., plateau 14, '1440: the smooth and the striated'.
146 Jameson, *The Political Unconscious*, p. 23.
147 Vincent B. Leitch, *Deconstruction: An advanced introduction*, London: Hutchinson, 1983, pp. 211–23.
148 Wright, *Psychoanalytic Criticism*, p. 174.
149 J. G. Merquior, *Foucault*, London: Fontana, 1985, pp. 12–13.
150 Brian McHale, *Postmodernist Fiction*, London: Methuen, 1986.
151 Deleuze and Guattari, *A Thousand Plateaus*, p. 215.
152 Ibid., p. 215.
153 Ibid., p. 213.
154 Ibid., p. 215.
155 Ibid., p. 208.
156 Ibid., p. 209.
157 Ibid., p. 222.
158 Ibid., pp. 204 and 217.
159 Ibid., pp. 216–17.
160 Ibid., p. 277.
161 Ibid., pp. 433 and 468.
162 Ibid., p. 461.
163 Ibid., pp. 227–30.
164 Ibid., p. 224 and Michel Foucault, 'Two lectures', 'Truth and power', 'Power and strategies' in C. Gordon (ed.), *Power/Knowledge*, Brighton: Harvester Press, 1980.
165 Dews 'Power and subjectivity in Foucault', *The Logic of Disintegration*, chapter 5; Jean Baudrillard, *Forget Foucault Semiotext(e)* (1986), pp. 17–47.
166 Deleuze and Guattari, *A Thousand Plateaus*, p. 224.
167 Ibid., p. 225.
168 Ibid., p. 227.

169 Ibid., pp. 226–7.
170 Foucault, in *Power/Knowledge*, esp. p. 142.
171 Deleuze and Guattari, *A Thousand Plateaus*, p. 469.
172 Foucault, in *Power/Knowledge*, p. 130.
173 Deleuze and Guattari, *A Thousand Plateaus*, p. 276.
174 Ibid., p. 353.
175 Ibid., pp. 351–2.
176 Ibid., p. 357.
177 Ibid., p. 360.
178 Ibid., pp. 354 and 360.
179 Ibid., p. 396.
180 Ibid., p. 416.
181 Ibid., p. 422.
182 Ibid., pp. 395 and 417.
183 Foucault, in *Power/Knowledge*, p. 123; Deleuze and Guattari, *A Thousand Plateaus*, p. 467.
184 Foucault in *Power/Knowledge*, pp. 114 and 145.
185 Deleuze and Guattari, *A Thousand Plateaus*, pp. 443–7.
186 Ibid., p. 444.
187 Ibid., p. 472.
188 Ibid., p. 500.
189 Ibid., p. 472.
190 Ibid.
191 Dews, *The Logics of Disintegration*, pp. xi–xvi.
192 Jameson, *The Political Unconscious*, p. 125, and 'Postmodernism, or the cultural logic of late capitalism'.
193 Ibid., p. 92.
194 Foucault, 'Intellectuals and power: a conversation with Gilles Deleuze', in Bouchard, *Language, Counter Memory, Practice*, pp. 206–7 (my emphasis).
195 Ibid., p. 208.
196 Theodor Adorno and Max Horkheimer, *Dialectic of Enlightenment*, London: Verso, 1973.
197 Dews, *The Logic of Disintegration*, p. xiii.
198 Baudrillard, *Forget Foucault*; Jean Baudrillard, 'The ecstasy of communication' in H. Foster (ed.), *Postmodern Culture*, London: Pluto Press, 1985, pp. 126–34.

3

THE IRREDEEMABILITY OF CHANGE

Action and structure in the late plays of Anton Chekhov

Steve Giles

> Reflection shows us that our image of happiness is thoroughly coloured by the time to which our own existence has assigned us. The kind of happiness that could arouse envy in us exists in the air we have breathed, among people we could have talked to, women who could have given themselves to us. In other words, our image of happiness is indissolubly bound up with the image of redemption.
>
> (Walter Benjamin, 'Theses on the philosophy of history')

Twentieth-century critics and theorists of drama have been united in the claim that modern drama is in a state of crisis, whose beginnings are generally located in the late nineteenth century. The most radical version of this claim holds that the very modernity of modern drama consists in its negating drama as traditionally conceived. The arguments underpinning such claims are varied, and sometimes contradictory. Antonin Artaud believed that Western drama and theatre were in terminal decline, thanks to the excessive and obsessive rationality of Western culture,[1] whereas Bertolt Brecht felt that the empathetic drama of the late bourgeois era was shot through with contradictions generating the need for a radically new form of theatre.[2] As far as critics of the genre are concerned, one of the few studies devoted to modernism in modern drama asserts – *pace* Artaud – that the crisis in drama is based on the rejection of rationality assumptions prevalent in Western culture since the Renaissance,[3] while Peter

166

Szondi's neo-Hegelian theory argues that modern drama is no longer dramatic.[4]

The claim regarding a state of crisis is only meaningful in the context of a set of theoretical assumptions defining the nature of drama, and disagreements between conflicting accounts of 'the crisis in drama' ultimately turn on their alternative specifications of what it is for a text to be dramatic. Traditionally, from Aristotle via Hegel down to Suzanne Langer, aesthetic theorists have defined drama in terms of action. Notwithstanding differences in these positions which will become clear later, it is possible to construct from them a traditional theoretical model of drama, whose core presuppositions have been articulated particularly effectively by Langer. Langer argues that the basic abstraction of drama is 'the act, which springs from the past, but is directed towards the future, and is always great with things to come'.[5] Any act, whether instinctive or deliberate, is normally future-oriented, and this factor is a prerequisite for the 'ominous forward movement of consequential action' which is essential to drama.[6] Drama can, therefore, only be sustained by a particular type of act capable of motivating further acts so as to generate integrated actions, and I shall refer to this mode of action as *generative* action. Clearly, action-based theories of drama must posit a tight link between individual and dramaturgical action, so that the specific nature of drama in such theories is determined by further assumptions about the nature of self, society, and their interrelation, which must be involved in any specification of individual action. Hegel's theory of drama, for example, assumes that action in drama is generated by the individual's inner volition and character; the individual freely decides on particular ends and makes these the practical content of his/her willing self.[7] At the same time, individual agents come into conflict, expressing their character and ends to one another through the medium of dialogue, thereby moving forward the action of the play. It should be noted, however, that the concept of generative action – which is central to traditional dramatic theory – does not entail a Hegelian model of the subject, and it is possible to conceive of other modes of human activity, such as game and ritual, which do not obviously satisfy generative criteria. If, however, drama is a mode of action, what are the implications for drama if *action itself* becomes problematic? If a play which fails to satisfy Hegel's criteria for individual action is also unable

167

to meet the structural and dramaturgical requirements implicated in his notion of action, can we no longer construe it as drama? In fact, the Hegelian model of the subject is contested by nineteenth-century dramatists working within a Hegelian paradigm, but when the assumptions grounding this paradigm come to be questioned, the edifice of drama founded on generative action itself begins to crumble.[8] At the turn of the twentieth century, the most radical threat to drama as traditionally theorized was posed by the late plays of Anton Chekhov, which shattered the concept of generative action and thereby abrogated the category of the dramatic.[9]

THE ACTION PROBLEM IN ITS GENERAL ASPECT

The problem of action at the individual level has not received systematic investigation in Chekhov criticism. Yermilov implicitly denies that there is a problem. He asserts of *Three Sisters* that the 'whole play affirms the arrival in life of the kind of people who know no break between word and deed, who are alien to everything vain and petty and are capable of realizing the dream of universal happiness'.[10]

Stroeva comments that people in *Three Sisters* are 'doomed to inaction',[11] while the English critic, Harvey Pitcher, feels that 'what Chekhov's characters *do* is important only in so far as their actions (or in the sisters' case, inaction) illustrate these emotional preoccupations, and in particular, as the expression of some inner emotional crisis'.[12]

Apart from the fact that critics have assumed too often that the Chekhov text may be taken at its face value – an assumption which is altogether dubious, as I shall indicate – they have polarized the concept of action into an opposition of action and inaction, in such a way as to preclude adequate analysis of the issues raised by the text. This section will therefore elaborate a theoretical model of the action problematic in Chekhov, in the context of a general debate on the nature of personal identity.

The process of self-definition occupies a central position in Chekhov's plays. Static concepts of personality are undermined by Dorn in conversation with Sorin in *The Seagull* when he says: 'After a cigar or a glass of vodka you're not Peter Sorin any more, you're Peter Sorin plus something. Your ego dissolves and you start thinking of yourself as "him", in the third person' (*S*, p. 88).

The principal agent of dissolution in Chekhov is not alcohol, however, but time. The consequences of existence in time are fragmentation and discontinuity, and consciousness of this fact generates a search for stability. The vicissitudes of the Treplev–Irina relationship are partly a function of Treplev's reminding his mother of her age. Irina is unable to come to terms with the reality of ageing – and its consequence, death – and so she attempts to deny the flow of time: 'And I make it a rule not to look into the future, I never think of growing old or dying' (*S*, p. 86). The fact that time is the monster of damnation, but never of salvation,[13] accounts for the negativity of the individual's experience of the present in Chekhov's plays, and the negativity of present experience produces two basic strategies under which other behavioural phenomena may be subsumed: escape into utopian speculation, and into habit. It is implied that such attempts are regressive and irrational; the negation of flux in structured forms of existence appears to be the prerogative of situations which are artificial or fictional, so that composition is not to be seen as a feature of everyday life, and stability remains alien to actuality.

Almost always in Chekhov, experience of the present moment is negative, and tends to be categorized as boredom. The physicality of the experience is emphasized as Sorin, for example, complains of feeling 'as stale as someone's old cigarette-holder' (*S*, p. 98). Sleep no longer replenishes, but devitalizes the individual, who wakes not to freshness and life, but to nightmare and death. The claustrophobic nature of Sorin's experience is mediated by the viscosity that characterizes his description of it; it is as if 'all that sleep had glued my brain to my skull or something' (*S*, p. 72). Unlike Treplev's, Sorin's self-obsession falls short of the morbid since he has a perspective on himself expressed in self-mocking laughter, but in opposition to his experience stands the sense of emptiness felt by Uncle Vanya:

> Oh my God, I'm forty-seven. Suppose I live to be sixty, that means I have still thirteen years to go. It's too long. How am I to get through these thirteen years? What am I to do? How do I fill the time?
>
> (*UV*, p. 48)

If, like Masha in *The Seagull*, Vanya knew where he came from, or what he was doing on this earth, if he had clear and definite goals, filling time would not perhaps present as many problems as it evidently does. Chekhov's late plays are marked by a preoccupation with the concept of happiness as a generalized end to be striven for. *The Seagull* opens with a brief and inconclusive discussion on the subject. Masha's claim that she is unhappy is countered by Medvedenko's inability to understand how this could possibly be the case. He implies a relationship between happiness and material well-being, yet suggests a disjunction between his own behaviour and his economic position – 'I don't go round like someone at a funeral' (*S*, p. 71) – and then denies Masha's subsequent observation that even a poor man can be happy. As he goes on to define his own material privation, Masha looks back at the stage, as if to imply a histrionic element in his behaviour (and also, ironically, in her own black melancholy): a mechanism of negations has emerged that undermines efforts to take what is said in the play at face value. Later, Sorin will claim that it's somehow better in the town than in the country, but his explanation does not match up to what he asserts, and his entire utterance is undercut, in any case, by Dorn's singing. Trigorin's idealization of young love, and fictionalization of the love object, is not only ironized by the central example of young love in Nina and Treplev, but also, implicitly, by his own claim that it 'sweeps you off your feet into a make-believe world' (*S*, p. 103), and the concrete image of happiness appears to subsist as illusion, or even delusion. Nina's experience indicates that the disintegration of one set of fictions on actuality precipitates the need for a replacement, in this case a Vignyesque ethic of knowing how to bear one's cross and have faith. Treplev is deluded into believing that she has found her road, while he has none, but her own confusion about her identity (equivocation relating to her seagull status, the excess in her statements on acting) knocks down this assumption, without denying the *need for* a goal. The problem is that the specification of goals by figures in Chekhov all too often involves absolute negation of the present, so that it becomes logically impossible for any such goal, and hence the state of happiness, to be realized.

If happiness is to be the prerogative of those that cross the horizon of the infinite future, present matters will acquire even greater urgency. Irina would rather learn a part than sit around doing nothing, a panacea which involves the composition of a false self which is structured, the creation of a fictive identity, as if only a fictive identity can be structured. Similarly, one might attempt to fix the self with reference to others, though one problem here will be that the public self is necessarily fragmented and unstable in its plurality. The great actress's relationship with Trigorin is an instance of this strategy. It might have been expected that since Treplev reminds her of her age, Irina's partial rejection of her son would infuse her attitude to Nina, who is both a professional and an emotional rival. However, unless her behaviour in Act II before Nina's affair with Trigorin has blossomed is the ultimate in mendacity, her attitude towards Nina is decidedly positive; indeed, Nina seems to assume the role in Irina's world of the little girl she never had. Crisis with respect to Nina occurs only when Trigorin threatens to go off with the potential starlet, and it is significant that Irina's attentions are not directed at her rival, but at the object of her love. Her terror and distress precipitate an attempt to repossess Trigorin, for her relationship to him is predicted on the assumption that the being of the loved individual is the prerogative of the lover, and must therefore be possessed. This is a manifestation of a more fundamental identity syndrome, as Treplev indicates. His suggestion that his mother needs to be praised implies that in her relationships she is constantly seeking confirmation and self-definition from without. However, as the Trigorin crisis shows, as soon as identity depends on the other it becomes precarious, since the other may withdraw his or her sanction at any moment. At a more superficial level, the opiate of flattery is not to be had in the country, yet the mere fact that its absence could be problematic is sufficient to confirm the danger inherent in Irina's strategy.

The efforts of the individual to achieve even limited aims in the present are frustrated by a disjunction of intention and action. This is emphasized by Sorin when he points out that neither of his two ambitions came off, and what he did get just happened. The realization of intention is also frustrated by the gratuitousness of the figures' motivations and decisions; Masha asserts that getting married will at least make a change, and in *The Cherry Orchard* even Lopakhin is affected by the disintegration of intention: 'I come out here specially so I can go and meet them at the station, then suddenly fall asleep and wake up too late' (*CO*, p. 59). The possibility of generative action is withdrawn, and the acts of the individual in Chekhov come to assume merely habitual status, as (in *The Seagull*) Masha repeatedly takes snuff,

Sorin combs his beard, Treplev constantly looks at his watch, and Trigorin obsessively takes notes. These habitual acts are at the same time, however, attempts to structure time, to impose a ritualistic order on it, a need summed up by Marina in *Uncle Vanya*, as present disaffection is to be eliminated by a return to former practices: 'We'll go back to our old way of doing things, with breakfast at eight o'clock and dinner at one' (*V*, p. 46). Moreover, the constant activity indulged in by Irina (which in her opinion keeps her looking younger) is a means of eclipsing consciousness of time, and if the ultimate in habit is game, it is not surprising that the habitual nature of activity finds expression in the frequency of games in Chekhov. Games are structured, rule-based forms of activity, whose repetition – itself sanctioned by tradition – has the aim of structuring the present in terms of the past, of fixing the present moment, and Gayev's relation to billiards in *The Cherry Orchard* may be taken as paradigmatic for the general significance of game in Chekhov. The most significant examples of the game theme in relation to Gayev occur in crisis situations:

(a) GAYEV (*somewhat embarrassed*): In off the right into the corner. Screw shot into the middle.

(b) My hands are shaking. It's a long time since I had a game of billiards.

(c) [Gayev enters weeping, and the stage-direction reads]: *The click of billiard balls is heard. . . . Gayev's expression changes and he stops crying.*

(d) GAYEV (*greatly distressed, afraid of bursting into tears*): The train. The station. In off into the middle, double the white into the corner.

(*CO*, pp. 69, 86, 99, 111)

Habit is the guarantee of a 'dull inviolability', 'a compromise effected between the individual and his environment'.[14] To take the argument a stage further:

the fundamental duty of Habit, about which it describes the futile and stupefying arabesques of its supererogations, consists in a perpetual adjustment and readjustment of our organic sensibility to the conditions of its worlds. Suffering

172

represents the omission of that duty, whether through negligence or inefficiency.[15]

The need for activity is equalled only by the need for words; the vacuum of silence is abhorred just as much as the emptiness of time: 'the silence frightens me when I'm on my own' (*CO*, p. 94). Language becomes yet another engine in the arsenal of habit, communion is strictly phatic, and the speech-acts of the characters assume the status of ends in themselves. Nobody seems to have anything to say, but, as Masha observes in *The Seagull*, 'When people can't think what to say they always hold forth about the young' (*S*, p. 85). The juxtaposition of Masha's remark with her own habitual snuff-taking invites the comment that 'holding forth' is simply another means of filling time. Shamrayev is especially prone to indulge in reminiscence in the form of declamation. His tendency to produce citation and recitation suggests that his stories from the past are implicated in the attempt to create a relationship to the past which is structured in fictional terms, an anecdotal identity. While this might once more imply the fictive status of structured identities, at the same time the process of narration itself has been inserted into a framework of doubt; the levels of meaning recall Masha's reflexive use of the cliché that 'Unhappy love affairs are only found in novels' (*S*, p. 107). The undermining of the text thus applies not only to its production of meanings through negation, but to the conventions of linguistic communication as such.

THE DIALECTIC OF HOPE AND DESPAIR IN *THREE SISTERS*

> I loathe our present life, but thinking about the future makes me feel really good. I feel so easy and relaxed, I see a light glimmering in the distance, I have a vision of freedom. I see myself and my children freed from idleness and drinking kvass and stuffing ourselves with goose and cabbage, freed from our after-dinner naps and this vile habit of trying to get something for nothing.
>
> (*TS*, p. 183)

Andrew's words in *Three Sisters* are ironically framed by Ferapont's account of a natural disaster in St Petersburg. His repudiation of the present has as its consequence escape into futuristic delusion, and through this situation the Chekhovian dialectic of hope and despair is articulated. However, fiction is contradicted by actuality, and sense and meaning appear to be extinct. Irina's feeling that the world made sense was a function not of some all-uniting transcendent experience, but of having a wash after getting up in the morning. Her idealization of work does not depend on some prior moral imperative, but is instead a reflex of her own non-work situation: this is emphasized by the metaphor she herself employs of drink and thirst. The ideal exists as antithetical to the present, as negation of the status quo. Irina's subsequent experience of work radically contradicts her idealized expectations, and in her account of work lurks the implication that it is impossible to satisfy a want that subsists as negative illusion: 'I must find another job because this one doesn't suit me. The things I'd hoped for and wanted so much – they're just what it doesn't give me. It's sheer drudgery with nothing romantic or intellectual about it' (*TS*, p. 147). The knock from the floor below does not shake her into veridical self-consciousness, and her later doubt that Moscow will ever be reached highlights the disparity between her consciousness and her situation, since it is an effect more of present dissatisfaction than of insight. Although she refers to her dreams of a Moscow lover as sheer foolishness, one observes a reassertion of the Moscow fantasy as Act III closes, since the *need* for such beliefs must, if necessary, swamp any potential realization of their actual status. Later, she tries to rationalize the impossibility of going to Moscow in terms of God's will, and just as the disintegration of one fiction necessitates the search for another, so the substitution of marriage for Moscow leads to the rehabilitation of the previous fiction, already discredited, of work.

Olga's idealization of Moscow occurs in the context of her endeavours to relate past and present. While the specificity of her temporal references, and the parallels between past and present, conspire in the identification of present and past, the attempt to relate the two situations serves none the less to emphasize the difference between them. Then, as the clock strikes twelve, as it had done a year previously, the forward flow of time is somehow arrested, and channelled into a current of static circularity: Olga's ostensible desire to integrate two different times is a manifestation of the convert aim of denying time. The effectiveness of this strategy is partly subject to the adequacy of memory, but this

is put in question later by Vershinin's inability to remember the
sisters as they were, by Masha's beginning to forget her mother's
face, and by Olga's own doubts about the power of her own
memory. Her escape into memory cannot, in any case, obliterate
the present, nor can it dissolve the necessity of acting in relation
to the future, though when it does come to facing up to a
situation or acting positively, her response, not surprisingly, is
one of procrastination. Her admitted reliance on memories
is juxtaposed later with her statement that 'Nothing ever works
out as we want it' (*TS*, p. 185). But she herself has become
headmistress almost by default: her denial of the present entails
the very disjunction of action and intention which her situation
illustrates.

In the preceding section I mentioned the significant role
played by habit in Chekhov's world; its supererogations are equally vital in *Three Sisters*, and are touched upon by Masha: 'A lot
depends on habit of course. After Father's death for instance it
was ages before we got used to having no orderlies about the
place' (*TS*, p. 145). The immanence of individual death adds
further strains to the process of readjustment. Chebutykin's entry
reading a newspaper, making notes, his hurried exit combing his
beard, stand against his observations on the theme of human
decay in his opening words. His existence is informed by a dialectic of consciousness and habit, the habit necessary to fill the time
left until the lesser end of retirement is reached, and counterpointed as he 'Puts his newspaper in his pocket and takes out
another' (*TS*, p. 175). The element of regression in his behaviour
is implied in his intention to be a good little boy, and the game
solution in general comes under attack when Marsha angrily
jumbles up the cards in Act II, in anticipation of the constant
shifts from socio-economic fact to game situation in the third act
of *The Cherry Orchard*. The problem of parting – the dilemma of
integrating the end of a relationship – coincides with the need
to drown the present in verbosity towards the end of Act IV,
when Vershinin speculates on past and present, the generations
of the past being no more: 'They've left a great gap behind them
and so far there's been nothing to put in their place, but people
are desperately trying to find something and in the end they're
bound to succeed' (*TS*, p. 185). Of course, people in the play
have found 'something'; but their solutions are inadequate to
their predicament. In Vershinin's case, habit and speculation

coincide, for his parting speech is yet another tirade, a declamation rather than a communication, as the pain of parting must be assuaged by holding forth. The suggestion that speculation is a mode of habit is confirmed in an earlier speech, where in the space of four sentences Vershinin moves from a report on present disaster, to comparison with the past, and to idealization of the future, in complete harmony with the dialectic previously defined:

> The children were standing by the front door in their nightclothes, the street was all red with flames, there was a most appalling din. It struck me that it must have been rather like this in the old days of sudden enemy invasions, with all that looting and burning. But what a difference between then and now, come to think of it. Before very long – in two or three hundred years, say – people will look back on our way of life with the same horror and contempt.
>
> <div align="right">(<i>TS</i>, p. 166)</div>

And life is going to be marvellous. Vershinin's faith in the future golden age is expressed in the context of the relativity of the present consequent upon the flow of time. What seems important today will be forgotten, or seen as insignificant, and yet it is also necessary to rationalize the present in terms of the future, to project meaning onto the contemporary situation via the myth of progress. Men now will have no part in the perfect future, but the meaning of their lives depends upon their role in bringing it about, so that both work and suffering may be harmonized through being integrated into a world-historical scheme. Even if the cultured few are gradually swallowed up by the crowd, ultimately their kind will prevail, and a new breed of men and women will arise. The status of Vershinin's act of faith is not easy to establish. It might be seen, for example, as no more than ideological compensation for the problematics of being that infect a moribund class.[16] However, the claim has been made that in fact Chekhov is expressing his own views through Vershinin, and not merely by Soviet critics wishing to retrieve the play into a progressive mythology. Harvey Pitcher, for example, writes as follows: 'Tuzenbakh's remarks are sometimes quoted as if they were distinctly "Chekhovian" and expressed the whole spirit of *Three Sisters*. That Chekhov's sympathies would have lain more with Vershinin can be inferred from the play in general.'[17]

Pitcher's argumentation does not justify this altogether dubious inference. He concedes that Vershinin's faith in the future might be read as mere rationalization, but wishes to solve the problem by seeing Vershinin as 'a character who is quite unequivocally emotion-centred',[18] rather than as a social type. Pitcher is right to point out that Vershinin is expressing a deeply felt faith in the future, but this cannot establish the claim that Chekhov himself is therefore writing from the heart, and in any case, it overlooks the contextualization of Vershinin's utterances, which repudiates even the most sophisticated attempts at identifying Chekhov with beliefs held by his characters. All Vershinin's speculations regarding the future are relativized when he points out that 'we can't possibly know now just what will be thought significant and important, or what will seem pathetic and absurd' (*TS*, p. 131). What is more, Vershinin's speculation is negated by Tuzenbakh's, as if to indicate that the truth-value of both is nil. This is also apparent in Act II, when the two men self-consciously consider what life will be like in two or three hundred years. The habitual status of their meaningless meanderings into the future is made crystal clear, for their discussion is juxtaposed with Irina's preparations for a game of cards, and it assumes similar ritualistic connotations. Indeed, even if their philosophizing were not completely vacuous, it would be discredited precisely because of the recurrence of the game motif. Like Olga's relapse into memory, Vershinin's escape into speculation may be seen as a regressive denial of the present, whittling away the possibility of concrete action in relation to the future, not least when he wonders in Act I 'what it would be like if we could start living all over again' (*TS*, p. 135). His own criteria of happiness are subjected to bathos when he argues that the remedy for his situation is embodied in flowers – 'Why, they're just what I've been missing all my life' (*TS*, p. 135) – and his own discussion of the concept of happiness will seem both pretentious and ironically perceptive. He alludes to the fact that the image of happiness subsists as negation of the present, that the sisters will not notice Moscow when they live there, and concludes, 'We have no happiness. There's no such thing. It's only something we long for' (*TS*, p. 152). To be sure, this argument is, as one might have expected, undermined in context as Tuzenbakh observes the absence of the chocolates, but his statement is of relevance to the problem of happiness in a general sense. The implicative force of Vershinin's allusion is

177

to discredit *all* striving towards happiness in the play, not least his own.

Once more, language does not exist primarily as a medium of communication; it also articulates the process of self-definition. Olga's opening words in Act I, while ostensibly addressed to Irina, mediate the longing to relate past and present, and are part of a strategy that wishes to evade consciousness of time, of the fact of growing old. Kulygin's Sunday speech, whose rationality is at best one of form and not of content, as it shifts from mothballs to Romans to the omniscience of the headmaster to Masha, curtains and carpets, defines its own significance: 'Our head-master says the important thing about life is its pattern or shape. A thing that loses its shape is finished, and that's true of everyday life as well (*TS*, p. 136). His own preoccupation with time indicates that the necessary structure must relate to time, and his repeated assertions that he is a schoolmaster would seem to justify the inference that his need to remind himself of his social identity reveals ontological insecurity. Any security Kulygin might have depends on rigid encasement in his role, and the idiom it demands:

> Why all the fuss? It's quite the thing these days, *modus vivendi* and all that. The head's clean shaven, so when I became second master I followed suit. No one likes it, but I don't care. I'm perfectly happy.

> (*TS*, p. 176)

Similarly, Natasha's repeated self-citations and extensions of her power over others have their roots in an identity crisis which is a direct result of the inadequacy of egoism in self-definition. Her preoccupation with her physical appearance implies a vanity which is precarious in its dependence on the reflecting confir-mations of the mirror. Her need to see herself is paralleled in the pleasure she derives from being seen, receiving sweet looks from her children, who may themselves be considered as consol-ing projections of the self. Natasha's condition illustrates the dangers involved in basing identity on consumption and subju-gation of the other, a method which is self-contradictory, since it presupposes the presence of the other but entails the other's destruction.

VALUES AND SOCIAL CHANGE IN *THE CHERRY ORCHARD*

The Cherry Orchard's presentation of the problems of action and time paves the way for a social account of individual predicament. The passing of time is described in socio-economic terms, the crisis of action is historically specific, and the individual's response to change in time is necessarily a response to social modifications. Furthermore, the attitudes to change conveyed by figures in the play are counterpointed and reinforced by the set.

The cherry orchard in Act I is a locus of paradox. The references to the season of the year and time of day focus on beginning, on the transition from winter to summer, from old to new. The concentration on transition expresses change and movement forwards, but the juxtaposition of bloom and frost emphasizes the paradoxical nature of change, in the same way that the scene on the ice in Pudovkin's film *Mother* reveals the ambiguity of thaw.[19] The set exposes the difficulty of evaluating change: the future orientation of its temporal images is balanced by the location of the action in the nursery, the place of regression. The movement outwards from the nursery, already suggested by the opening of windows in Act I, is completed by Act II, which is situated in open country. Now, however, although once more the time is one of transition, the set concentrates on images of the end: stones resembling tombstones, dark poplars, and a tumbledown chapel. The play's first visual statement of economic and social change – 'There is a row of telegraph poles in the distance and far, far away on the horizon are the dim outlines of a big town' (*CO*, p. 76) – is framed by metaphors of death. In terms of set, the final act of the play is the negation of the first, characterized by absence, emptiness and departure rather than arrival and return, and it takes place in October, not in May. While the emphasis is again on the ambiguity of transition, the emotive loading of the set, together with the destruction of the orchard, seems to imply the negative aspect of change, whereas Pudovkin's images of transition recognized the inopportunity of revolutionary action in 1905, but looked forward to a positive future. In *The Cherry Orchard*, though, the notion that change necessarily involves progress is controverted in the presentation of Trofimov. Trofimov's sense of crisis and his belief in progress are reflexively related, in accordance with the typical syndrome of hope and despair, and the multiplicity of responses to change may be exemplified further with reference to Lopakhin and Mrs Ranevsky. Lopakhin's attitude to time is radically different from that of the landowners. It is characterized by a sense of urgency which they do not share, and is summed up in his 'you can't put the clock back now' (*CO*, p. 100). Lopakhin's sense of time is future-oriented, and social change is assimilable in terms of it. Ranevsky, on the other hand, had related the process of arrival in Act I to the return to the past, and her attitude to time is condensed in her later response to the orchard: 'When I woke up every morning happiness awoke with me, and the orchard was just the same in those days. Nothing's changed' (*CO*, p. 71). The play indicates that her attitude is regressive. The linear movement of the play denies her claim that all is as it was, and facts about her own past experience imply that times gone by were typified as much by disaster as by happiness. Moreover, the movement in Act III from game situations to economic actualities ultimately involves the disintegration of game on the reality of change. However, while it is suggested that, as a strategy for coming to terms with change in time, regressive behaviour is inadequate, the appropriate response to the new is as yet unclear.

> Our father, God rest his soul, inflicted education on us. It's a funny thing, sounds silly in fact, but I must confess that since he died I've started putting on weight and in one year I've filled out like this, just as if my body had shaken off some kind of burden.
>
> (*CO*, p. 134)

The loss of paternal authority, thematized here in *Three Sisters*, and the consequent liberation of the individual, have ambiguous results in Chekhov's writing. Firs, the oldest figure in *The Cherry Orchard*, gives one possible explanation of the situations presented in the play by relating social conditions before and after the emancipation of the serfs: 'Yes, those were the days. The serfs had their master and the masters had their serfs, but now everything's at sixes and sevens and you can't make head or tail of it' (*CO*, p. 82). Social change as Firs describes it evidently involves deregulation, but he rejects the new order, and the emancipation is to be seen as the fall from grace rather than the realization of heaven on earth. While Firs's idealization of the past is questioned in context by Lopakhin's reference to floggings, his account of the effects of change is confirmed by situations in the play. As he observes, in the past their guests were generals, barons and admirals, but now they have difficulty in securing the favours even of the post-office clerk. This suggests both the decline in social status of the Ranevskys and the rise in importance of lower functionaries; increased social mobility is implied, and derigidification of class structure. Between 1861 and 1904, Russian society experienced fundamental change. While in the mid-nineteenth century its economy was overwhelmingly agrarian, with peasants – almost all of whom were serfs – forming three-quarters of its population, the years preceding the 1905 revolution were marked by rapid industrialization and fast growth of towns, and an urban proletariat developed.[20] The transformation of the economic base of society had consequences for value concepts, as the play indicates. Lopakhin sees the orchard solely in terms of its exchange value: 'The only remarkable thing about that orchard is its size. It only gives a drop every other year and then no one knows what to do with the cherries. Nobody wants to buy them (*CO*, p. 67). Similarly, he conceives of autumn in strictly pragmatic terms, and treats flowers as economic objects rather than natural ones. Lopakhin's concept of value is countered by its opposite: the significance of the orchard for Ranevsky and Gayev consists in the fact that it is interesting, remarkable, and mentioned in the Encyclopaedia. Likewise, the bookcase is no mere receptacle, but an object of cult value, whose continued existence over time has upheld traditional values and ideals, just as for Ranevsky the orchard is the locus of beauty, purity, innocence and happiness. The conflict of values which the play presents is directly related to the fact of socio-economic change. In the past, as Firs points out, the orchard was not problematic at all. Indeed, the changing status of the orchard can be described with reference to Benjamin's theory of the loss of aura that corrodes aesthetic objects given certain non-normative developments, and the fate of the orchard may be seen as an index of the fate of art: 'To pry an object from its shell, to destroy its aura, is the mark of a perception whose "sense of the universal equality of things" has increased to such a degree that it extracts it even from a unique object by means of reproduction.'[21]

This order of perception would appear to be the prerogative of the Lopakhins of the world. The rise of Lopakhin is evidently symptomatic of social change, and it is he who is most capable of acting effectively in terms of new developments. This is evidenced in his plans for the orchard, which take account of the social diversification produced by change, and contrast starkly with Gayev's aphasia concerning the status quo and the actions it entails: his response to Lopakhin's solution is 'That's all rubbish' (*CO*, p. 68). Lopakhin's purchase of the cherry orchard and the hysterical joy of possession he expresses indicate the victory of the values he represents, in terms of which beauty is economically quantifiable and its spoliation can be rationalized with reference to concepts of wealth and ownership. The former slave has risen up to wrest the symbol of oppression from its owners, and all that remains to complete his victory is the obliteration of the symbol.

To all intents and purposes, Lopakhin appears to be of a radically different constitution from other figures in this and in Chekhov's other late plays. On the face of it, he is a man of action, a successful pragmatist who achieves his ends positively through work. However, he too is affected by the general problem of identity in Chekhov, and while at one level he embodies the objective motions of History, this special status depends at least as much on subjective sickness. Work is significant for Lopakhin in that it is a panacea; just as work acts as a sedative for Tuzenbakh, so it has the function of habit for Lopakhin: 'When I work for a long time at a stretch I feel a bit calmer, and I too seem to know why I exist' (*CO*, p. 105). Indeed, Lopakhin cannot stand not working, and his description of the ridiculous way his arms flop about as if they belong to someone else is reminiscent of R. D. Laing's account of the schizoid mode of being-in-the-world.[22] His situation shows how activity in Chekhov may be defined as negation of work, but at the same time work does not appear to be a solution to the problem. The longing for work was thematic in *Three Sisters*, and the action problem as it concerns figures in that play is apparently accounted for by Irina: 'We must work, work, work. That's why we're so miserable and take such a gloomy view of things – because we don't know the meaning of work. We're descended from people who despised it' (*TS*, p.138). Irina's own experience of work could just as easily confirm this view as disconfirm it, but Lopakhin's situation implies that work is not a solution even for those who are descended from people who possibly did not despise it. Furthermore, Irina's words invite a Marxist reading of Chekhov, according to which the action problem is specific to a particular class. While there is justification for this approach if one looks especially at *Three Sisters*, the thesis suggested by *The Cherry Orchard* would appear to be that this issue and the related dilemma of identity affect all social orders. Indeed, the situation in *The Cherry Orchard* is a classic example of the anomic condition of society as defined by Durkheim.

In Durkheim's view, the satisfaction of those human needs which are not purely biophysical in character depends upon the existence of a set of moral rules. These rules act as a barrier or constraint on human passions, and can only be legitimized through a force external to the individual: society. As Durkheim believes that none of our ends has any absolute or intrinsic value, it is necessary for society to provide ideals and goals which can co-ordinate human activity and give life meaning. At the same time, societally given ends are inherently problematic, because, Durkheim continues, 'if ever we perceived that behind these relative ends there was only nothingness, the spell which draws us to them would be broken, and our life would be deprived of meaning and significance'.[23]

Clearly, any fundamental questioning of social values could precipitate a crisis of individual action and identity, and Durkheim argues that societal and individual dislocation is inevitable in periods of transition. Shifts in values are generated by economic changes, and if these are so radical that society's moral barriers collapse, then it is plunged into the condition of anomie, whereby

> the moral system which has prevailed for centuries is shaken, and fails to respond to new conditions of human life, without any new system having yet been formed to replace that which has disappeared. In a word, the former gods are growing old or are already dead, and others are not yet born.[24]

Even at this level of generality, there are clear analogies between Durkheim's account of change and, for example, the value problem in *The Cherry Orchard* and the notion of the present as vacuum in *Three Sisters*. However, still more precise parallels may be drawn. Durkheim suggested that when the moral barriers of society weaken, human forces tend to pursue ends that are constantly elusive; indeed, under certain conditions, the notion of the *infinite* appears, and he saw this malady as tormenting his own age.

His account of insatiable desires is clearly applicable to the predicament of individuals in Chekhov: 'Unlimited desires are insatiable by definition and insatiability is rightly considered a sign of morbidity. Being unlimited, they constantly and infinitely surpass the means at their command; they cannot be quenched. Inextinguishable thirst is constantly renewed torture.'[26]

Furthermore, Durkheim's depiction of the effects on action constituted by a collapse of reasons and norms is such that it provides a model for the negation of generative action in Chekhov:

> All man's pleasure in acting, moving and exerting himself implies the sense that his efforts are not in vain and that by walking he advances. However, one does not advance when one proceeds towards no goal, or – which is the same thing – when the goal is in infinity. Since the distance between us and it is always the same, whatever road we take, it is just as if we have not moved. . . . To pursue a goal which is by definition unattainable is to condemn oneself to a state of perpetual unhappiness.[27]

If it is true to say that the goal located at infinity is equivalent to no goal at all, then it may not be possible to speak of action at all in Chekhov's plays, as the behaviour of the individuals will fail to satisfy the central condition that action must be directed towards an end in the future. As this condition is incorporated in traditional dramatic theory's specification of individual action, it might no longer be legitimate to refer to Chekhov's plays as drama.

THE FORMAL FEATURES OF CHEKHOV'S LATE PLAYS

The nature of the dramaturgical action in Chekhov's plays has received frequent comment in Chekhov criticism, but no sufficient explanation. It is generally accepted, for example, that dialogue comes to be characterized more and more by what Pitcher has called 'deformalization', but the theoretical problems raised by this phenomenon have seldom been explored. Pitcher points out that 'Chekhov had to undermine the persistent dramatic convention, whereby dialogue is arranged in the kind of neat and rational sequence that is seldom to be heard in life itself'.[28]

184

However, his approach generally, like that of many critics, has the effect of deproblematizing the text. Even Peter Szondi, who is conscious of the threat to drama which is manifested in the relativization of language and action at the individual level, claims that Chekhov's drama does not utimately renounce those categories necessary for it to be dramatic. In terms of Szondi's *own* proposed categories, Chekhov's plays are indeed problematic, and Szondi is least adequate when he considers the status of dialogue: 'dialogue hardly ever becomes problematic in them, nor does their internal contradiction – between monological thematics and dialogical expression – lead to the explosion of dramatic form.'[29]

It certainly is not the case that dialogue only seldom becomes a problem in Chekhov's plays, and while drama may not be exploded, there are definite contradictions in the later plays at this level. It has been suggested that the composition of the 'Chekhovian play' is characterized by filling in between spiritual peaks, in the form of conversations which say nothing and silences,[30] and in a Formalist account of *The Cherry Orchard*, Balukhaty has indicated the *un*systematic way in which themes are articulated: 'Thus, the movement of themes through the acts is accomplished according to the principle of unorganized articulation, of a kind of *disintegration* of composition in which the devices of interruption, severance, and recurrence of themes clearly stand out.'[31]

Nevertheless, he argues, Chekhov's drama does not abandon compositional unity, since each act is characterized by a dominant theme. Chekhov's methods of structuring the text are, however, more manifold than Balukhaty implies, and the recurrence of themes which he cites as an agent of *dis*integration is one of them. The break-up of the generative model of action in Chekhov's late plays thus invokes a reciprocal attempt to structure the text, which sets up a contradiction within it; criticism has been all too ready to resort to similar strategies of retrieval. Corrigan, for example, concedes the dedramatization of the text, but he claims that Chekhov's abnegation of events – for example in the case of Treplev's suicide – may indeed be less theatrically exciting, yet 'is much truer to life and in the long run its impact upon us is probably more lasting and horrible'.[32] The rationalization of triviality and inconsequentiality in terms of a greater realism is echoed in Pitcher. He says that Chekhov 'tried to create on stage the impression of the casual, haphazard flow of ordinary conversation'.[33] Though there is some truth in this, salvaging 'deformalization' in this way can only involve Chekhov's plays still further in the self-contradictions of theatrical naturalism; ironically enough, Pitcher's argument is followed by implicit concession of the conventionality of Chekhov's representations, as he defines the audience as eavesdropper. Chizhevsky has tried to relate the particular character of Chekhov's realism to impressionism, but he fails to consider the full implications of this categorization, which could well clarify certain aspects of the plays: the atomization of objects in an impressionist painting consequent on the subjective refinement of naturalistic representation is analogous to the principle of conversational discontinuity that threatens dialogic convention in Chekhov's late plays. Chekhovian drama has been defined as one of atmosphere, of mood, of undercurrent, but this Stanislavskian type of retrieval has been rejected by Skaftymov, who points out that such a definition 'has only descriptive value. Furthermore, it has little concrete meaning.'[34] It has been conceded that the 'usual procedures of dramatic criticism' are defied by the Chekhov text;[35] it is time to show what procedures may legitimately be applied to it.

An apparently insignificant distinction between Chekhov's late plays and his earlier work *Ivanov*[36] is that, while in the earlier play the acts are divided into scenes, in the later plays they are not. This is not some sort of typographical eccentricity; it is a direct consequence of the way in which Chekhov composed his late plays. My discussion of this problem will concentrate on *Three Sisters*, and especially on the first act. Scenic divisions in *Ivanov* occur when a new figure joins one or more figures on stage, or, much less frequently, when a figure is left alone on stage; if one attempts to apply this principle of scenic division to *Three Sisters*, the identification of scenes becomes problematic. Furthermore, assuming that it has been possible to identify scenic units – albeit in a provisional manner – it will be noted that these too fragment. A major principle of composition in *Three Sisters* is interruption, but although the negation of dialectical flow within each act attacks the model of drama Chekhov has inherited, it does not ultimately explode it. Before he wrote his late plays, Chekhov structured his work in terms of the features of composition incorporated in the traditional model of drama. Although the scenes in *Ivanov* are a good deal shorter than scenes tend to be in

Ibsen's plays from *Pillars of Society* onwards, and even though there are signs of a break-up of the traditional model towards the end of Act II of *Ivanov*, it is generally the case that they are, in a structural sense at least, internally cohesive, as they are in Ibsen. However, the method of scenic composition in *Three Sisters*, and in *The Seagull* and *The Cherry Orchard*, anticipates techniques of filmic composition. In *Film Form*,[37] Eisenstein relates how the application of future methods of film composition to stage production necessarily involved the abandonment of the stage. Eisenstein's theory of film emphasizes the centrality of montage (which is exemplified in the 'comics' scene in *Madam Bovary*); montage is characterized by collision, and the dynamics of montage drive the film forwards. The camera carves out fragments of empirical reality which in themselves are neutral, but whose combination gives rise to new meanings and concepts possibly unplanned at the time of filming, together with modified perspectives: 'By combining these monstrous incongruities we newly collect the disintegrated event into one whole, but in *our* aspect.'[38] Furthermore, montage is a key factor in the antithetical relation of film and stage observed by Walter Benjamin.[39] While the stage actor presents his performance to his public himself in a definitive manner, the film actor's performance is presented by an apparatus that cuts him off from his audience and need not respect his performance as a totality. The film actor's performance is composed – or *re*composed – from a disintegrated sequence of episodes according to the principles of montage. Moreover, the illusory nature of film is radically different from that of the stage: 'Its illusory nature is that of the second degree, the result of cutting.'[40]

While cutting and montage in film are agents of recomposition, on the stage they involve discomposition; in terms of Brechtian theatre this would not be disadvantageous, but in the case of Chekhov's late plays the text exists in a state of contradiction, as Chekhov still appears to pay lip-service at least to realist dramatic convention.

At times in Chekhov's plays, dialogue disintegrates. The exchange between Chebutykin and Soliony during Act II of *Three Sisters*, while it may well exemplify the triviality and misunderstanding characteristic of everyday conversation, reveals the disjunction of discontinuous actuality and homogenizing conventional form.[41] The section of Act II extending from

187

Chebutykin's entry to the delivery of the letter for Vershinin is remarkable for its interruptions – Chebutykin's entry is itself an interruption – such as laughter, music, song, reading aloud, and silences. As soon as it seems possible that a dialogue sequence might get off the ground, it is undermined, for example when Vershinin's and Tuzenbakh's speculations are relativized in the ways suggested earlier, and by Masha's ambiguous laughter. Conversational flow is characterized by its *a*logicality; Fedotik's laying out of the cards is preceded by Rodé's interruption of his conversation with Nina, and followed in the space of little more than half a page by reference to the weather, an exchange on cards and Moscow that signals the interrelation of fictive speculation and habit, a reading from a newspaper, the announcement that tea is ready, Natasha's idealization of her son, Soliony's negation of her remark, and Masha's reference to Moscow (*TS*, p. 152). Of course, it might be suggested with some ingenuity that there is an underlying thematic unity here, in that the utterances of the characters refer to central problems in the play; however, this is to miss the point. The argument is not that the text disintegrates completely and lacks any unity whatsoever, but that the structure of the 'dialogue' is in contradiction with the requirements of the dramatic model Chekhov has taken over. Szondi was right to point out the monologic quality of much of Chekhov's dialogue, exemplified in the apparent conversation between Andrew and Natasha at the beginning of Act II, but it is not correct to say that the text sustains monologic intrusion. Indeed, when Natasha asks Andrew why he doesn't say anything, his reply is that 'There's nothing to say anyway' (*TS*, p. 143), but the conventional framework of the play demands that things be said, if only the repetition of the time to a deaf servant, and the event of identifying dialogue is itself deprived of its potential drama.

The conversation problem is exemplified in Act I of *Three Sisters* in the luncheon scene, where a similar surface fragmentation may be established. The difficulties involved in identifying scenic units are indicated in the section of the text that precedes the luncheon scene, starting from Kulygin's entry (*TS*, pp. 135ff.). This potential scene may be further subdivided into ten more segments, all but two of which are marked by an entry or an exit. On the basis of similar criteria, it is possible to argue that the opening section of the play, up to Chebutykin's hurried exit, is divisible into a further five segments. This process of focusing down on particles of the text invites the suggestion that Chekhov's theatre could be seen in Brechtian terms as being gestic, but the significant distinction is that, whereas Chekhov's theatre is implicitly gestic in structural terms, it is not gestic in that Chekhov does *not* conceive of scenic segments in terms of their social relevance, as Brecht did.[42] Indeed, the collection of gestures is not systematically integrated into any meaningful order. The difficulty of attributing precise semiotic values to the auditory leitmotivs in Chekhov's plays can be transcended, if one realizes that they defy decoding in order to thematize the problem of meaning which is also at the core of the private dilemmas which the plays depict. Montage and the absence of meaning then become internally related in the semblance of art, as Adorno has indicated:

> Ultimately, art is illusion because it cannot escape the suggestion of meaning in the midst of meaninglessness. The unity of works of art which negate meaning must, however, also be disrupted; that is the function of montage, which both disavows unity thanks to the accentuated disparateness of the parts, and yet produces it as a principle of form.[43]

Irony and negation are additional marks of the dilemma. Olga's opening speech, while apparently addressed to Irina, is interrupted by the striking of the clock, and by the pause that follows her response to this. Her reminiscing is questioned by Irina, who asks why she brings up old memories at all. Olga continues in the same vein as before, despite the fact that her interrupted monologue is encroached upon once more through the interpolation of Chebutykin's and Tuzenbakh's remarks:

CHEBUTYKIN (*to Soliony and Tuzenbakh*): Not a chance in hell.
TUZENBAKH: Absolute nonsense of course.

(*TS*, p. 123)

This implicit undermining depends upon the ambiguous reference of the utterances involved; but what, may one ask, is the relative status of Masha's whistling, which appears to exist as a comment on both? Later, the short conversation on Vershinin is curtailed by the entry of Soliony and Chebutykin. The seriousness of Tuzenbakh's report on Vershinin is juxtaposed with Soliony's comic syllogistic travesty, whose statement of human strength is countered by Chebutykin's reference to human decay in a quotation he reads from the newspaper. This tripartite juxtaposition relativizes the utterances by implicitly questioning the difference between sense and nonsense, citation and seriousness. In fact, Chebutykin's reading might be taken as a bathetic revocation of Tuzenbakh's presentation of human suffering, for what is the real difference between one's hair falling out, and one's spouse attempting suicide? The problem of discourse is encountered again and again in Chekhov, as any absolute status is denied to the utterances of the characters, and techniques such as ironic juxtaposition, interruption and parody are employed to generate alienating perspectives on the individual utterance in such a way as to defuse the attempt to attribute any special meaning to it. Sequential negation is a typical mode of Chekhovian irony. While irony may be based on discrepancy with a third term taken as objective, very often in Chekhov, if there *is* a third term, it would seem to be the application of a principle of negation as such. However, these negations do not form part of a triadic dialectical movement: the process is not the agent of an ultimate synthesis. Instead, it implies a critique of absolute claims to knowledge – though the grounding of such a critique is ambiguous between relativism and scepticism – and further controverts the status of the text.

At the same time the technical devices which may be subsumed under strategies of negation and relativization constitute a principle of textual composition. Although the logic of interruption is to fragment the text, the repetition of interruptive techniques may become not a discohesive factor but an agent of homogenization. In the same way, the habitual actions of the characters both undermine the status of the dramaturgical action, and also structure the text. The use of non-verbal signs may be taken as a further attempt at composition, rather than the manufacture of moods and atmospheres. *Three Sisters* is characterized by contrasting experiences of space and light. The play opens at midday, and the set expresses openness, as the drawing-room expands into the ballroom, and this sense of spaciousness is enhanced by the cheerful shining of the sun. In contrast, Act II opens in darkness, though the scene is the same as in the previous act. The absence of light is remedied as Natasha enters, but her candle, in addition to casting light, visually anticipates the fiery glow of Act III and Masha's accusation that 'The way she goes about you'd think it was she who'd started the fire' (*TS*, p. 170). Natasha's association with light is ambiguous, as at one level she embodies forces of destruction. Her crossing the stage is repeated towards the end of the act – as it is soon before the end of Act III – initiating the next stage in her appropriation of space. This is underlined, as Act III opens, by the inner movement of the set into the cluttered bedroom of Olga and Irina, their beds surrounded by screens, which involves an increasingly claustrophobic experience of space, intensified by consciousness of the world beyond their room. While in Act I the relation of the set to the world beyond was expansive, now the effect is to impose the sense of a prison-like contraction of the stage. Act IV opens in midday light, as did Act I. Darkness and fire had been reciprocated during Act III by the dawn, but it is a dawn of dispossession as Natasha is firmly ensconced within the house and remains inside. The relation of light and space no longer involves the expansion from inner to outer; rather, it counterpoints the separation of the inner and outer worlds of the set, which has, as it were, been turned inside out. Natasha's ominous act of crossing the stage is left to her husband, whose performance of his wife's action and fulfilment of her maternal role express the subjugation of the Prozorovs, and the denial of their values. The relation of the set from Act I to Act IV is less obviously antithetical than it is in *The Cherry Orchard*, but is suited none the less to the montage techniques applied by Krejca in his production of *The Seagull*.[44] But collision and contradiction, the driving forces of montage, still express relation, and the symbolic substructure of the text is characterized by a setting up of relations between contradictory notions and experiences: light and darkness, space and the denial of space, freedom and imprisonment, inner and outer, the set and the world. It has an essentially integrating force on a text which is notable for a conflicting pull towards discomposition; indeed, the effect of discomposition *depends on* its relation to a textual framework.[45]

The generative concept of action involves a precise relationship between action and time. The act which is necessarily end-directed, which makes explicit in the future what was implicit in the past, evidently drives forward in time. This is true of both individual and dramaturgical action; indeed, the dialectical movement forwards in time of a given dramaturgical action is a direct function of the nature of individual action. In his classic study of

191

time in drama, Peter Pūtz clearly conceives of action in generative terms: 'Action presupposes a temporal progression, by producing change and driving towards completion from the beginning.'[46]

I have suggested that individual action in Chekhov's plays is not generative; indeed, when Durkheim equates the infinite goal and having no goal at all, the concept of action is stretched to the limits of its applicability, since an end or goal located in the future is essential to it. Furthermore, dialogue, which in terms of Hegelian theory and the conventions Chekhov has inherited is the motor of drama, has become equally problematic. If the palsying of intention prevents the characters' actions from generating any ominous forward movement, and if their often habitual words and actions merely fill in time, what is the status of the dramaturgical action? Is it, too, no more than a spurious attempt at plugging the gap between present and future? Mrs Ranevsky suggests as much in Act III of *The Cherry Orchard*:

> And still no sign of Leonid. I can't think what he's been up to in town all this time. The thing must be over by now. Either the estate's sold or the auction didn't take place, so why keep us in suspense all this time?
>
> (*CO*, p. 91)

Chekhov's late plays abound in references to past and future events, to arrivals and departures. They are notable for the specificity of their references to chronological time; at the beginning of *Three Sisters*, the clock strikes twelve, Kulygin compares his watch with the clock and declares it to be seven minutes fast. There are precise mentions of the ages of the characters, precise definitions of the temporal relation between past and present. Act IV of *Three Sisters* seems at first sight to be temporarily structured in terms of the analytic technique, and to work out the effect of the past on the present: the past is revealed in piecemeal fashion until past and present coincide in Tuzenbakh's duel with Soliony. However, it is difficult to establish any causal relation between the actions of figures in the play and the materialization of future events. The references to the future at the beginning of *The Seagull*, which generate expectancy on the part of the audience through the relation of present and future they seem to set up, develop a time structure which exists apart from the actions of the characters, and when future events do materialize, they may do so independently of individual action. The textual segment framed by Treplev's announcement that the play is due to start in ten minutes, and the actual commencement of the play, fills in the space that separates these instants in time. When, as Nina departs later, all projected future events have come about, one may legitimately question the status of the subsequent section of dramaturgical action if one applies *generative* criteria. Moreover, when future events are realized, they are de-dramatized; this is the case with Treplev's suicide, and with the duel in *Three Sisters*. Once again, there appears to be a contradiction between the model of drama Chekhov has taken over and the nature of action in the text, and the creation of a self-sufficient time structure is an attempt to resolve this contradiction. However, the composition of such a time structure involves further problems concerning the reference of scenic time, problems underlined by Walter Benjamin in the context of his comparison between film and stage: 'a clock that is working will always be a disturbance on the stage. There it cannot be permitted its function of measuring time. Even in a naturalistic play, astronomical time would clash with theatrical time.'[47]

Chekhov's dramatic practice does not necessarily require the presence of a clock on stage – though his complaints about the Moscow Art Theatre production of *The Cherry Orchard* suggest that this might have been of help[48] – but it does involve the collision Benjamin describes. The problems of naturalistic theatre can only be aggravated by the specificity of time in Chekhov, as the plays attempt to fulfil Castelvetro's requirement that the time of the representation and the action should coincide, but the existence of temporal gaps between the acts is inconsistent with the convention that determines the composition of the acts themselves. The experience of time in Chekhov's plays involves less the timelessness that Corrigan finds characteristic, than a radical disjunction between the chronicity of the action they present, and the convention of *kairos* inherent in dramatic form.[49]

CONCLUSION

In structural terms, Chekhov's late plays embody the most radical assault on the Hegelian and traditional models of drama in Europe at the turn of the twentieth century. While the late plays of Strindberg explode the pretensions of naturalistic representation and are evident forerunners of expressionist drama, Chekhov's work initiates a crisis in traditional drama in such a way as to push the concept of drama to its very limits. Similarly, although the plays of other major nineteenth-century dramatists such as Büchner and Ibsen problematize or negate the terms of reference provided by Hegelian theory, it is still possible to argue that they are, in many ways, written *against* Hegelian assumptions; in Chekhov's plays, however, the final implosion of Hegel's model of drama is achieved: freedom, volition, decision and will are concepts which in Chekhov's dramatic universe have no sense. Furthermore, the collapse of reasons for action, the disintegration of any normative guarantee for action preferences, the consequent paralysis of agency expressed in the contingency of 'intention': all these factors combine to signify that the acts of individual agents (if it is legitimate to speak of 'act' or 'agent' any more) simply cannot generate traditional drama's consequential movement forwards in time. This process is grounded in an anomic upheaval that now engulfs the very possibility of meaning, and precipitates the reduction of dialogue – once the dynamic of drama, and medium of communicative interaction – to verbal gesticulation under the dubious aegis of habit. The former gods that Durkheim wrote of are finally dead, and the new ones are as yet unknown. Joseph Wood Krutch, writing in 1953, wondered what the effect upon drama would be if the theories and procedures of playwrights such as Chekhov (who abolished action) and Pirandello (who got rid of character) were universally adopted. His answer was as follows:

> [O]ne is tempted to suggest somewhat light-mindedly that whatever else we may or may not be able to predict about the future which lies across the chasm one thing seems fairly certain: There will not be any plays in it.[50]

A year earlier, *Waiting for Godot* had been published in Paris.

NOTES

1 See Antonin Artaud, *The Theatre and its Double*, New York: Grove Press, 1958. The best short introduction to Artaud's work in English is Martin Esslin, *Artaud*, Glasgow: Fontana/Collins, 1976.
2 See *Brecht on Theatre*, ed. and trans. John Willett, London: Methuen, 1982.
3 See Joseph Wood Krutch, *'Modernism' in Modern Drama: A definition and an estimate*, New York: Russell & Russell, 1962.

4 See Peter Szondi, *Theorie des modernen Dramas 1880–1950*, Frankfurt aM: Suhrkamp, 1971. A detailed critique of Szondi's model of drama is presented in Steve Giles, 'Szondi's theory of modern drama', *British Journal of Aesthetics* 27: 3 (Summer 1987), pp. 268–77.

5 Suzanne Langer, *Feeling and Form: A theory of art developed from 'Philosophy in a New Key'*, London: Routledge & Kegan Paul, 1963, p. 306.

6 Ibid., p. 307.

7 See G. W. F. Hegel, *Aesthetics: Lectures on fine art*, trans. T. M. Knox, Oxford: Clarendon Press, 1975.

8 See Steve Giles, *The Problem of Action in Modern European Drama*, Stuttgart: Heinz, 1981.

9 Page references will be made in the main text in abbreviated form using the following editions: Anton Chekhov, *Ivanov, The Seagull, Three Sisters*, trans. and ed. Ronald Hingley, Oxford: Oxford University Press, 1972; Anton Chekhov, *Uncle Vanya, The Cherry Orchard*, trans. and ed. Ronald Hingley, Oxford: Oxford University Press, 1970. The abbreviations *S*, *TS*, *UV* and *CO* will be used, followed by a page number.

10 Quoted in *Twentieth-Century Views on Chekhov*, ed. R. L. Jackson, Englewood Cliffs: Prentice Hall, 1967, p. 15.

11 M. N. Stroeva, '*The Three Sisters* in the production of the Moscow Art Theatre', in Jackson, *Twentieth-Century Views on Chekhov*, pp. 121–35 (p. 132).

12 Harvey Pitcher, *The Chekhov Play: A new interpretation*, London: Chatto, 1973, p. 9.

13 Samuel Beckett, *Proust*, London: Calder & Boyars, 1965, p. 11.

14 Ibid., pp. 18–19.

15 Ibid., p. 28.

16 Compare Georg Lukács's account of the function of the Nietzschean Superman in late bourgeois ideology in *Von Nietzsche zu Hitler, oder der Irrationalismus und die deutsche Politik*, Frankfurt aM: Fischer, 1966, pp. 27–39.

17 Pitcher, *The Chekhov Play*, p. 148.

18 Ibid., p. 149.

19 V. I. Pudovkin, *Mother: A film*, London: Lorrimer, 1973.

20 See H. Seton-Watson, *The Decline of Imperial Russia: 1855–1914*, London: Methuen, 1952, pp. 109ff.

21 Walter Benjamin, 'The work of art in the age of mechanical reproduction', in *Illuminations*, ed. Hannah Arendt and trans. Harry Zohn, Glasgow: Fontana/Collins, 1977, pp. 219–53 (p. 225).

22 See R. D. Laing, *The Divided Self: An existential study in sanity and madness*, Harmondsworth: Penguin, 1965, pp. 69ff.

23 Emile Durkheim, *Selected Writings*, ed. and introduced by Anthony Giddens, Cambridge: Cambridge University Press, 1972, p. 94.

24 Ibid., p. 174.

25 Ibid., p. 244.

26 Ibid., p. 175.

27 Ibid., p. 175.

28 Pitcher, *The Chekhov Play*, p. 21.

29 Szondi, *Theorie des modernen Dramas*, p. 37.
30 Dmitri Chizhevsky, 'Chekhov in the development of Russian literature', in Jackson, *Twentieth-Century Views on Chekhov* pp. 49–61 (pp.
   58–9).
31 S. D. Balukhaty, '*The Cherry Orchard*: A Formalist approach', in Jackson, *Twentieth-Century Views on Chekhov*, pp. 136–46 (p. 139).
32 R. W. Corrigan, 'The drama of Anton Chekhov', in *Modern Drama*,
   ed. Bogard and Oliver, New York: Oxford University Press, 1965,
   pp. 73–98 (p. 86).
33 Pitcher, *The Chekhov Play*, p. 21.
34 A. Skaftymov, 'Principles of structure in Chekhov's plays', in Jackson,
   Twentieth-Century Views on Chekhov, pp. 69–87 (p. 70).
35 Corrigan, 'The drama of Anton Chekhov', p. 86.
36 *Ivanov* was completed in 1889.
37 S. M. Eisenstein, *Film Form: Essays in film theory*, ed. and trans. Jan
   Leyda, New York: Meridian Books, 1957.
38 Ibid., p. 34.
39 See Benjamin, 'The work of art in the age of mechanical reproduction', pp. 231–2.
40 Ibid., p. 235.
41 See Georg Lukács, *Zur Ontologie des gesellschaftlichen Seins*, Neuwied:
   Luchterhand, 1971, pp. 53ff.
42 See Brecht, *Brecht on Theatre*, pp. 104–5.
43 T. W. Adorno, *Aesthetische Theorie*, Frankfurt aM: Suhrkamp, 1973,
   pp. 231–2.
44 See *Theater Heute*, Jahressonderheft 1972, p. 118.
45 Compare Adorno, *Aesthetische Theorie*, p. 237: 'In terms of its values
   in artistic language, asymmetry can only be conceived of in relation
   to symmetry.'
46 Peter Pütz, *Die Zeit im Drama: Zur Technik dramatischer Spannung*,
   Göttingen: Vandenhoeck & Ruprecht, 1970, p. 39.
47 Benjamin, 'The work of art in the age of mechanical reproduction',
   p. 249.
48 Balukhaty, '*The Cherry Orchard*', p. 146.
49 This terminology is taken from Frank Kermode, *The Sense of an
   Ending: Studies in the theory of fiction*, Oxford: Oxford University Press,
   1970, pp. 46ff.
50 Krutch, '*Modernism' in Modern Drama*, p. 87.

4

IN SEARCH OF TOTALITY

On narrative and history in
Fredric Jameson's *The Political
Unconscious*

Sara Danius

METACOMMENTARY AND THE INTERPRETATION OF HISTORY

Sometime in the early 1970s, Frank Lentricchia writes in *After the New Criticism*, 'we awoke from the dogmatic slumber of our phenomenological sleep to find that a new presence had taken absolute hold over our avant-garde critical imagination: Jacques Derrida.'[1] It is probably no exaggeration to claim that with the arrival of recent French critical thought on the American intellectual scene, for which the name of Derrida serves as the privileged emblem, the phenomenon which Fredric Jameson often refers to as the 'theoretical marketplace' began to take proper shape. During the 1970s, the ground was thus prepared for a radically new kind of critical awareness. Concepts like 'meaning', 'totality', 'truth' were problematized; even the concepts of 'interpretation' and 'history' became, it would seem, outmoded, at least as positive entities. As we know, the 1980s were to see a booming interest in critical theory, in particular within the field of academic literary criticism and scholarship. For two decades now, the publishing market has managed to produce, perhaps paradoxically, an overwhelming number of works considering various aspects of the so-called crisis of interpretation, and continues to do so. The student of literature is thus faced with an abundant number of theoretical options, all the way from New Criticism, myth criticism, structuralism, poststructuralism, deconstruction, psychoanalysis, feminism, Marxism, to the New Historicism – not to mention the numerous

197

subdivisions, and more or less happy marriages between various strands.

When Fredric Jameson published *The Political Unconscious: Narrative as a socially symbolic act* in 1981, he stressed that his intention was not to compete on the theoretical marketplace. Instead, his proposed Marxist metacriticism sets out to transcend the competition itself. Indeed, Jameson takes as his goal the highlighting of the theoretical pluralism and the provision of nothing less than the 'absolute horizon of all reading and all interpretation'.[2] Given the general hostility towards concepts such as totality, it does not, as Dominick LaCapra has rightly noted, 'take much acuity to decode Jameson's assertive use of notions of "absolute horizon" and of centrality as a polemical gesture'.[3]

The following is a critical examination of Fredric Jameson's conception of narrative and history, and, more specifically, how these ideas are elaborated into the construction of a Marxist hermeneutics in *The Political Unconscious*. The focus and ambition of this enquiry is thereby twofold. First, I wish to discuss Jameson's proposed interpretive programme, largely on its own terms, by concentrating on the notions of narrative and history. Second, I aim to discuss the principles underlying his readings in *The Political Unconscious*, with a rationale for choosing the reading of Joseph Conrad's novels. For although this book has been widely recognized as a crucial contribution to the conception of cultural studies in many English-speaking academic institutions, and although the number of review essays on *The Political Unconscious* is remarkable, there has been surprisingly little interest in Jameson's readings, either as 'applications', or as readings in their own right. Most commentators have found it sufficient to discuss what passes for the handy 'theory', which then is equated with the introductory hundred pages of the study, called 'On interpretation'.[4]

Jameson, himself, maintains in the preface, that he is content to 'have the theoretical sections of the book judged and tested against its interpretative practice', while warning that the practice should not be transformed into so many mere examples, buttressing the more rigorous theoretical statements. For Jameson it is not a question of maintaining the distinction between theory and practice; for him that dichotomy is transcended by Marxism. This is not the place to discuss the possible truth of that statement. But it is clear that with poststructuralism, the seemingly clear-cut distinction has been problematized. It is therefore all the more ironical that the readings have been neglected.

As far as the distinction between theory and practice in Jameson's study is concerned, I would like to propose that the readings are not mere applications. Rather, they may be seen as 'extended theory', not only because the readings of Balzac, Gissing and Conrad explicate and pursue the hermeneutical technique in more detail, but also because these analyses, by virtue of their supplementary relation to the introductory section and the intermediate chapter on the genre of romance, amount to an implicit historiography of the novel, a writing of the history of the bourgeois novel from a historical materialist point of view. This provides us with a second reason for approaching the book not as consisting of two separate parts, distinctively different from one another, but rather as a whole, as a narrative about historiography, which we could 'judge and test against' the more straightforward, explicit statements about narrative and history in the introductory section. I would therefore like to suggest that to discuss Jameson's proposed interpretive programme is ultimately at one with a discussion of his philosophy of history.

Jameson does not argue the priority of the Marxist perspective because it offers a 'better' hermeneutics, in the respect of being more faithful to the presumed intention or content of a literary work. Instead, he holds that the supremacy of the Marxist perspective derives from the fact that, as a rigorous philosophy of history, it is capable of historicizing various theories of interpretation by means of construing their conditions of possibility. The insights and blindnesses of these interpretive methods are thereby relativized, but Jameson does not repudiate them. They possess a limited authority which, he asserts, descends from 'their faithful consonance with this or that local law of a fragmented social life, this or that subsystem of a complex and mushrooming cultural superstructure' (p. 10). Marxism, however, is said to exceed all these interpretive methods because it is capable of showing how the enumerated theoretical schools rely on a so-called 'interpretive code' or 'master narrative', according to which a given text is rewritten. The illusion of universality and eternal truth, which the various deciphering techniques tend to project in one way or another, works to silence the cultural past and social significance of the text, and conceals ultimately the fact that the interpretive paradigm or set of theoretical assumptions underlying a technique of decipherment are historically specific as well. Relying on what Jameson claims to be a 'genuine' philosophy of history, Marxism, by contrast, seeks to open out texts onto history, to make them speak their past. Thus the Marxist technique of interpretation proposed by Jameson attempts to conceive under what conditions a text is or seems meaningful in the first place. History, then, is not a master narrative or an interpretive paradigm, but the ultimate condition for understanding. *The Political Unconscious* is consequently an argument for a philosophy of history and a proposal of a specific interpretation of literary texts all at once. The pressing question, therefore, is not so much 'What is literature?' but 'What is history, and how do texts and our understanding of them relate to history?'

To this end Jameson proposes the critical strategy of 'metacommentary', a method which presupposes that

> we never really confront a text immediately, in all its freshness as a thing-in-itself. Rather, texts come before us as the always-already-read; we apprehend them through sedimented layers of previous interpretations, or – if the text is brand-new – through the sedimented reading habits and categories developed by those inherited interpretive traditions.
>
> (p. 9)

The object of study is therefore less the text itself. Rather, what we handily refer to as 'the text' has now become 'the interpretations through which we attempt to confront and to appropriate it' (pp. 9f.).

Jameson's first comprehensive attempt to elaborate this metacritical strategy is to be found in 'Metacommentary'.[5] In this 1971 essay, he spells out what he takes to be the function of literary criticism in arguing for a restoration of the validity of the then disreputable notion of interpretation, made more or less obsolete due to the dominance of various formalistic approaches within literary criticism. It may be interesting to take a closer look at this essay, since it constitutes one of Jameson's earliest proposals of an interpretive technique.

'Metacommentary'

The essay 'Metacommentary' takes as its polemic point of departure Susan Sontag's influential anti-aesthetic in *Against Interpretation* which, as its title straightforwardly indicates, denounces the traditional *explication de texte*, i.e. the kind of literary criticism concerned with the question: 'What does it mean?' In her 1964 essay, Sontag argues that

> interpretation means plucking a set of elements (the X, the Y, the Z, and so forth) from the whole work. The task of interpretation is virtually one of translation. The interpreter says, 'Look, don't you see that X is really – or really means – A? That Y is really B? That Z is really C?'[6]

The immediate meaning of a text, i.e. that which a text appears to 'be about', is, Sontag argues, bracketed by the critic as mere quasi-content, disguising what is taken to be the true meaning lurking somewhere in the depth. The work of art is thus altered according to the interpretive standards of the critic, and in our time, Sontag argues, that means in most cases the paradigms of Marx and Freud. The reductionist manoeuvre which goes under the name of interpretation can only be met by a different critical strategy which implies a rejection of the problem 'what does it mean' and a shift towards *how* the work of art means. What is at issue for Sontag is therefore a kind of formalism, a celebration of stylistic devices and techniques, a critical strategy not necessarily theoretically underpinned. On the contrary, the work of art provides an almost sensuous experience which, Sontag asserts, art commentary should posit as its starting-point. In the companion essay 'On style', Sontag derives this crucial experience from the 'style' of the work, which even tells of the 'will' on the part of the author: 'In art, "content" is, as it were, the pretext, the goal, the lure which engages consciousness in essentially *formal* processes of transformation.'[7] The style of the work of art does not, therefore, evoke content, but is the expression of the experience of that content. 'In place of a hermeneutics', Sontag concludes, 'we need an erotics of art.'[8]

Ironically enough, however, it would seem that Sontag's proposal ends where interpretation as a problem begins. To conceive of the style, the form, or whatever is supposed to be 'sensual' or 'concrete' in a work of art, is as much a conceptual affair as the designation of that work's assumed content. The critic, it seems, is thus always obliged to resort to the fate of rewriting and, in a sense, translation.

Jameson confronts Sontag's discussion by throwing the argument onto another level. The immediate problem is, he claims, not the nature of interpretation; rather, what is at issue is the actual need for critical treatment – why is it that a work of art needs commentary in the first place? This strategy enables Jameson to put the problem of interpretation in a historical perspective:

> [What] initially needs explanation is . . . not how we go about interpreting a text properly, but rather why we should even have to do so. All thinking about interpretation must sink itself in the strangeness, the unnaturalness, of the hermeneutic situation; or to put it another way, every individual interpretation must include an interpretation of its own existence, must show its own credentials and justify itself: every commentary must be at the same time a metacommentary as well.[9]

Yet Jameson holds that content needs no interpretation. Content is instantly meaningful to the reader because it is concrete, being 'essentially social and historical experience'.[10] The problem, however, is that today this content is situated in the depth of the narrative text, as a latent message, which, Jameson suggests, has to pass some sort of censor, and therefore is forced to produce a manifest message. Accordingly, the task of the critic is not to interpret either the manifest or the latent substance, but to reveal the hidden content. This latter strategy calls for a hermeneutics concerning itself not with 'translating' content, but with investigating the formal relations and transformations between surface and depth: 'all stylization, all abstraction in the form, ultimately expresses some profound inner logic in its content and is ultimately dependent for its existence on the structures of the raw materials themselves.'[11] A rigorous commentary on formal features will therefore elicit the latent historical content, he argues.

It would seem, then, that the need for art commentary or interpretation is itself symptomatic of our historical predicament. It is a judgement on us as readers in history. Explaining this circumstance by sketching out a brief history of the narratological form of the novel, Jameson is obviously inspired by the early

George Lukács's *Theory of the Novel* (1916) and the notion of the epic age, located by Lukács in the Homeric era. Arguing that the Greece of Homer was a homogeneous world which knew no difference between appearance and essence, a world whose wholeness was reflected by the epic of the period, Lukács posited the epic as integration and plenitude, from which narrative was supposed to have fallen. As a result, the novel emerged:

> The novel is the epic of an age in which the extensive totality of life is no longer directly given, in which the immanence of meaning in life has become a problem, yet which still thinks in terms of totality.[12]

In similar fashion, Jameson argues that there was a time when the content of a novel was immediately meaningful, because it corresponded to and was somehow congruous with the concrete social conditions of that historical moment, which by virtue of its capacity to provide 'an ordering of events revealed itself to be a coherent totality'.[13] But Jameson's golden age is that of narrative realism, which is supposed to precede the fall. Fielding's *Tom Jones* is his axiomatic example of the novel of plenitude. Our satisfaction with the classical well-made plot is, he suggests, a sign of our satisfaction with that society as well, precisely because it was able to provide the very possibility of that plot. But when we reach the 'plotless' or modernistic novel, society has, since the emergence of the capitalist mode of production, gradually become a dismembered totality, and is thus no longer capable of offering the raw materials for a coherent plot. Hence, with the plotless novel, interpretation 'reasserts its claims with a vengeance'.[14]

Jameson's argument is primarily a cognitive one, since he holds that reason, confronted with the dissolution of the unity of action and character, starts to 'work unconsciously ... unable to cease making those intricate cross-references and interconnections that the surface of the work seems to deny'.[15] For beneath the amorphous surface of the modernistic novel there is always a message, a content, which is a type of '*Erlebnis,* or *expérience vécue,* a lived experience of some sort, no matter how minimal or specialized'.[16] This content, moreover, need not be interpreted; it needs dismantling only because it is already shaped and meaningful, being 'nothing more nor less than the very components of our concrete social life: words, thoughts, objects, desires, people, places, activities'.[17]

Discussing the plotless novel, Jameson appears to suggest that the mind is apt to reorganize the decomposed surface of this kind of novel so as to restore, if not a meaningful and coherent whole, then at least a temporal ordering which endows the events with meaning; and, further, that this cognitive reorganization proceeds from some sort of arche-structure which, moreover, accords with the way lived experience was offered shape in that particular social organism in which Fielding conceived his novel so successfully. In other words, Jameson seems to imply that we apply a kind of cognitive *Ur-form* when attempting to understand and confer meaning on our life stories, and that this form governs our readings of novels as well. In fact, Jameson even implies that this *Ur-form* corresponds to a narrative deep structure: 'The plotless work thus stands before us as a kind of rebus in narrative language, a strange kind of code written in events or hieroglyphs, and *analogous to primitive myth, or fairy tales.*'[18] We are thus not very far from the structuralist dream of finding the deep structural pattern of all narrative, that is, the narrative grammar generating all kinds of narrative utterances. For what Jameson appears to suggest is indeed that there is an essential structure common to both the plotless novel and the primitive myth, and, by implication therefore, all narratives. This structure, it seems, accords with the cognitive one; that is, the way in which reason is supposed to organize data.

Jameson therefore advocates the structuralist method, because in positing the binary opposition and relational values (e.g. identity/difference) rather than substance as its major categories, structuralism is concerned primarily with organization rather than content. However, he adds the crucial proviso that the basic structuralist categories need to be transformed into historical ones, because they are

> conceived by the structuralists to be ultimate and rather Kantian forms of the mind, fixed and universal modes of organizing and perceiving experience. . . . For structuralism necessarily falls short of a genuine metacommentary in that it thus forbids itself all comment on itself and on its own conceptual instruments, which are taken to be eternal.[19]

If this is so, then there is a peculiar sliding between two incompatible positions in Jameson's reasoning; on the one hand, a belief in some kind of cognitive *Ur-form* related to narrative structure, and on the other, the historical-materialist stance and the obvious refusal of Kantian idealism. In the concluding section of this chapter, I will argue that this tension informs the basic argument of *The Political Unconscious* as well.

Metacommentary, however, aims at resolving this dilemma by, as we have seen, problematizing the need for interpretation and construing the preconditions of the question 'What does it mean?', a strategy which perhaps seems like a detour but which actually contains within itself the point of departure of the interpretive act. Thus metacommentary 'directs the attention back to history itself, and to the historical situation of the commentator as well as of the work'.[20]

In conclusion, Jameson's proposed interpretive technique posits a model of the work of art, which draws on, first, a Freudian surface–depth metaphor, that is, the idea that there exists simultaneously a 'manifest and latent content ... disguise and message disguised', and second, the structuralist view of the work of art because of its stress on formal organization.[21] Thus structuralism provides the tools for describing and explicating the mechanisms of 'censorship', that is to say, the formal transformations of the original message.

Jameson's proposed interpretive technique can in this way be seen as a mixture of structuralism's anti-substantialism on the one hand, and classical hermeneutical belief in the Word as revealing (the Holy) Truth on the other. Or, by drawing on Paul Ricœur's well-known distinction, we could describe metacommentary as a twofold strategy: Jameson's hermeneutics sets out as one of suspicion in refusing to treat the surface message on its own terms, and, having demystified the apparent meaning of the text, it ends up as a positive hermeneutics, as one of sympathy, in aiming at restoring the 'original message' situated in the depth: 'the object forbidden'.[22]

History as absent cause

We have now seen how Jameson promotes an interpretive programme which presupposes something of a hypostatization of *Erlebnis* or *expérience vécue*. This notion of content as just being there in some irreducible essence is problematized by two

205

principal ideas. One is his own point of departure: historical materialism and the related idea that human cognition changes over time, all of which is, in the last instance, due to the prevailing material conditions in a given society. It follows, then, that the *Erlebnis* of a literary work can hardly be said to have a fixed meaning, as he seems to suggest. Ironically enough, Jameson appears to neglect the historical distance between text and interpreter.

The other idea is to do with the problem of representation. A novel is a text, constituted by signs. Here the Saussurean notion, radicalized by poststructuralism, most notably by Derrida, presents itself, namely the idea that a sign is always a question of cultural and historical conventions.[23] As is well known, Derrida has developed the view that the 'meaning' of a signifier, i.e. the relation between signifier and what is signified, is never fully present due to the fact that the signifier bears the mark of its difference from all other signifiers. As a result, the signifier becomes effective as a trace, since it is marked by all the possible absent meanings whose differences produce a particular signifier and its meaning-effect. There is, then, no one-to-one relation between representation and that which is being represented, between signifier and signified. Accordingly, the ontological difference between text and world makes clear that a text can scarcely be said to embody or make real 'essentially social and historical experience'. Clearly, poststructuralism poses difficulties for the notion of an immediately meaningful and fixed content, and indeed the idea of a content as such.

In *The Political Unconscious*, Jameson anticipates precisely the philosophical critique sketched out above. There is, to be sure, a great difference between the interpretive technique proposed in 'Metacommentary' and its implicit assumptions, and the full-fledged Marxist hermeneutics in *The Political Unconscious*, where Jameson comes across as a theorist in his own right. Generally speaking, the philosophical idealist tendency is now less pronounced, and the dialectical historical-materialist stance foregrounded. But there are similarities which need to be stressed. His prime concern in the latter work is still how to interpret and conceptualize historical content; likewise, his principal methodological proposals are very much in the spirit of structuralism and Freudian psychoanalysis, albeit slightly revised in the wake of poststructuralism and deconstruction. In a way, Jameson attempts to work out 'the Structuralist procedure' into 'a genuine *hermeneutics*', a critical project he proposed at the end of *The Prison-House of Language* (1972).[24] Such a project would ultimately 'reopen text and analytic process alike to all the winds of history' in seeking to reconcile 'synchronic analysis and historical awareness . . . structure and self-consciousness, language and history'.[25]

Taking into consideration the poststructuralist critique of the uses of the concepts of meaning and history, and the related attack on the traditional notion of interpretation understood as a matter of explicating content, Jameson is anxious not to posit the concept of history as a positive one, fully present to itself as it were, since this would entail that the concept of history assumes the position of a transcendental signified, a move which would undermine the powerful point of departure of Marxism. Rather, as the a priori 'untranscendable' horizon, history can never be subjected to representation, because, in Jameson's view, history is the ultimately determining instance. History is therefore what makes meaning, understanding and representation possible in the first place.

Indeed, *The Political Unconscious* can usefully be seen as a complex and multi-layered response to the poststructuralist stance which finds its epitome in Derrida's famous and often misunderstood phrase, 'Il n'y a pas de hors-texte.' Insisting on the primacy of the *hors-texte* or extra-textual, Jameson, for his part, aims at elaborating an anti-transcendental Marxist hermeneutics. This is no doubt an impressive task. Cornel West sums up Jameson's megalithic project by proposing that the general question haunting *The Political Unconscious* reads: 'How to take history, class struggle, and capitalist dehumanization seriously after the profound poststructuralist deconstructions of solipsistic Cartesianism, transcendental Kantianism, teleological Hegelianism, genetic Marxism, and recuperative humanism?'[26] For Jameson, the most striking insights into the problems to do with representation, hermeneutics and history are provided by Gilles Deleuze and Félix Guattari on the one hand, and Louis Althusser on the other. As we shall see, the former articulate the problems intertwined with interpretive activity in what for Jameson becomes a highly productive critique; the latter makes available a Marxist theoretical solution to the poststructuralist impasse: the exclusive focus on the signifier.

In *Anti-Oedipus* (1972), Deleuze and Guattari discuss the

interpretive technique of Freudian psychoanalytic criticism.[27] They argue that by means of postulating the sexual dynamics of the nuclear family as an interpretive paradigm and therefore as a myth of origin, Freudian psychoanalysis reduces the richness of everyday experience and mutilates the potentially multiple referentiality of the analysand's story, the literary text, or any other object treated as occasion of explication. Pursuing an allegedly repressed idea, content, or experience 'beneath' the 'surface' message, Freudian psychoanalysis conceives of the 'surface' text as the phenomenal appearance of a more fundamental and real level situated in the depth: Meaning itself. In other words, the surface level is rewritten in terms of the second, deeper level, whereby the former is reduced into the latter, seen as significance *per se.*

Freudian psychoanalysis, then, relies on a system of allegorical interpretation, for it treats the surface level as an allegory, since it is not conceived of as immediately meaningful in itself. To this end, the paradigm of the sexual dynamics of the nuclear family provides the privileged allegorical key because of its status as the ultimate level and source of meaning. The problem, however, is that the Freudian family narrative is itself another allegory. For when we realize that this holy family structure is a recent historical phenomenon, limited mostly to Western countries, then its universal significance is shattered; and, consequently, this family narrative is revealed as the very beginning and the very end of Freudian psychoanalysis: in a word, as a transcendental signified.

Following the critique raised by Deleuze and Guattari, Jameson sets out to argue that by positing a master discourse in order to designate the meaning of a specific cultural artefact or discourse, most interpretive techniques rely on a system of allegorical interpretation. This applies to such interpretive methods as the structural, the myth-critical, the ethical, the existential, the phenomenological, where the master discourse is constituted by, respectively, Language, the myth of the origin of all human behaviour, the greatness of human nature, anxiety and the fear of freedom, and, finally, Time (pp. 58ff.).

Jameson also maintains, however, that even Deleuze and Guattari, contrary to their intentions, project a new interpretive programme in its own right precisely by substituting the question 'What does it mean?' for 'How does it work?' (p. 22). It may be interesting to note that Jameson, by the same token, raises a similar critique against other major proponents of the so-called anti-interpretive theoretical current.[28] Deleuze and Guattari none the less provide him with a productive perspective, in particular because of their politicized notion of interpretation.

By situating the emergence of Freudian psychoanalysis in late nineteenth-century bourgeois life in Europe, Jameson argues that we are thus able to recognize that there are ideological reasons for the privileged status of the nuclear family. In taking this type of family for granted, Freudian psychoanalysis can be said to operate within the structural limitations imposed upon Freud by his epoch. What we have encountered is, in other words, the tacit ideology of Freud's interpretive apparatus. From the present perspective, then, ideology works by way of closure, or, in Jameson's words, as a 'strategy of containment'.

There is, however, a second difficulty which Freudian psychoanalysis overlooks, or rather conceals, by virtue of its specific technique of decipherment, a theoretical difficulty which is crucial to Marxism. This is the problem of causality and mediation. For instance, let us suppose that a case of female hysteria is traced back to the sexual dynamics of that woman's childhood; here the suggestion would be that the hysterical behaviour is a symptom of repressed childhood experiences. When, however, this behaviour is explained in terms of the Freudian family narrative, the analysis not only collapses the manifest level into the latent level, it also implies a form of causal relation between the manifest level and the alleged proto-level without reflecting on the very nature of that presumed causality. This causal relation often tends to assume a specific guise, a privileged trope, commonly that of homology or some sort of formal identity. In other words, the juxtaposition of similar forms solves as it were a causal problem, and neglects the mediating relations between the two phenomena, separated by, for instance, time.

Time creates difference, a fact which the interpretive operation described above not only disregards, but also effaces. A reflection upon the etymology of the term 'homology' speaks for itself: from Greek *homologia* (agreement), from *homologos* (agreeing), from *homo* + *legein* (to speak); thus, the homology speaks the same. Hence, the surface structure and the deep structure of a text, or, similarly, the manifest and the latent message, are seen as ultimately speaking the same; and as a result, the interpretation/analysis happily confirms its own underlying theoretical assumptions by virtue of having discovered its own conceptual paradigm in the surface level of the text or discourse in question.

Causality and determination are issues central to Marxism, particularly Marxist cultural criticism, which must attempt to conceptualize the mediatory relations within the social totality. It therefore remains to be seen how Jameson avoids the fallacy of the master discourse when setting out to propose an antitranscendental Marxist hermeneutic which posits history as the untranscendable horizon and ultimately determining instance. It is here that the French Marxist philosopher Louis Althusser proves to be of vital importance. His critique of various forms of so-called effectivity in *Reading Capital* (1966) amounts to a conception of totality, history and causality which can be said to offer a point of transition, a theoretical relay, enabling Jameson to elaborate a hermeneutics which seems capable of respecting the epistemological firmament of Marxism without turning the economic into a master discourse.

Althusser's interpretation of Marx's *Capital* is a critical and restorative project all at once: he seeks to question the way in which the relations between base and superstructure have been theorized by leading Marxist theorists, and does so in order to rid Marxism of its idealist, teleological and historicist tendencies. In short, Althusser sets out to criticize what he takes to be the prevailing understanding of Marx's theory: the Hegelian interpretation of Marx. Discussing the problem of mediation and totalization, he distinguishes and criticizes two models of causality, the mechanistic and the expressive, the only models available to what he calls classical philosophy. He then proceeds to advocate a third model: that of structural causality. The mechanistic model of causality refers to the uncomplicated cause-and-effect phenomenon. For Althusser, this model has no validity in the elaboration of an acceptable conception of the concrete totality and the mediatory relations between its semi-autonomous levels. Expressive causality is also denounced by Althusser. This model, he writes, 'dominates all Hegel's thought'.[29] It denotes a holistic view which posits the whole as possessing an inner essence, to which the component parts of the whole relate by way of mere reflection, that is to say, they are conceived of as expressions of that inner principle which for Hegel is the Absolute Spirit. Very schematically, Hegelian history is the dialectical unfolding of a *Wesen*, the total movement through time and space encompassed by the superior intentionality of the Absolute Spirit, whose realization, which is at one with the world's coming to consciousness of itself as being endowed with this divine intentionality, constitutes the *telos* of history. What Althusser objects to in Hegel's conception of totality is, as Martin Jay has pointed out, 'its reduction of the whole to the alienated exfoliation of an original simple unity. All of the elements in the totality were thus merely manifestations or "moments" of the essential genetic principle underlying the whole.'[30] The Hegelian conception of causality is therefore intertwined with the idea of a teleological history, both of which are features which, according to Althusser, have retained a far too powerful hold over Marxist thinking. Setting out to rectify Marxism in a rereading of Marx, he claims that a new model of causality, entirely unrelated to the Hegelian one, was under way in Marx, and with that an unprecedented conception of the world-as-totality. Althusser's interpretation of Marx thus assumes the form of a proposal of the model of structural causality, for he repudiates the notion of a base determining the superstructure. To be sure, he insists on the priority of a holistic perspective, but, and this is a crucial point, this whole comprises several semi-autonomous levels, and is essentially decentred. As Norman Geras has pointed out, Althusser conceives of the social totality 'as a hierarchy of practices or structures, genuinely distinct from one another, and although, amongst them, the economic is causally primary, the others are relatively autonomous, possessing a *specific effectivity* of their own and, in some degree, independent histories'.[31] Althusser thus invented the concept of structural causality to denote the causality of the social formation as a 'structure-in-dominance', i.e. the determination of a structure by a structure. The structure, however, is present only as an immanence in its effects: '*the whole existence of the structure consists of its effects*, in short . . . the structure, which is merely a specific combination of its peculiar elements, is nothing outside its effects.'[32] The causality of the structure is thus constituted by the sum of the various effects immanent in the various parts of the structure. Hence, as an instance of effectivity, the structure is absent as such, present only in its effects.

By means of positing class struggle as the true site of historical development and change, Marx assigned, according to Althusser, a primordial status to antagonisms and contradictions, which thereby become the motor of history. The idealist notion of a superior intentionality encompassing the movements of history is thus displaced. Or, to put it another way, the Hegelian notion of essence is replaced by a different paradigm – that of contradiction or relation. Marxist history, Althusser contends, 'is a process without a *telos*'.

It is here that Althusser has proved important to Marxism in general and Marxist cultural criticism in particular. As Jay has emphasized, one of the central implications of Althusser's work 'was the displacement of the economy from its causally central role as the motor of history'.[33] Given the fact that culture traditionally belongs to the superstructure, the question of how to conceive of the mediating relations between base and superstructure becomes an immediate problem for Marxist cultural criticism if it is to avoid treating culture in an instrumental fashion, which results in the conflation of base and superstructure, of economy and culture. To construe culture as an effect, or as a reflection of the economic mode of production, is to construe culture as an expression of the economic. That is to say, it is not only to rewrite culture according to the allegedly fundamental paradigm of the economic, a move which collapses the semi-autonomous status of culture into the economic, but it is also to assign a transcendental status to the economic, which thus becomes the master discourse of Marxism.

It is easy to see that the various hermeneutical models criticized by Jameson and Deleuze and Guattari are pinned down precisely by this tendency to posit a whole of which the parts become reducible to a hypothesized inner essence, be it the nuclear family, God's almighty power and everpresence, or the language system itself. This inner essence becomes the master narrative, the fundamental source of meaning, according to which all kinds of narratives are rewritten and explicated.

We are now in a better position to understand why Jameson holds that history is the a priori 'untranscendable' horizon. However, it is important to stress, as Geoff Bennington has remarked, that in Jameson's reading of Althusser's structural causality, 'the mode of production is not a level among others but the structure itself'.[34] Indeed, for Althusser, the mode of production was merely one of the levels within the whole, albeit the most crucial one. Now, Jameson does not only equate the structure with the mode of production, but also with the whole, the absent cause, and history (pp. 35f.). In the following pages, we will examine how

Jameson's appropriation of Althusserian structural causality enables him to elaborate a negative and a positive hermeneutics simultaneously. Drawing on Althusser, Jameson thus suggests that

> history is *not* a text, not a narrative, master or otherwise, but that, as an absent cause, it is inaccessible to us except in textual form, and that our approach to it and to the Real itself necessarily passes through its prior textualization, its narrativization in the political unconscious.
>
> (p. 35)

To say that history is the absent cause is to claim that history is the fundamental and remote background against which we read, perceive and conceive all kinds of phenomena in the world. History, then, is what makes interpretation possible. Consequently, interpretation is a question of trying to establish the links between the text and the intractable horizon of history.

We have now seen how Jameson is able to insist on the *hors texte* by means of positing the mode of production as an absent cause. Thus he restores the validity of the concept of history. In this way, Jameson's position saves the Althusserian priority of a holistic perspective, and polemicizes at the same time against poststructuralist views of history as deferred discourse.

The problem of mediation

Althusserian Marxism redefines determination in terms of structural causality, and rethinks the totality as a structured complex unity. For Marxist cultural criticism, therefore, the pressing question is how to conceive of the level of culture in relation to the other relatively autonomous levels within the social totality. To be sure, Althusser repudiated the traditional Marxist way of conceiving of the mediatory relations between base and superstructure. Jameson argues, however, that Marxist cultural criticism is vitally dependent on the notion of mediation as an analytical device. He asserts, moreover, that Althusser rejected the notion of mediation because he understood it exclusively as a homological operation, by means of which the various levels of the superstructure were to be transformed into mere expressions of the economic base (p. 39). Jameson therefore suggests a rewriting of the concept of mediation as a process of *transcoding*, which should be conceived as the invention of a set of terms, the strategic choice of a particular code or language, such that the same terminology can be used to analyze and articulate two quite distinct types of objects or 'texts', or two very different structural levels of reality.

(p. 40)

The notion of transcoding is fundamental to the elaboration of the Jamesonian hermeneutics. This critical operation is supposed to relate as much as it separates. But in the final analysis, Jameson asserts the primacy of totalization and of the whole, for 'social life is in its fundamental reality one and indivisible, a seamless web, a single inconceivable and transindividual process' (p. 40). Transcoding, then, aims to restore what he takes to be the lost unity of social life, with the essential proviso, however, that in the course of the analysis the concepts of identity and difference must consistently be seen as depending on and defining one another.

Jameson's Marxist hermeneutics posits three widening 'semantic horizons', through which a given text is supposed to pass in order to 'come out onto' history. Each level or horizon generates the next, and in this way, the text will eventually 'speak its past'. In this context, Jameson is in fact inspired by medieval exegesis and its fourfold sequence of interpretive levels, where the final level, the anagogical, is seen as the story of the 'destiny of the human race'. Thus, Jameson does not perceive his own theoretical model of interpretation as relying on an interpretive code which, as in the case of Freudian psychoanalysis, will reveal itself to be an allegory, but rather as a comprehensive system of allegorical operations, which code one level onto another by using the device of transcoding.

The first level is the 'narrowly political or historical' horizon. Here, as on the other two levels, Jameson conceives of the text as a 'symbolic act', and draws on Lévi-Strauss's suggestion that myths are imaginary resolutions of real social contradictions. He argues, moreover, that this symbolic act can be grasped in terms of the analytical device developed by the French structuralist Greimas. Jameson refers to Greimas's 'semiotic rectangle', which was elaborated in order to model the 'elementary structure of signification', the supposedly rudimentary structure of thought. It assumes the form of a four-term homology, relating an item to

214

both its converse and its contrary, e.g. black:white: :non-black: :non-white.

In a crucial move, Jameson rewrites Greimas's semiotic rectangle as a mapping out of the 'limits of a specific ideological consciousness'. Further, it is said to mark 'the conceptual points beyond which that consciousness cannot go, and in between which it is condemned to oscillate' (p. 47). In this way Jameson is able to argue that an antinomy or an aporia in a text is at the same time an ideological expression and an imaginary resolution of a real social contradiction. He conducts such an analysis in the chapter on Balzac, which roughly corresponds to the first semantic horizon.

The second semantic level is the 'social' horizon. The text is here read in terms of the 'essentially antagonistic collective discourses of social classes', in which it is seen as a *parole* or utterance. The object of study is the 'ideologeme', the smallest intelligible unit in such class discourses (p. 76). In his reading of George Gissing's novels, Jameson detects the ideologeme of *ressentiment*. It denotes the ethical binary opposition of good and evil, which according to Jameson is 'one of the fundamental forms of ideological thought in Western culture' (p. 88). In the case of Gissing, the ideologeme of *ressentiment* is a not only a 'raw material' but also a narrative paradigm, which goes back to the genre of romance, plotted explicitly in terms of good versus evil, where the Other is evil, not because he (for it is most often a male) is evil, but simply because he is other. In Jameson's view, the ethical binary of good and evil is an ideology informing the struggle between classes.[35]

The third level, finally, is the most comprehensive semantic horizon, addressing the text in terms of 'the ideology of form' (p. 76). Jameson's reading of Joseph Conrad is a great endeavour in such a critical genre. How Jameson conceives of the mediatory relations between mode of production and Conrad's particular form of modernism, how history can be said to determine the plots of *Lord Jim* and *Nostromo*, and whether he manages to avoid positing a historical master narrative – these are questions that will be dealt with in the following.

Marxism as narrative

The totalizing objective is, as we have seen, one of the features which in Jameson's view makes Marxism superior as a hermeneutics. He asserts also that a Marxist interpretive framework is unsurpassed because of its 'semantic richness' (p. 10). Finally, he argues the priority of the Marxist perspective in terms of narrative capacity. Marxism is said to offer the necessary comprehensiveness for understanding historical and contemporary phenomena, and to enable the human subject to map out not only his or her individual life context and the larger social context of that historical moment, but also their crucial interrelations. Marxist history thus tells a story by organizing the record of the heterogeneous historical events into a meaningful narrative, which makes the random and manifold social phenomena intelligible. Thus it is thanks to its narrative capacity that Marxism achieves its great strength. Because the 'essential *mystery* of the cultural past', and the long-forgotten messages and matters of remote historical moments can

> recover their original urgency for us only if they are retold within the unity of a single great collective story; only if, in however disguised and symbolic a form, they are seen as sharing a single fundamental theme – for Marxism, the collective struggle to wrest a realm of Freedom from a realm of Necessity. . . .
>
> (p. 19)

Narrative is without doubt the central category in *The Political Unconscious*; indeed, Jameson even goes as far as setting out to

> restructure the problematics of ideology, of the unconscious and of desire, of representation, of history, and of cultural production, around the all-informing process of *narrative*, which I take to be (here using the shorthand of philosophical idealism) the central function or *instance* of the human mind.
>
> (p. 13)

This argument, reminiscent of the one we found in our account of Jameson's discussion of the plotless novel in 'Metacommentary', is related to what I would call Jameson's cognitive idealism. The argument is akin to the idea of a 'narrativization' agency in the political unconscious (see above, p. 213), an idea which brings to mind Kant's transcendental categories of understanding. We will return to this issue in due course, but first we must discuss Jameson's insertion of Conrad's narratives into the third semantic horizon, a critical move which itself tends to assume the form of a narrative, motored by the mediating category of rationalization and reification.

CONRAD AND THE THIRD SEMANTIC HORIZON

In his reading of Conrad, Jameson aims at a complete analysis. The third semantic horizon is supposed to make the text open out onto the 'whole complex sequence of the modes of production' (p. 76). This level thus demands a considerable transformation of the traditional notion of the content of a text, for the semantic framework pursued here is nothing less than the 'ultimate horizon of human history as a whole' (p. 76), the idea being that literary forms bear the traces of the mode of production in which they were seen to emerge. Thus, by inserting the text into this semantic framework, the critic is intended to reveal the ideology of form. Jameson explains:

> I will suggest that within this final horizon the individual text or cultural artifact ... is here restructured as a field of force in which the dynamics of sign systems of several distinct modes of production can be registered and apprehended. These dynamics ... make up what can be termed *the ideology of form*, that is, the determinate contradiction of the specific messages emitted by the varied sign systems which coexist in a given artistic process as well as in its general social formation.
>
> (pp. 98f.)

Jameson sees the mode of production as a dynamized totality, a structure containing within itself vestiges and anticipations of all modes of production. It is, to recall Althusser's proposition, the principally reigning features produced by a structure-in-dominance which constitute what we would call, say, the feudal mode of production.

It may be valuable to add that Jameson, although it is never fully spelled out in *The Political Unconscious*, understands the capitalist mode of production not as one monolithic unit but as an ever-dynamic structure, whose principal changes have hitherto settled, as it were, in three distinct moments. Capitalism, he writes in a 1976 essay, constitutes a heterogeneous mode of production, 'in which a persistence or an identity of the underlying system is maintained throughout moments of expansion'. These expansions are felt as 'the emergence, particularly in culture and the superstructures, of a radically new existential and cultural logic'. These moments are, first, classical or national market capitalism; second, monopoly capital or imperialism; and finally, after the Second World War, multinational or late capitalism. Jameson maintains moreover that to each of these moments corresponds realism, modernism and postmodernism respectively, which, however, should be conceived not as 'styles' but as cultural 'dominants'.[36]

However, the mode of production is not immediately available to us but as an always already textualized phenomenon. Jameson suggests therefore that the conflicting structures within the mode of production make themselves felt as conflicting sign systems. Furthermore, there are crucial links between those forms determining social life and those embedded in a literary work or other cultural artefact.

Following the Danish linguist Louis Hjelmslev's notion of the 'content of the form', Jameson argues that essentially formal processes within a text can be said to accommodate a 'sedimented content in their own right' (p. 99). He rewrites Hjelmslev's strictly linguistic description in terms of narrative in the following manner (p. 147):

FORM	*expression:*	the narrative structure of a genre
	content:	the semantic 'meaning' of a generic mode
SUBSTANCE	*expression:*	ideologemes, narrative paradigms
	content:	social and historical raw material

The notion of genre is crucial to the revealing of the ideology of form; it provides a useful mediatory code, enabling the critic to juxtapose the 'history of forms' with 'the evolution of social life' (p. 105). The generic study offers in Jameson's view the simplest and most illustrative set of methodological tools for the investigation of the content of form. His reading of Conrad will, furthermore, follow roughly the Hjelmslevian schema, whose various levels are conceived of as allegorical planes, each generating one another into ever-widening circles, moving towards that ultimate level, the untranscendable horizon.

Meditating on the historical destiny of the genre of romance,[37] Jameson goes some way towards explaining the relation of mode of production to literary genres. In order to elucidate this correlation, he evokes that remote moment belonging to a precapitalist mode of production wherein narratives were orally transmitted. Oral narration, he maintains, was a form of concrete social relationship: story-teller, public, and narrative raw materials were part of the performance situation itself. The referential frame of the narrative may therefore be seen as having been determined by the immediate social context of the narrative utterance. With narration being transformed into writing, however, the performance situation vanishes, and with that the deictic 'I', 'we', or 'here'. From now on, deictics must be made intrinsic to the narrative, that is to say, what used to be a 'natural' frame must reoccur within the text. At this moment something of a history of narrative forms begins to emerge. Given the fact that every mode of production generates a structurally unprecedented social formation with a specific class set-up and specific forms of mutually antagonistic social sign systems, we may appreciate the extent to which not only literary forms such as the epistolary novel or the picaresque are historically produced but also our understanding of them. In the narrower sense, then, the genre is a device which arouses and delimits the reader's expectations all at once; it works to frame the narrative, to seal off a number of potential interpretations and uses of it. Thus Jameson argues, like so many Marxists before him, that genres are essentially 'literary *institutions*, or social contracts between a writer and a specific public, whose function is to specify the proper use of a particular cultural artifact' (p. 106). This may explain how the genre, as a form, is intrinsically ideological, and hence, that it is possible to speak of the content of form. As we shall see in a moment, Jameson is particularly interested in generic discontinuities, as these are indexes of the conflicting sign systems within the mode of production.

With these preliminary remarks, we are in a better position to grasp how Jameson begins when conceiving of the relation between mode of production and literary form. This is not the place to account for how he theorizes this correlation in more detail. Briefly, his genealogical sketch of the history of the romance posits the problem of the subject as the crucial category, which thus serves to assess the emergence of various literary genres against the appropriate historical situation. In what follows, however, I will discuss how the mediatory relations between Conrad's stylistic practice and the capitalist mode of production are conceived of.

The content of form

Jameson's piece on Conrad is the longest and most comprehensive reading in *The Political Unconscious*, and stretches over seventy-five dense pages. None of the readings, however, is a programmatic application of the theoretical proposals outlined in the introductory section. Like the Balzac and Gissing readings, the piece on Conrad emerges, for better or worse, as a well-nigh self-contained exegesis. The route it seems to take is, as I have suggested, from the content of form to the form of content, a truly acrobatic dialectical performance.

Jameson is primarily concerned with two of Conrad's novels, *Lord Jim* (1900) and *Nostromo* (1904). The former endows him with a point of departure for a narrative within the general narrative authored by Jameson in *The Political Unconscious*, for which the latter novel serves as the twin or double closure. Thus the movement from *Lord Jim* to *Nostromo* signifies, to begin with, a 'developmental' passage within Conrad's authorship as such, whose various stylistic features and multiple narratological shifts make up for competing and incommensurable interpretations even in this day and age. On the level of the history of literary forms, the passage from *Lord Jim* to *Nostromo* also marks the transition from premodernism to the threshold of high modernism. According to Jameson, it therefore tells the story of the traces of the concrete totality being gradually and visibly diffused, transformed slowly into an absent totality, present only in its effects. In this way, *Nostromo* constitutes a denouement, closing Jameson's brief history of the novel. Concluding his reading of Conrad with what is by now a virtually classical formulation, Jameson states that

> After the peculiar heterogeneity of the moment of Conrad, a high modernism is set in place.... The perfected poetic apparatus of high modernism represses History just as suc-

cessfully as the perfected narrative apparatus of high realism did the random heterogeneity of the as yet uncentered subject. At this point, however, the political, no longer visible in the modernist texts, any more than in the everyday world of appearance of bourgeois life, and relentlessly driven underground by accumulated reification, has at last become a genuine Unconscious.

(p. 280)

Jameson argues, as we have seen, that there is a correlation between mode of production and literary form. With modernism onwards, whose occurrence coincides with the emergence of monopoly capital and imperialism, we have, as so many sociologists of literature have observed, the hitherto unknown phenomena of high culture and popular culture. It is partly in this respect, Jameson holds, that the span of Conrad's authorship proves to be of the utmost interest. Tracing a generic discontinuity in Conrad, something which applies first and foremost to *Lord Jim*, he maintains that the authorship of Conrad can be said to display this very transitional period. Conrad marks, as no other writer, the gradual emergence of 'two distinct cultural spaces': on the one hand, that of high culture, to which corresponds, crudely speaking, his impressionistic style, and on the other, that of mass culture, to which corresponds the generic mode of romance and melodrama. Henceforth, Jameson argues, the particular style which Conrad was elaborating becomes a literary practice in its own right, soon to be institutionalized and canonized as literary modernism. Romance, for its part, comes to flourish in the 'half-life of the subliterary genres of mass culture' (p. 107).

Conrad is also rather fond of the story-telling situation itself, which is to be found in both *Heart of Darkness* and *Lord Jim*, thus adding still another generic mode to the notable heterogeneity of his works. This heterogeneity, Jameson notes, has caused some disarray when it comes to the reception of Conrad's novels. It has given rise not only to 'the "romance" or mass-cultural reading of Conrad as a writer of adventure tales, sea narratives, and "popular" yarns', and, on the other hand, the view of Conrad as a 'practitioner' of what Jameson terms the 'properly "impressionistic" will to style' (p. 208). It has also given rise to a huge number of interpretive approaches such as the structural, the myth-critical, the deconstructionist, and others. These apparently conflicting and incompatible notions correspond to what constitutes, in Jameson's eyes, 'discontinuities objectively present' in Conrad's works (p. 208). For Jameson, the various interpretations of Conrad provide a 'network of leitmotifs within the reading of *Lord Jim* and *Nostromo*', whose 'formal levels' help to construct a 'model of Conrad's text' (p. 209). Crucially, his analysis aims to deconstruct precisely those formal levels in order, thereafter, to (re)construct Conrad's text as an event in history. This kind of reading, then, sets out as a metacritical activity, proceeding with a double objective: it is both a commentary on other readings and a hypothetical description of the prototype of Conrad's text.

Jameson's first step towards the deconstruction of *Lord Jim* is to discuss how the novel, as it were, frames itself on the level of sentence production and of genre; that is, how it establishes a ground or conceptual boundary, inviting certain interpretations while excluding others, and thereby containing within itself a kind of ideological closure. It is first of all the sea, that obvious and seemingly natural element in Conrad, which attracts Jameson's attention. The motif of the sea, he asserts, is ambiguous. The sea is on the one hand a place of labour, constituting a 'place of real business' in being the 'very element by which an imperial capitalism draws its scattered beachheads and outposts together' (p. 213). But, on the other hand, the sea is the principal instance of the strategy of containment, because the novel posits life at sea as existing completely on its own terms, outside the 'concrete places of work and life' (p. 213). In so doing, however, the novel displaces the determinate conditions of society as totality, and neglects the fact that the very possibility of the motif of the sea is structurally dependent on the imperialist power structure as well as on the colonized countries, and beyond that, of course, the logic of capitalism. The privileged place of the sea, therefore, is the prime example of a strategy of containment, framing as it does the 'narrative totality' (p. 216). To let the sea frame the narrative is to frame Jim's existential crisis: only in this way can Jim's complex of problems emerge in all its 'formal purity'.

Nevertheless, it is precisely because of the emergence of imperialist capitalism which, as we have seen, creates something of a *coupure* in culture and the superstructures and therefore a 'radically new existential and cultural logic', that Conrad is not capable of, as it were, writing the totality, for the raw materials for such a depiction no longer exist. In this way, according to Jameson, the ambiguity of the motif of the sea marks out Conrad as ' "nascent" modernism', as does the coexistence of romance and impressionistic style.[38]

Strategies of containment, Jameson adds, do not only work by way of exclusion, as in the example above. Framing devices also occur as forms of 'repression in some stricter Hegelian sense of the persistence of the older repressed content beneath the later formalized surface' (p. 213). In order to illustrate this statement, Jameson quotes what he takes to be a central passage in *Lord Jim*. For him, this passage visualizes precisely the Hegelian 'repression'. He uses it to signal his purposes and hypotheses as to the reading of Conrad; in fact, he takes the passage quoted below to epitomize not only the entire authorship of Conrad, but also the classical modernist novel:

> Above the mass of sleepers, a faint and patient sigh at times floated, the exhalation of a troubled dream; and short metallic clangs bursting out suddenly in the depths of the ship, the harsh scrape of a shovel, the violent slam of a furnace-door, exploded brutally, as if the men handling the mysterious things below had their breasts full of fierce anger: while the slim high hull of the steamer went on evenly ahead, without a sway of her bare masts, cleaving continuously the great calm of the waters under the inaccessible serenity of the sky.
>
> (quoted in Jameson, p. 214)

This, says Jameson, is a 'virtual allegory of manifest and latent levels in the text' (p. 214). Before exploring this statement, however, it may be valuable, for the sake of contrast, to juxtapose it with a purely formal description of the passage, bearing in mind, though, that such a description can never be exhaustive. Conrad's depiction contains so many explicit spatial markers such as: above, below, ahead, under, depths, sky; in addition to these there are implied horizontal markers such as: cleave-float-waters, and implied vertical markers such as: slim high hull-masts. These are virtual co-ordinates mapping out the vertical and horizontal dimensions of the majestic image of the voyage. But we have lost the essentially dynamic feature of this image if we fail to emphasize the play of the numerous oppositions generating the tension of the passage (incidentally a tension which the narrator proceeds to, as it were, interpret, in adding 'as if' the men down in the boiler room were 'full of fierce anger'). First of all, we have the various spatial oppositions enumerated above, but also, we have the ones to do with movement and sound, e.g. explode–calm, sigh–clang, scrape–slam, all of which we may sum up in the serene–violent and silent–loud oppositions.

Now, our formal description works by way of reduction; it has served its purpose if it will make clear that when Jameson proceeds to interpret the passage, he presupposes homologous relations, and that his reading works by way of allegorization. For strictly speaking, Conrad's depiction of the voyage can be seen as an allegory of the alleged manifest and latent levels in the text only on condition that one has an a priori conception of these levels and their function within the text. Needless to say, it was precisely this conception that Jameson was supposed to arrive at in his reading. Seen in this way, his move may seem peculiar, if not downright paradoxical. What needs to be stressed here, however, is not that Jameson enters his analysis through the back door, beginning with what was supposed to be the terminus, but that he is forced to. Neither the analysis nor its champion set out as a *tabula rasa*; rather, the critic brings to the work a specific kind of cultural competence: preconceptions, reading habits, thought conventions, expectations, etc. Like a literary work, criticism employs framing devices, which tend to assume, explicitly or implicitly, the form of a dualistic framework. Jameson is of course well aware of this constitutive circumstance, and we will return to this issue in a moment. It is enough to say that the statement that Conrad's vision of the ship 'is a virtual allegory of latent and manifest levels in the text' is less a proposition concerning the nature of Conrad's narrative than a hint towards Jameson's own interpretive standards. If the image of the voyage can be said to be an allegory at all, then it is obviously an allegorization of Jameson's own technique of decipherment. Consider the commentary on Conrad's passage:

Ideology, production, style: on the one hand the manifest level of the content of *Lord Jim* – the moral problem of the 'sleepers' – which gives us to believe that the 'subject' of this book is courage and cowardice, and which we are meant to interpret in ethical and existentializing terms; on the other, the final consumable verbal commodity – the vision of the ship – the transformation of all these realities into style and the work of what we will call the impressionistic strategy of modernism whose function is to derealize the content and make it available for consumption on some purely aesthetic level; while in between these two; the brief clang from the boiler room that drives the ship marking the presence beneath ideology and appearance of that labor which produces and reproduces the world itself, and which, like the attention of God in Berkeleyian idealism, sustains the whole fabric of reality continuously in being. . . .

(p. 214)

We are now able to sort out preliminarily how Jameson's hermeneutics is constructed. It models its notion of the text on a Freudian paradigm, combined with the traditional Marxist base/superstructure metaphor. For, the presumed manifest level is evidently equated with the 'surface' of the text, that which the narrative appears to be about, conceived of as a symptom of what is assumed to be one or several repressed ideas. This is also the level of framing devices and, therefore, of ideology. Likewise, what is taken to be the latent essence, i.e. 'the reality of production', is situated by Jameson in the depth (p. 215). This is the place of concrete content and truth, displaced by 'appearance' and repressed by ideology.

Furthermore, Jameson argues that by 'rewriting' the various realities encompassed by Conrad's image of the ship in terms of the aesthetic and of sense perception, those realities are 'derealized'. This is what the 'impressionistic strategy of modernism' consists of. It is obvious, however, that Jameson's statement presupposes that for something to be 'derealized', it must have the potential capacity of being real. Similarly, the claim that something is being framed presupposes a prior notion of that something. To put it another way, Jameson's reasoning implies an ideal norm against which to assess the degree of 'derealization', in much the same way as he has to posit that which is not impressionistic in order to designate an 'impressionistic strategy'. In fact, Jameson is almost explicit on the point. The transition from realism, Balzac and Gissing to modernism and Conrad, he asserts in a subordinate clause, is the transition of the 'naive

naming of the outside world in realism to the presentation of
the image ... to modernism and impressionism' (p. 212). By
claiming that Conrad's depiction of the voyage is a 'sonorous
inscription of a reality you prefer not to conceptualize' (p. 215),
Jameson opposes the conceptual to the sensory, the plain naming
to the elaborated image. Thereby he posits realism as the fundamental frame of reference. The 'naive naming' of realism is
assigned the status of being a full term. Indeed, in Jameson's
narrative it becomes the origin, from which writing and reading
is supposed to 'fall', a myth not unlike the Lacanian story of the
child leaving the symbiosis with its mother to pass through
the mirror stage which in turn makes way to the symbolic order.
Also, we recognize some of the ideas put forward in the essay
'Metacommentary', where the realist narrative was opposed to
the plotless novel.

It should be clear by now that the idea of the whole and the
concept of totality are fundamental to Jameson's remarks on
Conrad and the motif of the sea. Legitimized by the ontological
assumption that 'social life is in its fundamental reality one and
indivisible, a seamless web, a single inconceivable and transindividual process' (p. 40), the concept of totality works as a methodological tool, functioning to detect that 'fundamental reality'
lurking behind a world of appearances. In the context of Jameson's reading of Conrad, moreover, the concept of social totality
becomes an ideal totality, for he must posit an ideal totality as
some kind of a priori in order to claim that Conrad's 'narrative
totality' is *de facto* 'recontained'. This becomes abundantly clear
when the function of the sea in Conrad's novels is said to motivate
and legitimize 'the boundary which seals off all of the social
totality this narrative model can deal with' (p. 269). In Jameson,
there is thus a preconceived notion of a normative totality which
performs the function of a yardstick.

Finally, it should also be apparent that when he draws the
conclusion that 'this ground bass of material production continues underneath the new formal structures of the modernist
text' (p. 215), the possibility of the vertical surface–depth metaphor is founded on an allegorization of Conrad's image, which,
as we have seen, not only led Jameson to project onto the text
the Freudian manifest–latent model, but also to conflate this
model with the surface–depth metaphor. In other words, what
began as an interpretive attempt to open out Conrad onto history,

ends up positing Conrad as an allegorization of Jameson's already conceived notion of the diachronic dynamics of the capitalist mode of production.

Conrad's will to style

Let us now look at how Jameson illustrates the complex mediatory relationships of imperialist capitalism and Conrad's specific version of modernism. In this context he puts to work the Weberian notion of rationalization and the Lukácsian one of reification, which he in fact equates. These notions constitute the mediatory code that Jameson chooses to apply to Conrad's *Lord Jim* and *Nostromo*.

Prevailing long before the emergence of capitalism, rationalization denotes a manifold and all-informing process, culminating with capitalism.[39] It is founded on a goal-oriented, means/end logic, which in modern society is made visible primarily by the production process and its reorganization into ever smaller and more manageable units. The end is of course the satisfaction of the inexorable and inexhaustible requirements for profitability and economic growth. Rationalization has consequences not only for the production process and the organization of labour, but also makes itself felt in, for example, the domain of bureaucratic organization, which gradually becomes reorganized in the interest of productivity. In creating a calculable external environment, the rationalization process invades what used to be ways of living in precapitalist society, including the organization of social groups, religious activity, institutional values, and various forms of social solidarity.

Contrary to Marxists, however, Weber did not argue that the cause of the various processes of rationalization was to be found in the emerging capitalist mode of production. Instead he maintained that the development of modern capitalism could not have come into being had not people already been subjected to an inner rationalization, which transformed traditionalistic attitudes towards work. Rogers Brubaker has clarified the point in a commentary on Weber: 'the independent rationalization in the sphere of religion and ethics created a disciplined, work-centered inner orientation that turned out, by a great irony of history, to be superbly "adapted to the peculiarities of capitalism." '[40] As is well known, Weber traced back this crucial precondition to ascetic

Protestantism, but emphasized that the advent of a monetary economy entailed hitherto unprecedented possibilities of calculability, an utterly important key factor in the emergence of an entirely rationalized Western culture. Capitalism, then, actualized rationalization, and was the onset of an irrevocable process.

In *History and Class Consciousness* (1923), Lukács drew on Weber's ideas, and combined them with Marx's theory of commodity fetishism in *Capital*. Lukács rewrote rationalization as reification, a term he introduced to describe the fundamental experience of bourgeois life. Schematically, he argued that because of reification and the related momentous calculability, the world begins to appear as a relation between things and commodities, which conceals the fact that the essence of reality is to be found in the relation of humans to nature, and between human beings. We will expand this notion in a moment. Interestingly, Lukács also argued that human consciousness, too, becomes susceptible to the effects of rationalization, for people gradually start to experience their activities in terms of reification and commodity fetishism. Consequently, rationalization has implications for the individual's structuration of 'lived experience'.

Now, as we have pointed out, Jameson posits reification and rationalization as the privileged mediatory code in order to establish the relations between the two (semi-)autonomous levels of capitalist mode of production and Conrad's textual production. The purpose of this transcoding operation is to 'restore, at least methodologically, the lost unity of social life, and demonstrate that widely distant elements of the social totality are ultimately part of the same global historical process' (p. 226). Once again we see the validity of the totality as a crucial methodological point of departure. Also, we recognize yet another allusion to the assumed fall from an original unity.

By using rationalization as a mediatory code, Jameson hopes, first, to juxtapose Conrad's stylistic practice with 'the organization and experience of daily life during the imperialist heyday of industrial capitalism' in order to show not only that they are related to one another, but ultimately determined by the mode of production (p. 226). In the last instance, Jameson aims at delineating Conrad's 'will to style' as a 'socially symbolic act' (p. 225). Second, he seeks to demonstrate how rationalization is a necessary precondition for that other formal level in *Lord Jim*, that is, the form of content: plot and character system. Jameson's analysis of this latter level will be dealt with later; for now I will discuss the transcoding of Conrad's style and sentence production.

We have already noted that Jameson, in the context of the vision of the voyage, maintains that Conrad transforms a number of realities of production into a 'verbal commodity' by means of rewriting them in terms of sense perception. He justifies this argument precisely by referring to the phenomenon of rationalization. Drawing on Marx's suggestions in *Economic and Philosophical Manuscripts*, Jameson argues that rationalization even reaches down to the organization of the human sensory apparatus, and that it thus makes way for radically different kinds of aesthetic gratification. Indeed, Marx maintained that the organization and functions of the human senses were not naturally given once and for all; quite the reverse, the five senses have a history as to their structure and refinement, as have all kinds of human activity, and the essence of this history is to be found in man's relation to nature:

> Only through the objectively unfolded wealth of human nature can the wealth of subjective *human* sensitivity – a musical ear, an eye for the beauty of form, in short, *senses* capable of human gratification – be either cultivated or created. For not only the five senses, but also the so-called spiritual senses, the practical senses (will, love, etc.), in a word, the *human* sense, the humanity of the senses – all these come into being only through the existence of *their* objects, through *humanized* nature. The *cultivation* of the senses is the work of all previous history.[41]

Prior to capitalism, then, aesthetic gratification is intertwined with the crucial awareness of the object in question being humanly produced. There is an immediate appreciation of the amount of work involved, and a fair notion of the scale of the production process. With capitalism and the related rationalization process, however, human beings are estranged from the products of their labour, and therefore in a sense from themselves. Reality ceases to appear as a relation between human beings and nature. In this reified world, human activity becomes subordinated to the new, seemingly natural laws of society.

Sense perception and aesthetic gratification are subjected to the same basic process, Marx maintains. As the world becomes increasingly rationalized, the human perceptual apparatus undergoes a gradual differentiation as well. For if the cultivation of the human senses runs parallel to the history of man's relation to nature, and if aesthetic gratification is directly related to this history, it follows that man, confronted with the effects of rationalization, is no longer able to experience various objects as 'humanized nature'; accordingly, the functions of the human senses will henceforth be organized in a quite different way. Visual perception, Jameson argues, is a case in point. It becomes an activity in its own right, separated from the other sense perceptions and, as it were, self-conscious. Consequently, the all-invading process of reification makes way for hitherto unprecedented possibilities of aesthetic gratification, which is quite literally illustrated by recent paths of fine arts. Jameson explains:

> The history of forms evidently reflects this [reification] process, by which the visual features of ritual, or those practices of imagery still functional in religious ceremonies, are secularized and reorganized into ends in themselves, in easel painting and new genres like landscape, then more openly in the perceptual revolution of the impressionists, with the autonomy of the visual finally triumphantly proclaimed in abstract expressionism.

(p. 63)

He argues, thus, that the emergence of impressionistic painting must be thought of together with the ongoing rationalization process, prior to which landscapes without people were more or less unthinkable, or at least conceived as meaningless. Similarly, it is only at this moment that colour, light, geometrical shape, and the like, may take on, as it were, an abstract value.

Importantly, Jameson holds that it is against this background that Conrad must be understood, not only because the author lived during the period when rationalization made itself most dramatically felt, but above all because his style may be seen as a counterpart to impressionist painting. As we saw in our discussion of Conrad and the motif of the sea as a strategy of containment, Jameson asserts that Conrad, by means of foregrounding sense perception, derealizes 'the reality of production'. This 'aestheticizing strategy', he concludes, is the impressionistic strategy of modernism. Thus impressionism constitutes another significant framing device in Conrad: it seeks to '*recode* or *rewrite* the world and its own data in terms of perception as a semi-autonomous activity' (p. 230; italics added). At its most intense, Jameson points out, 'what we will call Conrad's sensorium virtually *remakes* its objects, *refracting* them through the totalized medium of a single sense, and more than that, of a single "lighting" or coloration of that sense' (p. 230; italics added).

It is no accident that Jameson repeatedly uses the prefix 're-'. These formulations would seem to imply that Conrad's world and its data are already written, coded, or made, lest Conrad could not be said to rewrite, recode, or remake these realities.[42] Leaving aside this problem for a moment, we will bring up another train of thought which appears to contradict the statement that Conrad 'remakes' the objects of his depiction. As we have seen, Jameson proposes that with the advent of capitalism the external, concrete world is fragmented due to the prevailing rationalization process, and that our way of perceiving this world also undergoes a rationalization, inscribing itself in our sensory apparatus. As a result, the aesthetic of the 'abstract' image becomes possible. However, these two phenomena, Jameson argues, the new ideology of the image and the objective fragmentation of the outside world

> are rigorously identical: in order to be read or seen *qua* image, to be grasped as a symbolic act which is image-production, or, following Sartre's account, derealization, such transformations of the world into images must always be marked as the reunifications of data which were originally chaotic or fragmentary.
>
> (pp. 232f.)

Now, Jameson asserted earlier that 'social life is in its fundamental reality one and indivisible'. Accordingly, he argued that the purpose of the transcoding operation is to make whole and to reunify that which appears as separated, because the

> realm of separation, of fragmentation, of the explosion of codes and the multiplicity of disciplines is merely the reality of the appearance: it exists, as Hegel would put it, not so much *in itself* as rather *for us*, as the basic logic and

fundamental law of our daily life and existential experience
in late capitalism.

(p. 40)

In the latter quote, Jameson appeals to an original, irreducible
unity, which thus motivates a transcoding operation. This, then,
would be the world in itself. None the less, Jameson appears to
posit another, equally original level of reality wherein the data of
the world are 'chaotic or fragmentary'. This is the world as it
exists for us. Of course, these quotations refer to two different
realms, but they ultimately meet in one and the same epistemological problem. On the one hand, Jameson seems to propose
that the various sensory signals and stimuli hitting the human
perceptual apparatus are essentially non-ordered and therefore
meaningless, but that the mind selects and interprets a given
number of these stimuli in order, then, to confer meaning on
them, and that this last, essentially cognitive act seeks to unite
the interpreted data into a meaningful whole. On the other
hand, Jameson seems to suggest that there is a fundamental unity
underlying the fragmentary appearance of our experience, that
is to say, that there is an essential unity existing prior to its
appearance. In both cases, it is clear that Jameson operates with
an ideal notion of unity, be it assigned to the being of the world
or our thinking of the world.

It would seem at least plausible to assume that Conrad's alleged
rewriting of the world and its own data is less a matter of Conrad
actually rewriting a received way of perceiving the world than an
appeal to Jameson's own ideal norm. This norm is the standard
which he must posit in order to be able to claim that Conrad's
sensorium rewrites the objects of perception, i.e. that standard
which must be established so as to make visible that Conrad's
codification of reality is different. The fact that Jameson appears
to project this ideal standard onto Conrad's writing is obvious
even if we accept his reasoning on its own terms: if sense data
are originally chaotic and fragmentary, then they need unification
only, not reunification; and, perhaps needless to say, this unification is an interpretive act in itself.

Be that as it may, Conrad's aestheticizing strategy, his
impressionistic style, is no doubt ideologically informed in Jameson's view: 'modernism is itself an ideological expression of capitalism, and in particular, of the latter's reification of daily life'

(p. 236). It should be noted, however, that Jameson does not, like Lukács, use reification as a normative category, that is to say, as a way of sorting out good and bad novels.[43] Jameson's is a twin perspective: to be sure, impressionist painting, he argues, finds its conditions of possibility in reification, but at the same time, impressionism could be seen as a Utopian compensation for all that reification entails. Fragmentation, which emerges in the wake of rationalization, provides in fact hitherto unknown areas and objects open to perception and libidinal gratification, and so it is that things are virtually seen in a new light:

> it is precisely this new semi-autonomy and the presence of these waste products of capitalist rationalization that open up a life space in which the opposite and the negation of such rationalization can be, at least imaginatively, experienced.
>
> (p. 236)

The Utopian compensation, Jameson asserts in a truly dialectical fashion, is

> the place of quality in an increasingly quantified world, the place of the archaic and of feeling amid the desacralization of the market system, the place of sheer color and intensity within the grayness of measurable extension and geometrical abstraction.
>
> (pp. 236f.)

In this way, Conrad's projected sensorium is a socially symbolic act, a significant gesture within its immediate social context. It is produced by social contradictions, to which it is at the same time a complex response. *Lord Jim*, like all works of art, accommodates Utopia and ideology all at once.

The form of content

In the preceding pages we have seen how Jameson deals with the content of form. We will now turn to that other formal level in Conrad, the form of content: 'the unavoidable false problems which are named character, event, plot, narrative meaning, and the like' (p. 242). Here Jameson aims, first, to construct the semic system which generates the typology of character in *Lord Jim* and *Nostromo*. This system is at one with the deep structural level of narrative. Second, Jameson focuses on the plot construction. Again he finds Weber's analysis of the rationalization process useful. Attempting to make a case for Conrad's character system being determined by rationalization, Jameson's reading, however, comes across less as an exegesis of Conrad's character system and plot construction than of Weber's theory of value. Indeed, I will try to show that he rewrites *Lord Jim* quite literally in terms of Weber's thoughts on value, whose suggestions become conclusions imposing themselves on the presumed character system, which Jameson takes to map out the 'limits beyond which [the] consciousness cannot go' (p. 47).

Initially, Jameson sets off with a typological operation, and distinguishes certain categories of character in order to discern the contours of a differential system. He argues that one immediately visible difference is that between anonymous masses and isolated monads; in short: the collective versus the individual. A strategical place to look, then, is at the beginning of the novel, where the *Patna* ship and the embarking people are described at length. Jameson chooses to dwell on the motif of the eight hundred pilgrims bound for Mecca, who are depicted going on board. At this moment the German skipper says, 'Look at dese cattle', an utterance which Jameson understands as marking out the difference between the pilgrims with their 'lack of "individualism"' and the Europeans. By testing and rejecting potential replacements, he concludes that the Muslim pilgrims are absolutely necessary and impossible to replace: they are not, as it were, reducible to this narrative function. Certainly, the pilgrims are in one sense a mere 'narrative device', for these people are, among others, the ones Jim will leave behind himself when he, against all rules, abandons the ship, thereby putting their lives in danger, all of which is the 'pretext' for his subsequent moral self-examination. But the motif of the pilgrims is also seen as having a 'substantive meaning in its own right, which is constitutive for the text' (p. 246). In Jameson's view, the plot is dependent on this motif; a European lot, for instance, would not submit to the kind of conduct of which Jim is an exponent, nor would various kinds of Asian crowds be able to fulfil the narrative function, because that would signal 'commerce and business motives' rather than sheer faith. 'So at length', he contends, 'we find ourselves interrogating, as though it were the fundamental concern of this sea story and adventure tale, the clearly secondary and marginal phenomenon of religion and religious belief' (p. 247).

The presence of the Muslim pilgrims is evidently a sufficient reason for Jameson to assign the 'nineteenth-century ideologeme of aesthetic religion' to Conrad, a feature which lays the ground for the whole edifice of the analysis. Again Jameson comes to think of Weber, Conrad's 'virtual contemporary' (p. 248). Having devoted some seven pages to expounding Weber's theory of value, Jameson is ready to confront *Lord Jim*'s character system. What, then, does the presence of the pilgrims signify, and how does Weber enter into the picture?

Weber argued, as Brubaker has summarized it, that the 'social world is composed of a number of distinct provinces of activity, each having its own inherent dignity and its own immanent norms'.[44] He called these autonomous realms 'value spheres', maintaining that one of the two fundamental sources for value conflict in the Western world is to be found in the 'objective differences in the inner structure of different forms of social action'.[45] The other source of value conflict is easier to grasp, and is constituted by individual and subjective value-orientation. Neither of these conflicts, Weber argued, may be rationally resolved. As the rationalization process becomes ever more influential in the social system as a whole, value conflicts, especially among value spheres, become ever more acute.

Jameson finds Weber's observations useful, not to say pivotal to his analysis. But he is eager to emphasize that Weber's object of study can come into being only when it has already emerged as deeply problematic. According to Jameson's Marxist reading of Weber, the study of the notion of value presupposes a level of abstraction which did not exist prior to the advent of capitalism and the rationalization process. In precapitalist societies, as Weber maintained, professions and vocations were for the most part inherited, and their norms and values were thus interwoven with the profession in question; in other words, norms and values were not yet visible as such. But the emergence of the capitalist mode of production cuts into these older ways of living and working. It dissolves traditional values, such as the fundamental ideal of *caritas* or brotherly love, brought forward by virtually every religion, and which could coexist easily with the tradition-oriented vocational systems in older societies. Weber explains:

There is no possibility... of any caritative regulation of relationships arising between the holder of a savings and loan bank mortgage and the mortgagee who has obtained a loan from the bank, or between the holder of a federal bond and a citizen taxpayer.[46]

With the introduction of a money economy and rational calculability, the virtue of *caritas* is in other words doomed to be replaced by the quite different virtue of rationally regulated self-interest. 'The material development of an economy on the basis of social associations flowing from market relationships generally follows its own objective rules, disobedience to which entails economic failure and, in the long run, economic ruin,' Weber maintains.[47] At this moment, Jameson argues, values cease to exist, and, similarly, it is only now that the notion of value can become an object of study. He concludes therefore that 'the study of value is at one with nihilism, or the experience of its absence' (p. 251).

It is precisely here that Jameson finds the one term which makes up for that looked-for antinomy assumed to exist in Conrad's text. 'Value', thus, is the one term, and 'activity' is, as we shall see, posited as the other. For according to Jameson, the experience of the loss of value, which is at one with the abstraction of value, coincides with one of the 'most active periods in human history':

it is only in the most completely humanized environment, the one most fully and obviously the end product of human labour, production, and transformation, that life becomes meaningless, and that existential despair first appears as such in direct proportion to the elimination of nature, the non- or anti-human, to the increasing rollback of everything that threatens human life and the prospect of a well-nigh limitless control over the external universe.

(p. 251)

During this period a number of influential authors and philosophers emerge who thematize an existential meaninglessness. Nietzsche is a case in point. Weber's theory of value and Nietzsche's eloquent nihilism: these are, Jameson asserts, 'clearly the absolutes with which Conrad's own private pessimism has its "family resemblance"' (p. 252). This is also the background against which Jameson maintains that 'the ideological meaning of aesthetic religion' must be understood. For, we recall, it is the occurrence of the eight hundred pilgrims on *Patna* which sparks off this meditation in Jameson. The logic of their insertion into the plot of *Lord Jim*, or more correctly, the logic of what these pilgrims are assumed to represent, namely the ideologeme of aesthetic religion, is thus explained in terms of a Marxist reading of Weber's theory of value:

> Religion is the superstructural projection of a mode of pro-
> duction, the latter's only surviving trace in the form of
> linguistic and visual artifacts, thought systems, myths and
> narratives, which look as though they had something to do
> with the forms in which our consciousness is at home, and
> yet which remain rigorously closed to it. Because we can no
> longer think the figures of the sacred from within, we trans-
> form their external forms into aesthetic objects.
>
> (p. 252)

The ideological vocation of religion in the nineteenth century, Jameson argues, is to provide the means for going beyond the instrumental logic culminating with capitalism; or, to put it another way, in the course of the reification process, the function of religion is being transformed into something of a compensa-tory discourse, which, in all its nostalgia, seeks to transcend the rising contradictions of that brave new world by means of an imaginary resolution.

However, this is the closest Jameson ever comes to an expli-cation of the motif of the pilgrims. It needs to be emphasized that the link between, on the one hand, the novel and its plot, and the knowledge that is brought to bear on it on the other, is remarkably weak. In spite of their marginal position in the plot, Jameson takes the sheer presence of the pilgrims to provide the crucial key to the deep structural system in *Lord Jim*.

Having made a detour via Weber, who buttresses him with the opposition between activity and value, Jameson thus returns to *Lord Jim* with the intention of 'reinvesting' its language with 'something like its original ideological and semantic content' (p. 253). Because Conrad writes about the imperialist periphery, where precapitalist forms of living coexist with capitalism, Jame-son presumes that 'the term value is still able to have genuine social and historical substance' (p. 254). This, then, together with the motif of the pilgrims, is Jameson's only justification for constructing the opposition between activity and value, on the basis of which he elaborates a semiotic rectangle. He warns that if the construction of this particular opposition should be objected to, if it seems to have moved away considerably from the paradigms of a Greimas or a Lévi-Strauss, who would elaborate strictly logical oppositions and relate an item to both its converse and its contrary, then, he claims, it must be stressed that the value–activity opposition exists as a *symptom*: 'the opposition between activity and value is not so much a logical contradiction, as rather an antinomy for the mind, a dilemma, an aporia, which itself expresses – in the form of an ideological closure – a concrete social contradiction' (p. 254).

It should be noted, however, that the immediate dilemma is less that the posited 'binary' opposition is not a logical one, less that the statement presupposes a homologous relation between the distinctly different phenomena, but that Jameson scarcely constructs this opposition on the basis of Conrad's text. Rather, it is derived from Weber. Surely, it is not at all unthinkable that the opposition between value and activity 'underlies' Weber's discourse, and that it marks out the conceptual limits beyond which Weber could not move. But it is not equally convincing in the case of Conrad. Indeed, it is uncertain whether this opposition has anything to do with Conrad's text at all. For, drawing on Weber, Jameson evidently begins with a description of a social contradiction, proceeds to assert that a similar 'opposition' exists in Conrad, only to conclude that the 'antinomy' expresses the very social contradiction which he started out with. In other words, Conrad's narrative system is the mere pretext for Jameson's happy confirmation of the already posited theoretical point of departure: thus, what Conrad's assumed antinomy expresses is quite simply Jameson's own conceptual paradigm.

Nonetheless, Jameson constructs an ideological deep structure taken to underlie *Lord Jim* (see figure 1). By combining and synthesizing each semantic node, he finds that this semantic combinatoire indeed generates the character system; or, if you like, that the characters fit in extraordinarily well (see figure 2). The characters, according to Jameson, are a surface phenomenon produced by the deep structure, the 'combinatoire'. At the same time, however, each character marks an attempted resolution of each 'local' antinomy in question. In addition to this, the

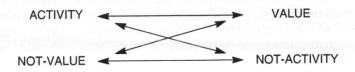

Figure 1 Jameson's construct of the ideological deep structure underlying
Lord Jim

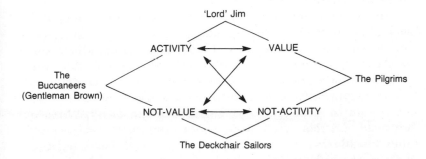

Figure 2 The generation of the character system from the deep structure
in *Lord Jim*

characterological schema as a whole maps out 'the imaginary
resolution of this particular determinate real contradiction',
which is that between activity and value. In this way, the schema,
like the character slots, accommodates an ideological and a Utopian impulse simultaneously: it seeks to resolve a contradiction,
but it also serves, as Jameson has it, to 'imagine away' the same
contradiction.

Now, this high structuralist way of construing a deep structure
of a plot is obviously not capable of accounting for the function of the characters within the plot, nor can it account for the
narrative as a movement in time. It collapses diachrony into a
synchronic system, and neglects the dynamics of the reading
process. Jameson is of course aware of this dilemma, and therefore sets out to rectify this problem by means of a commentary
on the plot construction of *Lord Jim*, a commentary which assumes

the form of analysing the framing of the 'event' of the novel. Jameson asserts that the ' "event" in *Lord Jim* is the analysis and dissolution of the event' (p. 257). He argues in fact that the novel is an 'interrogation of a hole in time', because the thematic focal point – Jim's decision to abandon *Patna* and the actual jump – is never properly depicted. What Jameson underscores, though, is not that it should have been delineated, but that it could not. The axis around which the entire narrative seems to rotate – the jump – is absent, because an act as such is assigned significance only at the moment when its consequences are possible to construe, which means that the pure act – in the present tense – is not only meaningless but also impossible, and cannot be subject to representation. Thus, he argues, we are always before or after the act in *Lord Jim*. The act is in other words crucially dependent on being framed.

The whole moral complex and existential analytic which occupies Jim throughout the novel, before as well as after the jump, is in fact an interrogation into the possibility of a meaningful act, and thus also an enquiry into the potential resolution of the opposition between activity and value. For the eventual jump is a structural repetition of a former situation, where Jim was faced with roughly the same difficult choice. He then failed to jump, a decision which turned out to be the wrong one. This time he succeeds, but this decision, too, proves to be the wrong one. Hence, what really concerns Jim, Jameson argues, is not so much the ethical questions haunting him even in that remote place called Patusan, where Jim is both honoured and successful; this moral soul-searching is

> something like a structural pretext for the quite different examination of what an act and what a temporal instant really are: when does the act happen, how much preparation is necessary, how far do you have to go in it before it suddenly 'takes' and becomes irrevocable, is it then infinitely divisible like the sprint-lengths of the hare, or of Zeno's arrow, and if not, then . . . how could that single hard ultimate indivisible atom which is the instant of action ever come into being in the first place?
>
> (p. 262)

As we have seen on so many occasions, Jameson's reading does not deal with Conrad's narrative on its own terms. It does not aim to explicate the various problems and issues which the novel purports to be raising, such as the quasi-philosophical enquiry into the structure of temporality. Instead, Jameson repeatedly insists on throwing light on the historical grounds of possibility. Conrad's enquiry into the nature of a meaningful act presupposes a specific experience of temporality which in turn presupposes an abstraction of temporality. In other words, the moral issues confronting Jim over and over again can come into being only when 'activity' and 'value' are, as we saw above, lifted out of their traditionally social spheres. Likewise, the possibility of a meaningful act can emerge as an existential problem only when 'temporality' begins to disengage itself, and the 'older traditional activities, projects, rituals through which time was experienced, and from which it was indistinguishable, have broken down' (p. 261). Jameson here clearly refers to the reification process, which, again, serves to mediate between Conrad's text and the mode of production.

This, then, is the way in which Jameson claims to have restored 'the whole socially concrete subtext of late nineteenth-century rationalization and reification of which this novel is so powerfully ... the expression and the Utopian compensation alike' (p. 266). Apparently, all other readings of *Lord Jim* must be misreadings. Jameson explains this circumstance with a reference to a 'built-in-substitute interpretive system' existing in the text, a strategy of containment ensuring 'the structural displacement' of concrete content (p. 266). Even though Conrad is aware of the broader historical and social situation, he is, none the less, subjected to resorting to the structural limitations of his epoch, and this is why what is taken to be the concrete content is not immediately visible to the reader. There are two strategies of containment surfacing in *Lord Jim*, both of which Jameson perceives as proper ideologies. Both 'aim to recontain the content of the events of Jim's narrative by locating "responsible parties" and assigning guilt' (p. 267). First we have the metaphysical strategy, denoting the framing device whereby nature and the elements, especially the sea, are consistently described in anthropomorphic terms. This invites the reader to interpret Jim's battle as an individual's ethical fight against an evil Nature. But the 'real issues' are elsewhere, Jameson maintains. They are to be found in a fundamentally social situation, which above all bears the marks of the historically produced contradiction between activity and value.

The second strategy is that of melodrama, most visible in the second part of the novel, the romance part, where 'the malevolent agency of Nature is replaced by that of man' (p. 267). As in the example above, Jim's battle presupposes another term, that which is to be fought so that he can prove himself and remain a 'hero'. Here Jameson holds that the ideologeme of *ressentiment* affects the character system, subdividing it into good and evil terms, into 'our man' and the Other(s).

We have now seen how Jameson proceeds when 'reinvesting' the language of *Lord Jim* with 'something like its original ideological and semantic content'. Before attempting to sort out some of the underlying assumptions informing this kind of 'reinvestment', however, I shall give a brief account of how Jameson goes about the reading of *Nostromo*. As I suggested earlier, *Nostromo* constitutes the denouement of the Jamesonian narrative about the passage from realism to modernism. Set in South America, in the fictitious country of Costaguana, this historical novel about violent revolution, silver mining, and the inauguration of a new society puts a full stop to Jameson's discussion of the nineteenth-century novel. But, for all the forceful emphasis on the extra-textual, the historical, and the crucially political dimension of literary texts and interpretive activity, this final moment of Jameson's reading none the less hovers securely within the boundaries of Conrad's authorship. *Nostromo* is read less against what would be its appropriate historical moment, nor is it seen, as one could have expected, as the imaginary resolution of a social contradiction. Rather, it is read against *Lord Jim*, in relation to which the later novel achieves its meaning and significance. Consequently, Jameson argues that *Nostromo* is a 'dialectical intensification and transformation of the narrative apparatus of *Lord Jim*', thereby signalling the hermeneutical principles (p. 269). Jameson will accordingly argue that the sheer absence in *Nostromo* of features which are present in *Lord Jim* is highly significant. *Nostromo*, then, is not framed by the sea, 'that basic masking device', nor is it contained by the melodramatic or the metaphysical strategy. Commenting on this negative significance, Jameson draws the conclusion that we can 'anticipate a formal transformation of Conrad's narrative line of the greatest interest in illuminating the determinant relationship between ideology and the production of form' (p. 271). Nevertheless, for all their differences in this respect, *Nostromo* is, like *Lord Jim*, the 'interrogation of a hole in time, an act whose innermost instant falls away – proving thus at once irrevocable and impossible, a source of scandal and an aporia for contemplation' (p. 264). The central act or event in *Nostromo* is 'the expedition of Decoud and Nostromo to the Great Isabel and the saving of the treasure, which is at one with the founding of the separatist Occidental Republic of Sulaco' (p. 272). This is the hidden axis: it is, as Jameson puts it, the aporia which the novel contemplates. Unlike *Lord Jim*, however, 'the contemplation of *Nostromo* is a contemplation on History' (p. 264). This is due partly to the fact that *Nostromo* is framed in terms of the collective and the collective destiny, rather than the existential fate of an individual.

In order to explain this, Jameson elaborates a semiotic rectangle, whose point of departure is constituted by the alleged opposition of Decoud and Nostromo, both of whom are, first, taken to be one *actant*, and the central one, for they are both essential to the foundation of the province of Sulaco. Nostromo and Decoud constitute an alliance of, respectively, 'body and mind, the man of action and the intellectual, the bearer of a personal, quasi-physical vanity and the lover of the ideal' (p. 273). But it should be stressed that Jameson also treats them as occasions for yet another allegorical interpretation, for, he remarks, the founding of Society obviously demands more than the achievement of two individuals. So it is that Nostromo and Decoud are seen as representatives of something that widely transcends their individual scope and importance in order for Jameson to legitimize his reading. He therefore transfigures the two characters, turning them first into representatives of two different groupings of characters and destinies. The one character-grouping 'descends from the mine owner Charles Gould', the other from 'the Italian immigrant and Garabaldino Viola'. These groupings are in turn transformed into another set of representatives, for seen in this way, according to Jameson, they

> sort themselves out into an immediately identifiable opposition: they correspond to the two great forces of nineteenth-century history – industrial capitalism, expanding into its imperialist stage, and 'popular' (that is, in the strictest sense, neither peasant nor proletarian) revolution

243

of the classic 1848 type, of which the heroic figure of Garib-
aldi is both the Lenin and the Che, and the only leader of
a successful revolution which founds an independent state.

(pp. 273f.)

Clearly, the figures of Nostromo and Decoud are here treated as
allegories. They are coded onto an overt and preconceived notion
of history, i.e. that which Jameson conceives as the significant
historical forces during the nineteenth century. The problem is
not so much that this history is preconceived – that is an irreducible necessity and indeed a constitutive hermeneutical 'prejudice'
– but that the two characters of Nostromo and Decoud end up
as allegorizations of Jameson's historical master narrative. This
narrative is, as we have seen, the story of the succession of the
various structures-in-dominance within the mode of production:
'nascent' capitalism (the moment of Balzac), classical capitalism
(the moment of Gissing), and, finally, imperialist capitalism
(Conrad). Thus, *Nostromo* is rewritten according to this (hi)story,
and it remains to be seen whether this history is, as Terry Eagleton
has put it, 'more one of closure than of horizon'.[48]

The characters of Decoud and Nostromo are, as we noted
above, seen as articulations of the 'ultimate opposition which
codes the narrative'. Rewriting the combination of Decoud and
Nostromo as the opposition between Ideal and Self, Jameson
argues that Decoud/Ideal embodies that phenomenon, which in
the name of idealism, moral concerns, humanism, civilization,
and the like, brings 'order' to the 'natural' or 'primitive' remote
regions in the world, an order that is synonymous with the introduction of capitalism (p. 275). Nostromo/Self, on the other
hand, is the opposite of Ideal. If Ideal bears within itself transcendence, then Self is congruous with immanence: it is the idea
of a self-contained society, where, as Jameson has it, *Wesen* and
Leben are one and the same; it is therefore something of an
'immanent' nationalism and populism, all of which is embodied
by Nostromo, a man of action and instinct. This, then, is the
fundamental opposition, that 'impossible synthesis or complex
term' which the novel is presumed to contemplate and ultimately
resolve. Indeed, realized by Nostromo and Decoud and their
joint expedition, this synthesis consists of the 'foundation or new
inauguration of society which will lift us out of fallen history'
(p. 277). But, crucially, this Ideal Act never happens in *Nostromo*,

244

we are always before or after it, as in *Lord Jim*: it proves to be that hole in time around which the entire narrative rotates. The reader, Jameson implies, is therefore led to imagine the very act; and this circumstance, it seems, renders *Nostromo* profoundly Historical, hence also Utopian. For, by insisting 'to the end on everything problematical about the act that makes for genuine historical change' (p. 277), *Nostromo*

> finally achieves its end by unravelling its own means of expression, 'rendering' History by its thoroughgoing demonstration of the impossibility of narrating this unthinkable dimension of collective reality, systematically undermining the individual categories of storytelling in order to project, beyond the stories it must continue to tell, the concept of a process beyond storytelling.
>
> (p. 279)

Thus Conrad's authorship, and in particular *Nostromo*, is seen as marking out the threshold to modernism. For henceforth, Jameson asserts, History and the political go underground, no longer visible as concrete content:

> *Nostromo* is thus ultimately, if you like, no longer a political or historical novel, no longer a realistic representation of history; yet in the very movement in which it represses such content and seeks to demonstrate the impossibility of such representation, by a wondrous dialectical transfer the historical 'object' itself becomes inscribed in the very form.
>
> (p. 280)

From now on concrete content is transformed into form, Jameson concludes. What was once immediately recognizable as the 'ground-bass' of material production is henceforth 'ultimately detectable only to the elaborate hermeneutic geiger counters of the political unconscious and the ideology of form' (p. 215).

Jameson's narrative and its beginnings

We have now seen Jameson arguing that Conrad's *Lord Jim*, on the stylistic level, is a rewriting of the concrete reality of production by means of having transformed this reality into aesthetic objects and images; second, that the character system in the same novel is generated by the value–activity contradiction; and third, that the closure of the plot construction presupposes an abstract structure of temporality and a likewise abstract notion of value, both of which constitute a framing device whereby Jim's crisis is staged as a purely individual dilemma. All these strategies of containment are taken by Jameson to be 'determined' by the rationalization process, which, in its turn, is increasingly fuelled by capitalism. To paraphrase Althusser, we may say that History is present in *Lord Jim* only as an immanence in its effects. Within the narrative, these strategies work to displace the historical and social reasons for the specific 'problematic' represented by Jim. At the same time, however, Jameson sees the various strategies of containment as imaginary resolutions of the very social contradiction which produces them.

Having abandoned the categories of the individual subject, *Nostromo*, by contrast, emerges as a great historical novel in Jameson's account. For, paradoxically, in failing to represent historical change (the foundation of society and the advent of capitalism in Sulaco), which amounts to the novel's pivotal event that, as we noted, implodes into that hole in time, *Nostromo* manages to register History. Indeed, Jameson seems to suggest that this void opens out the narrative onto History as absent cause. As the ultimately determining instance, History is what makes Conrad's narrative possible. But, crucially, History as such can never be subjected to representation, for, like Lacan's Real, it 'resists symbolization absolutely' (p. 35). Thus, History is accessible to us not as a thing in itself but as always already textualized, as traces and vestiges. Or, as in the case of *Nostromo*, History can be evoked negatively, by means of a kind of *via negativa*. History is in other words present in its absence. For Jameson, then, the move from *Lord Jim* to *Nostromo* describes the last moment of the passage from history as concrete totality to History as absent cause, because the former novel was at least partially a realistic depiction of life and labour at sea, which constituted something of a reality of production in itself, whereas in the latter novel, we are invited to see the final 'structural breakdown of the older realisms', entailing the transfiguration of content into form (p. 207).

It should be apparent that Jameson tells a narrative, which, among other things, illustrates how Conrad cannot but operate within the structural limitations imposed upon him by his epoch, and that, therefore, his strategies of containment are ideological.

But how is it that Jameson is able to reveal these strategies which Conrad himself could not see? In other words, what allows Jameson's perspective to be superior, and lay claims to having restored to Conrad's language 'its original and semantic content'? If Conrad had to recontain his stories in one way or another, it follows that all discourses, including Jameson's, are subject to resorting to these structural limitations. For, in order to tell the story of Conrad, Jameson needs to posit a point of departure, that is to say, a beginning; and this beginning, furthermore, comes to frame his narrative. Obviously, Jameson must frame his own discourse in order to demonstrate how Conrad frames his.

There are, as we have noted, at least two immediately visible beginnings in Jameson's reading of Conrad, and both ultimately merge into one. One is the zero degree against which Conrad's assumed rewriting of history becomes possible to assess. This zero degree is equated with the 'naive naming of realism' and its principal conceptualization of the world. The realist moment, therefore, is the full term to which Jameson appeals in order, literally, to assign meaning to Conrad and modernistic writing, thereby turning it into a distinct moment within his own historical narrative. This relational move enables Jameson to answer the question 'What does *Lord Jim* mean?' Having been endowed with this meaning, or, as Jameson would put it, the preconditions for this meaning, *Lord Jim* becomes the new full term, in relation to which *Nostromo* is understood as a dialectical transformation. Clearly, it is only when *Nostromo* is inserted into this Jamesonian narrative that it begins to signify.

The other beginning employed by Jameson is implicated by the concept of reification, based on a notion of the organic wholeness of precapitalist society and related forms of lived experience. The zero degree in this case, then, is the non-reified or the not-yet-reified, to which Jameson, throughout the analysis, refers as yet another full term, as that essentially whole society, possible to experience as an immediately concrete totality.

Hence, Jameson's narrative about Conrad's textual production is plotted in terms of the whole versus the fragmented, the concrete versus the abstract, and the collective versus the individual, oppositions in which the first term constitutes the privileged beginning. Clearly, the notion of the totality constitutes Jameson's arche-beginning. Not surprisingly, this is a traditionally Marxist dualistic framework. The question, however, is whether the way this framework it constructed is compatible with the theoretical pursuit we outlined at the outset of this discussion.

ON THE PRIORITY OF HISTORY

We can assume and assert nothing dogmatically; nor can we accept the assertions and assumptions of others. And yet we must make a beginning: and a beginning, as primary and underived, makes an assumption, or rather is an assumption. It seems as if it were impossible to make a beginning at all.

(Hegel)[49]

Beginning, totality, truth: the concept of totality is fundamental to Jameson's Marxist hermeneutics. It is the constitutive essence of his dialectical method, and, in a sense, the touchstone of truth. Both explicitly and implicitly, the concept of totality possesses different meanings in *The Political Unconscious*. First, it is posited as the ultimately determining instance – the absent cause. Second, it denotes the ontological assumption that the social totality is one and indivisible. Third, it suggests a methodological principle, an ideal standard, allowing Jameson to assess how a given text frames itself. Related to this methodological use of the concept of totality is the holistic perspective which argues the priority of the whole over the parts; that is to say, the parts achieve their meaning in relation to this preconceived whole.

But Jameson is, as we have seen, anxious not to posit the totality as an expressive one, where the parts are reducible to an inner essence of the whole. He therefore seeks to emphasize difference, heterogeneity, discontinuity, and the semiautonomous status of levels within the social totality. Likewise, he attempts to elaborate an accurate notion of mediation, which separates as much as it relates. To this end he proposes the method of transcoding. Accordingly, he valorizes the concept of allegory rather than that of symbol,[50] because allegory stresses the difference between levels where symbol entails unification and identity. This is partly why Jameson is inspired by the medieval system of allegorical interpretation. Its emphasis on the multiplicity of distinct levels within the object text underscores the essentially figural nature of the (biblical) narrative, whose potentially multi-layered allegorical character entails, in Jameson's view, a Utopian dimension. For the patristic sequence of allegorical levels brings with it the possible projection of the story of a collective destiny. On another plane, moreover, the sequence of allegorical interpretive operations, mediated by means of transcoding, reconciles the synchronic analysis with a notion of temporality. It is clear, then, that the concept of allegory is initially congenial to Jameson's hermeneutics of history. For, as Paul de Man has argued, 'in the world of allegory, time is the originary constitutive category'.[51] If symbol results in simultaneity, spatialization, and the Same, thus conflating the distinctly different levels in some illusory unity, then allegory evokes difference, and primarily a temporal one due to the distance between the allegorical level and its origin. As de Man maintains, it remains necessary,

> if there is to be allegory, that the allegorical sign refer to another sign that precedes it. The meaning constituted by the allegorical sign can then consist only in the *repetition* (in the Kierkegaardian sense of the term) of a previous sign with which it can never coincide, since it is of the essence of this previous sign to be pure anteriority.[52]

Now Jameson does not conceive of his technique of decipherment in terms of interpretation in the narrower sense, that is to say, as an allegorical operation, whereby, as in e.g. structuralism and Freudian criticism, a given text is rewritten according to a supposedly timeless interpretive paradigm. His Marxist reading method, by contrast, assumes the form of a metacommentary, which construes a given text as always already read, seeking to reveal the conditions of possibility of its received meaning. But he assigns a 'local' validity to the notion of allegory within the interpretive framework, for the semantic horizons addressed by the mediatory codes can be seen as just such allegorical levels.

Jameson's version of metacriticism derives its alleged superiority from the 'untranscendable horizon' called Marxism and its totalizing objectives. Initially, his hermeneutics aims to deconstruct the seemingly unified text, which, after patient treatment on the part of the suspicious critic, will disclose gaps, ruptures and rifts. The text's appearance of unity will be disclosed as ideological. But Jameson also attempts – and this is a crucial point – to reconstruct the text as an event in history. For having passed through the ever-widening semantic horizons, the text is supposed to come out onto that final and untranscendable level: History itself. At this moment, presumably, the text assumes its real meaning. To make the text whole again, however, means to restore it in 'the mode of structural difference and determinate contradiction' (p. 56). Jameson's hermeneutical enterprise seems thus rather equivocal, as my abbreviated discussion of totality and allegory suggests. For, the question is how far Jameson, when reconstructing the text, will allow the concept of allegory and the dispersal of meaning to extend themselves. There is indeed, as Dominick LaCapra has remarked, 'an unclear relation between totalization and decentering in Jameson's own approach'.[53] Jameson, himself, claims that his readings have been able to respect 'the methodological imperative implicit in the concept of totality' while simultaneously staging a ' "symptomal" analysis' of the pseudo-unified text (p. 57). LaCapra accredits this twofold feat to the readings, but argues that how it is that Jameson 'is able to do so remains mysterious on a theoretical level'.[54]

LaCapra is, to be sure, absolutely right when it comes to the theoretical level. As regards Jameson's readings, however, I have tried to show that the attempt to reconcile a negative hermeneutics with a positive one creates problems there as well. My discussion of the Conrad reading makes clear that the metacommentary quite quickly slips into a restorative project, and that the symptomal analysis is performed against the background of the primacy of totalization. Jameson's reading thereby tends to come across as a well-nigh traditional Marxist explication, which, contrary to his intentions, ends up answering the question 'What does it mean?', an interpretive exercise which will reveal itself to be dependent on a historical master narrative.

We have seen, for example, that when Jameson seeks to construe the necessary conditions of possibility of meaning, he makes repeated appeals to a notion of precapitalist organic unity. This applies equally well to his discussion of the ideology of form and the generic study, in which he evoked the distant past of oral narration, as to his immanent analysis of Conrad's style and the character system. In this context, it may be useful to add that Jameson is anxious to conceive of this kind of historical narrative neither as teleological nor as a quest for the origin. He would rather call it a 'linear fiction' or 'diachronic construct' (p. 136),[55] and conceive of this model of historical analysis as a genealogical one, which, in the Nietzschean spirit, is a history of the present, and which departs from 'a full-blown system . . . in terms of which elements of the past can "artificially" be isolated as *objective precondition*' (p. 139; italics added). Reification, Jameson acknowledges, is the full-blown system which *The Political Unconscious* begins with (p. 139). Genealogy, then, 'has the essential function of renewing our perception of the synchronic system as in an X-ray, its diachronic perspectives serving to make perceptible the articulation of the functional elements of a given system in the present' (p. 139; see also p. 218). When this elucidation has been accomplished, however, such diachronic constructs can 'be abandoned like so much scaffolding' (p. 145).

Now, a number of questions present themselves here. Advocating a genealogical approach, Jameson none the less seems to smuggle in problematic notions of objectivity and positivity. For how can a genealogical analysis possibly reveal the 'objective preconditions' of the present? And if the synchronic system in question takes on significance in relation to its diachronic elements, therefore in a sense being produced by them, how is it that the 'diachronic construct' can be 'abandoned' without the synchronic system changing at the same time? Jameson's proposition appears indeed to give way to a dangerously formalistic approach, positing the present 'system' as some closed and self-contained structure, simply being 'there'. However, if our experience of the past is vitally dependent on the present, as Jameson repeatedly argues, it follows that our reconstruction of the past will out of necessity involve a projection of our own social formation and related epistemological and ideological assumptions. The (study of the) past is therefore always a function or effect of the present. Genealogy scarcely claims objectivity, nor some absolute truth – it is a contradiction in terms. This is partly why Foucault, besides, preferred to call his later work genealogical. In the early and structuralist study *The Order of Things* (1966), Foucault attempted to theorize the epistemological a priori specific to the body of scientific thinking in a number of historical periods up to the present day. But he failed to lift himself by his epistemological bootstraps: he implicitly posited his own thought as untainted by the powerful structures he sought to conceptualize. Briefly, his own archaeological method tacitly claimed to operate outside history. Realizing the irreducible impossibility of arriving at such positivity, since that would require the theory to objectify the conditions which make objectification

possible, Foucault instead came to pursue a genealogical method-
ology, the idea being, schematically, that genealogical study would
thematize its taking place in history, thus allowing for the theor-
ist/the author to be situated and located within the discourse.
This kind of historical study would recognize its relativity. In a
commentary on Nietzsche, Foucault wrote that the

> purpose of history, guided by genealogy, is not to discover
> the roots of our identity, but to commit itself to its dissi-
> pation. It does not seek to define our unique threshold of
> emergence, the homeland to which metaphysicians promise
> a return; it seeks to make visible all of those discontinuities
> that cross us.[56]

Now, even if we accept what Jameson's 'diachronic construct'
purports to be doing, there are still numerous occasions where
he neglects the charge inherent in the conception of genealogy.
We have noted, for instance, that he claims to have 'reinvested'
Lord Jim with its 'original ideological and semantic content', and
to have 'restored' the 'whole socially concrete subtext of late
nineteenth-century rationalization and reification' to Conrad.
Obviously, he can do so only by means of having abolished the
historical distance between the present and Conrad's moment,
thus turning Conrad into a contemporary. This, furthermore, is
a prime example of a hidden, but of course symptomatic, shift
in Jameson's study. From the outset, he undertook to study 'the
interpretive codes through which we read and receive the text in
question' as opposed to 'the nature of the "*objective*" structures
of a given cultural text' (p. 9; italics added). Not only does
Jameson, in the Conrad reading, seem to end up with the latter
alternative, but when he says that the elements of the past can
' "artificially" be isolated as objective preconditions', he has evidently forgotten the original quotation marks around the word
'objective', thus appearing to claim objectivity and positivity, and
believe in the permanency of the past.

As regards reification conceived as the full-blown system, that
crucial starting-point of the 'diachronic construct', it becomes
clear that reification as beginning is always already an allegory.
Jameson cannot make as it were a fresh start with the *system* or,
for that matter, the *concept* of reification. To paraphrase Jameson,
we may say that reification conceived of as system is nowhere
fully present as such, neither as beginning nor as an instant – it

is a hole in time. Like the absent pivotal events in *Lord Jim* and *Nostromo*, reification must be framed in order to become visible and intelligible. Thus, rather than beginning with the 'system' of reification, Jameson has to begin with the *story* of reification, based on a notion of the organic unity of precapitalist society. Hence reification becomes, or, more correctly, has always been an allegory. For it will be noted that the method of metacommentary in a sense merely postpones the problem of interpretation and the master discourse. Instead of confronting a given problem on its own terms, instead of trying to answer the question 'What does it mean?', Jameson will, as we have seen, always focus on the historical grounds of possibility of that very problem, and proceed, crucially, to explain these conditions of possibility. To be sure, this critical strategy is inherent in the notion of metacommentary, but Jameson's particular version of metacommentary directs our attention to two problems.

The first problem is to do with the historicization of concepts and notions. As we have seen in relation to Conrad, Jameson historicizes Weber's concept of value by arguing that it can emerge as a concept only when it has lost its concrete status, which is to say that the study of value is at one with the loss of value. Likewise, Jameson historicizes the experience of abstract temporality found in *Lord Jim*, an experience which, like the notion of value, is ultimately determined by the advent of capitalism. Crucially, however, Jameson then goes on to employ these notions as positive entities in his reading. He inscribes 'value' in the narrative deep structure, and *Lord Jim* is said to be an interrogation into a 'hole in time'. In this way, he accepts into his discourse the very problems he sought to historicize. A parallel example can be found in Derrida's essay on Lévi-Strauss, where Derrida shows that the critique of ethnocentrism is the very condition for ethnology, and that 'the ethnologist accepts into his discourse the premises of ethnocentrism at the very moment when he denounces them'.[57] By the same token, Jameson's discourse comes to incorporate the premises that make 'value' and the 'experience of time' possible. As a true dialectician, he does not denounce these notions. It is clear, however, that in so far as Weber's theory is ultimately an expression of capitalism as 'always-already' there as a precondition, Jameson's project may be historicized in much the same way. But this is scarcely a revolutionary point. The point is that the 'untranscendable horizon' of Marxism becomes indeed transcendable – by history itself.

The second problem regarding the method of metacommentary as a way of explaining the historical conditions of possibility is that this explanation is and must be structured like a narrative. Indeed, Jameson's categorical imperative, which reads 'Always historicize!', urges a story. In *The Political Unconscious*, this (hi)story assumes the form of the chronological unfolding of the various structures-in-dominance within the capitalist mode of production. In short, it is a chronicle of the passage from precapitalism (unity) to imperialist capitalism (reification and fragmentation) to the threshold of late or multinational capitalism, to what he calls 'our schizophrenic moment'. The Jamesonian metacommentary, then, is dependent on a master narrative. And it is this particular historical narrative which will serve to explain why Conrad has been constantly misread, how it is that the specific received understanding of Conrad's novels has emerged, and, finally, how all interpretation of Conrad has hitherto operated within the structural limitations called ideology. This, then, is the deconstructive and metacritical part of Jameson's analysis. But, and even more importantly, the subsequent reconstruction of Conrad's novels will also be based on this historical narrative. In other words, Jameson's restorative interpretive act seeks to reinvest Conrad's authorship with its allegedly proper meaning precisely by means of rewriting these texts according to the privileged interpretive code of the story of reification. And this code is yet another allegorical level, waiting in vain for the revelation of that always already anterior origin of meaning.

This, then, is the sense in which history, as Terry Eagleton has argued, is 'more one of closure than of horizon'. For as I have argued in my analysis of the Conrad reading, there is a peculiar and probably characteristic gliding away from History as absent cause to history as a meaningful narrative with a Utopian *telos*, which is the recuperation of the whole. Or, to put it another way, History as absent cause appears to masquerade as the alibi for the reintroduction of an expressive totality. Eagleton derives this circumstance partially from the fact that 'the passage through and beyond Althusser is never really effected'.[58] Also, it could be argued that Jameson has to misread Althusserian structuralism in order to be able to elaborate a positive hermeneutics. For in his reading of Althusserian causality, Jameson is eager to assert that Althusser's structuralism is one

> for which only *one* structure exists: namely the mode of production itself, or the synchronic system of social relations as a whole. This is the sense in which this 'structure' is an absent cause, since it is nowhere empirically present as an element, it is not a part of the whole or one of the levels, but rather the entire system of *relationships* among those levels.
>
> (p. 36)

This means, however, that if there is only one structure, there cannot be a structure-in-dominance, that key concept which Althusser postulated in order to designate the dynamics and changes within the system. Jameson's reading of the Althusserian effectivity is a synchronic one, and tends to efface the dynamic aspect of the system of structures by equating the concept of structure with the mode of production. It is a move which allows Jameson partially to recuperate the Lukácsian expressive totality, which runs the risk of conceiving culture and the superstructures as mere expressions of the economic. However, a proper discussion of Jameson's reading of Athusser would lead too far in the present context. It should be enough to point out that, as we have seen previously, Althusser's social totality comprised several structures, each relatively autonomous, and that Jameson's appropriation of the absent cause is somewhat arcane. In his view, it seems, the mode of production is the structure is the totality is the absent cause. As LaCapra has contended, Jameson's mystifying use of the concept of absent cause often tends

> to become a secular surrogate for a missing divinity, open to negative theology and other ideological investments that indicate the hoped-for presence of some ineffable 'transcendental signified'. This is especially the case when the 'absent cause' seems to designate an empty but paradoxically crowded space wherein a number of concepts meet or even fuse with one another: the Real, History, Utopia, totality, and the 'political unconscious' itself. These concepts are all discussed in the same terms – terms that appear to make them highly labile substitutes for one another. At these points, Jameson seems quite close to 'identitarian' Hegelian

Marxism in the 'mystical' form of higher immediacy, for he furnishes a vision of a night in which all sacred cows are gray.[59]

The fact that the absent cause seems to replace that final warranty for meaning called God is not a coincidence. As Perry Anderson among others has pointed out, Althusser's notion of the absent cause is a secularized version of Spinoza's conception of God as *causa immanens*.[60] Thus, by way of the conflation mentioned above, the Althusserian absent cause at length becomes an idealist concept in Jameson. It works to legitimize his historical master narrative and *telos*: the totality. But since History and the totality are absent, Jameson has to elaborate a methodological totality which operates with a notion of an ideal whole. This notion, however, will always be a mere metaphor for the totality, that is to say, it will stand in for a pure beginning: the origin.

And so, because of the irreducible impossibility of an absolute beginning, Jameson is forced to posit a wholly different kind of solution, which gives part of his project a well-nigh Kantian spell. The Kantian doctrine that there are a priori propositions ordering our experience of the world posits a subject endowed with transcendental categories of understanding. Briefly, these categories were a necessary precondition for the experience and knowledge of reality which, however, was not accessible as a thing-in-itself. Only by positing a transcendental consciousness and investigating its categories could the philosopher attain knowledge of how knowledge of the phenomenal world is produced.

Cast in the abyss between subject and object, history and History, *Leben* and *Wesen*, Jameson postulates precisely a transcendental category: that of narrative – 'the central function or *instance* of the human mind' (p. 13). The narrativization agency in the 'political unconscious' is evidently a category of understanding, which may register History and totality. Thus, narrative is the means by which we can get a glimpse of History and totality. In Jameson's view, this is so partly because narrative form is sedimented content, i.e. multiple layers of historical content gradually transformed into formal features, which is why there is a correlation between narrative forms and mode of production; and partly because narrative is a process in Time, and that the mind, through a 'narrativization' of the events and raw material of history, will impose a temporal order on them in order to make them intelligible, and sort out why and how they happened the way they did. This refers to what I have previously called Jameson's cognitive idealism. Moreover, narrative is, we recall, the 'all-informing process' around which he set out to 'restructure the problematics of ideology, of the unconscious and of desire, of history, and of cultural production' (p. 13). Thus I have in a sense merely dismantled his original intention. At the same time, however, I have shown that Jameson's narrative about Conrad, about the passage from realism to modernism, and about reification as a crucial instance in this part of the history of the novel must rely on a master discourse, which of course is at odds with the other original intention: to provide the untranscendable horizon of all reading and all interpretation.

It seems as though Jameson is able to transcend poststructuralist views of history only by means of positing narrative as a transcendental category of understanding. Like Lévi-Strauss's structuralism, Jameson's enterprise could in this respect be called a Kantianism without a transcendental subject, a fact which makes his project vulnerable not only to poststructuralist critiques. For being forced to ground some of its vital presuppositions in the transcendental realm, Jameson's hermeneutics opens itself to a historical-materialist critique as well.

But we must not, however, content ourselves with having pointed out the various inherent problems in Jameson's theoretical enterprise. Because at the very moment he sets out to advocate the Marxist perspective in terms of its 'untranscendable horizon', he demonstrates perhaps better than anyone else that interpretation and hermeneutics are always a matter of rewriting and translation, bound to resort to the linguistic system and its conceptual boundaries which, probably, constitute the 'real' untranscendable horizon. So, in the end, it would seem that interpretive activity is not at all about faithful and true readings, but strong readings, and, to some degree, strong misreadings. I have discussed a number of blind spots in Jameson's theory and practice, and, to echo Paul de Man, they point out that blindness which makes possible Jameson's great insights into the nature of reading and the politics of theory, and, above all, their profound historicity.

The very greatest critics of our time, Jameson once remarked, are those who give priority to history rather than reading, those who have construed their role as the teaching of history, as the telling of the tale of the tribe, the most important story any of us will ever have to listen to, the narrative of that implacable yet also emancipatory logic whereby the human community has evolved into its present form and developed the sign systems by which we live and explain our lives to ourselves.[61]

He thought of Lukács and Leavis, but, it seems to me, this description applies equally well to his own intellectual enterprise. So it is that the blind spots and mysteries create an exemplary reader and historian.

NOTES

1 Frank Lentricchia, *After the New Criticism*, London: Methuen, 1983, p. 159. The present chapter is a slightly modified version of my M.A. thesis written in 1989. I would like to thank Douglas Tallack, Bengt Landgren and Stefan Jonsson for their useful and constructive comments on an earlier version of the thesis. I am also grateful for the intellectual support given to me by Fredric Jameson, with whom I have had the pleasure to work since the completion of this chapter.

2 Fredric Jameson, *The Political Unconscious: Narrative as a socially symbolic act*, London: Methuen, 1983, p. 17. Further references to this study are given after quotations in the text.

3 LaCapra, Review article on *The Political Unconscious, History and Theory* 21: 1 (1982), p. 85.

4 Thus Geoff Bennington writes:

It would, I think, be pointless to rehearse the detail of Jameson's analyses, which are undoubtedly rich and dense, either with the churlish aim of quarrelling over details, or with the aim of holding up samples for admiration (although there is much to admire).
(*Diacritics* (special issue on Fredric Jameson and *The Political Unconscious*) 12: 3 (1982), p. 26)

Hayden White holds that:

Nor is this the place to subject these readings to any kind of 'empirical' test. In spite of the fact that Jameson indicates his willingness to let his theory stand or fall on its capacity to generate insights into the structures of literary works, any objection to a given reading would simply indicate the presence of an alternative theory or presuppose a reading of the text in question that was simply more 'valid' than Jameson's account of it.
(*The Content of the Form: Narrative discourse and historical representation*, London: Johns Hopkins University Press, 1984, p. 164)

William C. Dowling, too, in his *Jameson, Althusser, Marx: An introduction to 'The Political Unconscious'*, London: Methuen, 1984, finds no reason to deal with the readings, nor even to survey them, since his intention is to have readers 'go on to read Jameson for themselves' (p. 14). Dominick LaCapra, by contrast, acknowledges that it

> would be incorrect to see these chapters as mere arabesques or finger exercises illustrating Jameson's hermeneutics of 'phases', for the very diversity and complexity of critical commentary in them both substantiates his larger claims and contests them in subtle ways.
>
> (p. 101)

LaCapra therefore devotes some two pages to an account of the Balzac reading (Review article on *The Political Unconscious*, pp. 83–106).

Michael Sprinker, in his review article in the *Diacritics* special issue, discusses Jameson's Conrad reading over two pages, and uses it primarily as a 'practical' example of metacommentary. There are, however, no principal remarks concerning Jameson's readings. See 'The part and the whole', pp. 57–71. Nor does S. P. Mohanty, in another *Diacritics* review article, pursue a critical analysis of the Balzac and Gissing readings accounted for in the article; these readings are treated sympathetically, as mere applications of Jameson's more theoretical statements. See 'History at the edge of discourse: Marxism, culture, interpretation', pp. 33–46. Jerry Aline Flieger sticks to a strictly theoretical discussion, which deals with Jameson's adaptation of psychoanalytic theories in particular, and does not consider any of the readings at all. See 'The prison-house of ideology: critic as inmate', *Diacritics* special issue, pp. 47–56. Terry Eagleton, like Flieger, is not concerned with the readings. Eagleton sets out to discuss Jameson's style as a 'dialectical figure'. See 'Fredric Jameson: the politics of style', *Diacritics* special issue, pp. 14–22.

John Frow, in his book-length study entitled *Marxism and Literary History*, London: Basil Blackwell, 1988, accounts for the theoretical section of *The Political Unconscious* in terms of Marxism versus (post)structuralism. There is a brief discussion of Jameson's 'practice of mediation' in the Conrad reading (see pp. 39f).

Cornel West, finally, is content with the 'theory', and focuses on the 'philosophical concerns and ideological aims' in *The Political Unconscious*. See 'Fredric Jameson's Marxist hermeneutics', *Boundary 2* (1982), pp. 177–201.

5 Jameson, 'Metacommentary', in *The Ideologies of Theory: Essays 1971–1986* vol 1: *Situations of Theory*, Minneapolis: University of Minnesota Press, 1988.

6 Susan Sontag, 'Against interpretation', in *Against Interpretation and Other Essays*, New York: Farrar, Straus & Giroux, 1966, p. 5.

7 Sontag, 'On style', in *Against Interpretation and Other Essays*, p. 25.

8 Sontag, 'Against interpretation', p. 14.

9 Jameson, 'Metacommentary', p. 5.

10 Ibid., p. 14.
11 Ibid.
12 Georg Lukács, *The Theory of the Novel*, trans. Anna Bostock, London: Merlin Press, 1988, p. 56.
13 Jameson, 'Metacommentary', p. 9. See also Jameson's discussion of Georg Lukács's *Theory of the Novel* in *Marxism and Form. Twentieth-century dialectical theories of literature*, Princeton: Princeton University Press, 1971, pp. 163–82.
14 Jameson, 'Metacommentary', p. 10.
15 Ibid.
16 Ibid., p. 14.
17 Ibid.
18 Ibid., p. 10; italics added.
19 Ibid., p. 13.
20 Ibid., p. 5.
21 Ibid., p. 13.
22 Ibid., p. 16.
23 Jacques Derrida, 'Différance', in *Speech and Phenomena*, trans. David B. Allison, Evanston, Ill.: Northwestern University Press, 1986, esp. pp. 140–1.
24 Jameson, *The Prison-House of Language: A critical account of structuralism and Russian formalism*, Princeton: Princeton University Press, 1974, p. 216.
25 Ibid.
26 West, 'Fredric Jameson's Marxist hermeneutics', p. 178.
27 Gilles Deleuze and Félix Guattari, *Anti-Oedipus*, vol. I: *Capitalism and Schizophrenia*, trans. Robert Hurley, Mark Seem and Helen R. Lane, London: Athlone Press, 1985.
28 Jameson maintains that Foucault, Derrida, Baudrillard, Lyotard and Kristeva, in spite of their general anti-interpretive stance, have generated new hermeneutics in their own right, whose master discourses, Jameson suggests, would read: 'the archaeology of knowledge, but also, more recently, the "political technology of the body" (Foucault), "grammatology" and deconstruction (Derrida), "symbolic exchange" (Baudrillard), "libidinal economy" (Lyotard), and "sémanalyse" (Julia Kristeva)' (*The Political Unconscious*, p. 23n.). See also Lentricchia's convincing discussion of the Yale Derrideans and their striking tendency to treat the aporia and the 'abyss' as positive events in literary texts, thus ending up positing them as transcendental signifieds. Lentricchia, *After the New Criticism*, pp. 177–88.
29 Louis Althusser and Etienne Balibar, *Reading Capital*, trans. Ben Brewster, London: Verso, 1979, p. 186.
30 Martin Jay, *Marxism and Totality: The adventures of a concept from Lukács to Habermas*, Cambridge: Polity Press, 1984, p. 406.
31 Norman Geras, s.v. 'Althusser', in *A Dictionary of Marxist Thought*, ed. Tom Bottomore, Oxford: Blackwell, 1985, p. 17.
32 Althusser and Balibar, *Reading Capital*, p. 189.
33 Jay, *Marxism and Totality*, p. 390.
34 Bennington, 'Not yet', p. 28.

35 The theory of *ressentiment*, besides, is assigned an impressive task in *The Political Unconscious*, intended to displace Derrida's critique of metaphysical thought. Thus Jameson suggests that

> it seems paradoxical to describe the ideologies of the decentered and serialized society of consumer capitalism as metaphysical survivals, except to underscore the ultimate origin of the binary opposition in the older 'centered' master code of theocentric power societies. To move from Derrida to Nietzsche is to glimpse the possibility of a rather different interpretation of the binary opposition, according to which its positive and negative terms are ultimately assimilated by the mind as a distinction between good and evil. Not metaphysics but ethics is the informing ideology of the binary opposition.
>
> (p. 114)

For a forceful critique of Jameson's move, which presupposes analogical features in epistemology and ethics, see West, 'Fredric Jameson's Marxist hermeneutics', pp. 188f.

36 See 'The ideology of the text', in *The Ideologies of Theory*, vol. 1, p. 67. This idea is further developed in the 1983 essay 'Cognitive mapping', where Jameson proposes that these three historical stages of capital 'have each generated a type of space unique to it', and that these spaces harbour three various kinds of 'cognitive mapping' respectively. Indeed, the transition from the early stages of classical capitalism over imperialist to multinational capitalism marks the transition from the possibility of the individual's experience of a concrete totality to the increasingly abstract and confused experience of the totality as an 'absent cause', this last feature finding its analogue in the American urban experience. See 'Cognitive mapping', in *Marxism and the Interpretation of Culture*, ed. Cary Nelson and Lawrence Grossberg, London: Macmillan Education Ltd, 1988, esp. pp. 348–53.

37 See *The Political Unconscious*, pp. 103–50. This section is a methodological proposal and a call for the restoration of the generic study. It assumes primarily the form of a critical re-evaluation of Frye's, Propp's and Greimas's respective conceptualizations of the genre of romance.

38 Jameson describes this phenomenon at length in the essay 'Cognitive mapping', in *Marxism and the Interpretation of Culture*. There he writes that with 'the passage from market to monopoly capital, or what Lenin called the "stage of imperialism" ' there is a

> growing contradiction between lived experience and structure, or between a phenomenological description of the life of an individual and a more properly structural model of the conditions of existence of that experience. . . . The truth of that limited daily [individual] experience of London lies, rather, in India or Jamaica or Hong Kong; it is bound up with the whole colonial system of the British Empire that determines the very quality of the individual's subjective life. Yet those structural coordinates are no longer

261

accessible to immediate lived experience and are often not even conceptualizable for most people.

Jameson argues moreover that the emergence of the various modernisms must be seen as a response to this rift (pp. 349f.).

39 Weber's use of the concept of rationalization refers to different regions of human life: it is linked to the notion that human action is instrumental or goal-oriented, and takes place within a cultural hierarchy of norms; second, it denotes the metaphysical and religious conceptions of cosmic and ethical orders developed by man in a given historical period; third, it also refers to the existential interpretation of these conceptions and man's willingness to live all aspects of his life in accordance with these ideas. Weber also elaborates a notion of economic rationalization. See *The Sociology of Religion*, trans. Ephraim Fischoff, Boston: Beacon Press, 1974, pp. 30f., 216f.

40 See Rogers Brubaker, *The Limits of Rationality: An essay on the social and moral thought of Max Weber*, London: George Allen & Unwin, 1984, p. 27.

41 Karl Marx, 'Economic and philosophical manuscripts', in *Early Writings*, trans. Rodney Livingstone and Gregor Benton, Harmondsworth: Penguin, 1984, p. 353.

42 It is possible that Jameson echoes the interesting and highly speculative suggestion in the essay 'Beyond the cave' (1975), an attempt to sketch out a 'supracultural model' for juxtaposing 'primitive storytelling, precapitalist literatures, bourgeois realism, and the various modernisms of the present postindustrial world of late monopoly capital' in order, ultimately, to see that all these literary modes are transformations of a 'common structure'. Drawing on Deleuze and Guattari's *Anti-Oedipus*, Jameson therefore proposes that there is an a priori 'primordial schizophrenic flux' which the various social forms will have to structure in one way or another, i.e., social life 'codes' this *Ur-flux*. Briefly, Jameson puts forward the idea that 'the savage state' simply codes the flux; next, 'barbarism' overcodes it; thereafter we have the period of capitalism, realism, Enlightenment and the related disenchantment of the world, in which the *Ur-flux* is decoded; and finally, late capitalism and modernism: our moment, subject to resort to a 'recoding of this henceforth decoded flux – by *attempts* to recode, to reinvent the sacred, to go back to myth' ('Beyond the cave', *The Ideologies of Theory: Essays 1971–1986*, vol. II: *Syntax of History* Minneapolis: University of Minnesota Press, 1988, pp. 124ff.). Clearly, Conrad's rewriting operation would, according to this view, be seen as the recoding of an essentially decoded world produced by realism. Yet this view, too, runs into problems as my concluding discussion makes clear. It should also be noted that the notions of a 'common structure' and a 'proto-flux' are fundamentally idealist ones, and end up as transcendental categories, which is obviously at odds with a historical-materialist stance.

43 Lukács argued that the prime criterion of great literature in the capitalist era is its capacity to produce a narrative which depicts

the social totality – in spite of the reification process. See e.g. 'Narrate or describe', in *Writer and Critic and Other Essays*, ed. and trans. Arthur Kahn, London: Merlin, 1978, pp. 110–48.

44 Brubaker, *Limits of Rationality*, p. 6.

45 Ibid.

46 Weber, *The Sociology of Religion*, p. 217.

47 Ibid.

48 Eagleton, 'Fredric Jameson: the politics of style', p. 19.

49 *Hegel's Logic*, trans. William Wallace, Oxford: Oxford University Press, 1975, p. 3.

50 This is especially clear in the 1986 essay 'Third-World literature in the era of multinational capitalism', where Jameson suggests that all Third-World texts are 'national allegories' (p. 69). Interestingly, Jameson takes the priority of the symbol over the allegory to be a symptom of the historical predicament of Western readers. He also maintains that in the Third World, narratives are *de facto* read as allegories – and as national allegories. Jameson therefore conceives of allegory as a kind of 'mapping process' (p. 73), designating two modes of how to think political life. 'In the west,' he proposes, 'political commitment is recontained and psychologized or subjectivized by way of the public–private split' (p. 71). In the Third World, by contrast, a narrative centring on the individual will always have an immediately political significance, precisely by way of the allegorical 'reading habit' (*Social Text* 15 (1986), pp. 65–88).

51 Paul de Man, 'The rhetoric of temporality', in *Blindness and Insight: Essays in the rhetoric of contemporary criticism*, 2nd edn, rev., London: Methuen, 1986, p. 207.

52 Ibid.

53 La Capra, Review article, p. 95.

54 Ibid., p. 96.

55 See the chapter 'Hegelian literary criticism: the diachronic construct', in *Marxism and Form*, pp. 309–27.

56 Michel Foucault, 'Nietzsche, genealogy, history', in *The Foucault Reader*, ed. Paul Rabinow, Harmondsworth: Penguin, 1987, p. 95.

57 Jacques Derrida, 'Structure, sign and play in the discourse of the human sciences', in *Writing and Difference*, trans. Alan Bass, London: Routledge, 1986, p. 282.

58 Eagleton, 'Fredric Jameson: the politics of style', p. 19.

59 LaCapra, Review article, pp. 97f.

60 Perry Anderson, *Considerations on Western Marxism*, London: New Left Books, 1976.

61 Jameson, 'Symbolic inference; or, Kenneth Burke and ideological analysis', in *The Ideologies of Theory*, vol. 1, p. 152.

INDEX